A DIGITAL GUIDE

MICROSOFT EXCEL®

This is a Starfire Book
First Published in 2002

02 04 05 03

1 3 5 7 9 10 8 6 4 2

Starfire is part of
The Foundry Creative Media Company Limited
Crabtree Hall, Crabtree Lane, Fulham, London SW6 6TY

Visit the Foundry website: www.foundry.co.uk

Copyright © 2002 The Foundry

ISBN 1 903817 94 3

A copy of the CIP data for this book is available from the British Library

Printed in China

Special thanks to: Michelle Clare, Vicky Garrard and Tom Worsley

A DIGITAL GUIDE

MICROSOFT EXCEL®

Carol Elston, Rob Hawkins and Sue Orrell

GENERAL EDITOR: S.A. MATHIESON

CONTENTS

HOW TO USE THIS BOOK

This book is a mine of information for everyone interested in Excel, regardless of experience; so whether you are a beginner, relatively familiar with Excel, a whiz kid with spreadsheets or are simply after some hot tips and hot web sites, this is definitely the book for you. We also supply practical information, teaching you 'How To' use Excel to organize your everyday life and provide Case Studies, which demonstrate how Excel can be used to its full potential in real-life situations.

By using the icons (illustrated in the blue box below), which tag each entry, you can read the entries that are specifically of interest to you.

1. Designed in an A–Z format for ease-of-use, you can simply look up the information that you are interested in by using the Contents List on page 4, or by flicking through the book. Please note that some entries are obvious (e.g. Adding and Subtracting) but others are more descriptive and may need some searching.

2. You can interrogate the book by use of the categories tagged throughout. We have provided eight categories: Easy, Intermediate, Advanced, How To, Case Study, Hot Tip, Hot Web Site and Beyond Excel, each represented by an icon (see below). So, if you are just beginning you can flick through the pages and read only the information which is tagged by the Easy icon. If you already know more than the basics then you can read only the entries tagged by the Intermediate icons and if you are an experienced user you can concentrate on those entries tagged by the Advanced icons. If you want practical examples of how to use Excel you can look up the Case Study entries (which follow a particular entry on that subject, e.g. the Features for those with Disabilities entry is followed directly by the Features for those with Disabilities Case Study) and How To categories. Hot Tip, Hot Web Site and Beyond Excel categories have been created for users of all levels. By using the icons all the information that you need is at your fingertips.

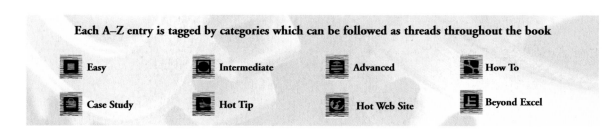

Each A–Z entry is tagged by categories which can be followed as threads throughout the book

Easy   Intermediate   Advanced   How To

Case Study   Hot Tip   Hot Web Site   Beyond Excel

3. The pages at the back of the book provide you with further, more detailed information to give you everything you need to use Excel. Two of the most important sections are:

- **Frequently Asked Questions** This section provides answers to the questions most asked by people who use Excel, whether it is solving an error that has been made or providing solutions to difficulties that they have encountered.

- **Functions** Excel provides literally hundreds of built-in functions. Some you may use on a daily basis, others only occasionally. The majority you will probably never use but there may be the odd occasion when it is just what you need. This section provides a complete list of all the functions available with Excel.

There are two types of pages throughout the book: the main A–Z entries and feature spreads (within the A–Z order), which focus on major topics and often present step-by-step information

Main A–Z entries

Feature Spreads

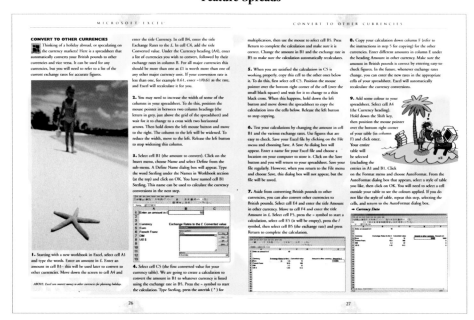

INTRODUCTION

Many pieces of software on your computer mimic existing technologies. A word processor turns your computer into what a curmudgeonly character from a Stephen Fry novel calls 'a socially ambitious type-writer'. The Victorians had the earliest form of a world-wide email system: it was called the telegraph network, and even the World Wide Web bears a resemblance to the Teletext systems available through televisions for decades.

Of course, computer software does the job of its mechanical predecessors much more efficiently, but a spreadsheet does things that an individual really couldn't do before, except with pen, paper, a mathematical mind and much, much more time. The software's real-world inspiration was large blackboards of calculations, used by large companies, which required a team of skilled mathematicians to run.

A spreadsheet can be used to organize text; Excel includes spell-checking, the chance to play with fonts, sizes and alignments and a text-finding facility similar to that of a word-processor. But it also lets you go further – the software can rearrange a list into alphabetical order and the grid lets you place text exactly where you want it.

But it's with numbers that spreadsheets, really, excel. They can act as sophisticated calculators, and Excel has a range of mathematical functions far greater than that available on a scientific calculator. The real beauty, however, is that you can get a spreadsheet to take the input for these maths from other cells.

Why is this the best thing about spreadsheets? Let's say you're working out your accounts on paper. You get to the end, and then realise you've made a mistake – perhaps you missed out just one thing, which means a total is wrong. That total feeds into several other totals so you'll have to rework the whole thing.

Or perhaps you're planning a budget. What would happen if you decided to splash out on something? How much would that leave you with later? Or what if you saved a little bit each month? What would that mean?

On paper, changing things within an inter-connected web of numbers is a slow, tedious and error-strewn process. But in a spreadsheet, once you've got that web woven, you can

play with it. Change one number in the spreadsheet, and everything else connected to it is automatically updated in an instant. That's the great thing about spreadsheets: you can play with numbers. You can correct mistakes or see what happens if you change something – all with the greatest of ease.

In producing this book, we've tried to provide you with several ways to explore the potential uses of spreadsheets. About half of the text is made up of guides to the different functions available within Excel: it's a huge piece of software, and there's always something new to discover. We've grouped these entries into Easy, Intermediate and Difficult (some of which have Case Studies), and all aim to provide you with a clear, step-by-step guide to using the function in question.

A further chunk of entries contain Hot Tips, which deal with specific subjects to help you improve your use of Excel. We don't pretend to list every last function within the program, but we reckon we've covered most things.

Then we've written 16 'How to' entries. These are designed to put Excel's functions into action, through practical suggestions of how you can use it to do your taxes, keep track of a sports league, run an address book, keep a library and a dozen more.

Backing these up are a chunk of entries on web sites you can use to find data for such tasks, and also for further assistance in getting the most from your software.

Finally, we've written some entries that take you beyond Excel. These give you a brief history of spreadsheets, the legal situation on storing data and issues regarding different versions of Excel. We've also included entries on other spreadsheets, namely Lotus 1-2-3, Claris Works, Epoc Sheet and StarOffice and there is an entry on Excel as used on the Apple Macintosh.

Spreadsheets have been around for two decades now, and they all look very similar in terms of their basic functions. Most of the functions and ideas discussed here for Excel will work equally well for other software packages. StarOffice is just as good as Excel for many purposes and is available free online. It also includes a word-processor, drawing and presentation software, and anyone who does not own Excel or another spreadsheet should consider downloading StarOffice and trying it first.

However, this book is written with Excel in mind, specifically the version provided in Microsoft Office 2000 used on a personal computer running Microsoft Windows 98 or later.

This isn't a text-book designed to be read from beginning to end. Dip into it to get help with specific problems, new ideas for using your software, or further information.

Rather as spreadsheets help you play with numbers and words, expanding your ideas of what you can do, we hope this book will help you play with your spreadsheet.

NB: In some versions of Excel, when you click on a menu at the top of the screen (as mentioned in many entries in this book), you might not see the full list of options – just the more popular ones. For the full list, move the cursor over the small, double-downward arrow at the bottom of the abbreviated list, then the full version will appear.

S.A. MATHIESON, GENERAL EDITOR

ADDING AND SUBTRACTING

Simple calculations. The basic purpose of a spreadsheet is calculation. It can of course do much more, but the essence of any spreadsheet is the ability to

add, subtract, multiply and divide. Excel provides a number of tools to make simple arithmetic as easy as possible. The first step is to enter your data. With most spreadsheets, numbers are entered in rows or columns to make it easier to perform calculations. To enter a column of numbers, use your mouse to point to the first cell in which you want to type a number and click the left mouse button to select the cell. The selected cell will be displayed edged by a black border. Type the first number and then press the Enter key or the Down Arrow key. The cell frame will automatically move down to the cell below. You can then repeat the process until you have entered all the numbers.

If you enter a column of data in this way, you will end up with the cell frame positioned on an empty cell directly below the column of figures. To add up the column, simply double-click on the AutoSum button (circled on the screen shot on your left) on the Standard toolbar. If the Standard toolbar is not displayed, right-click on the current toolbar, deselect it and select the Standard toolbar instead. The result is instant and accurate, no need to double-check with a calculator.

The only time you will have to take care is when the column or row of figures contains a blank cell. Cells containing zero do not cause a problem, but if the range of cells contains an empty cell the AutoSum tool will only

sum up to, or across to, that empty cell. If the range does have one or more empty cells, single-click on the AutoSum button rather than double-clicking. Instead of automatically placing the result in the current cell, Excel will show you the cells it intends to include in the calculation. It does this by enclosing the range of cells with a dashed line, often referred to as marching ants. Its official name is a marquee! The range will only extend up to, or across to, the first blank cell. To extend the range of cells to include all the values, click and drag your mouse across the required cells. Click on the Tick button in the Formula bar or press the Enter key to confirm.

Another method of adding the contents of cells is to create a formula. This is particularly useful if the numbers you want to add together are stored in cells that are non-adjacent.

To enter a formula to add cell values, first, click on an empty cell. Formulae always start with an equal sign (=). Type = and then use the mouse to point to and click on the cell containing the first number you want to include in the calculation. The cell you have pointed to will now have a marquee around it. You will also notice that the address of the cell you are pointing to is displayed in the cell you started from, the result cell. Now type a plus sign (+). The pointer will jump back to the cell containing the result. Point to the cell containing the second number to be added. If you want to add further numbers, type a + and point to the next cell. When you have completed the calculation, click on the Tick button in the Formula bar. The result will be displayed in the selected cell and the formula will be displayed in the Formula bar.

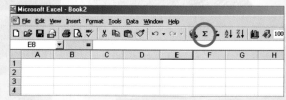

If you want to subtract the values held in cells, the process is similar. Start the formula with =, click on the first cell to be included in the calculation and then press the minus sign (-). Point to the second cell and click on the Tick box or press the Enter key to complete. You can, of course, include addition and subtraction within the same formula. For example, =B3+B7-C11.

The same process can be used to add or subtract values held in different sheets. Select a cell to hold the result and type = to indicate a formula. Create the formula as before. When you get to the point where you want to add or subtract a value from another sheet, type the + or – symbol and click on the sheet tab at the bottom of the screen to take you to the selected sheet. Click on the required cell. Type a + or - to continue the formula and select the sheet that contains the next cell to be included in the calculation. When the formula is complete click on the Tick box on the Formula bar. Excel will jump back to the selected cell on the original sheet and display the result. The current cell will contain the result of the calculation and the Formula bar will display the formula.

➡ *Functions, Multiplying and Dividing, SUMming up*

ADDING COLUMNS AND ROWS

Changing the design. When creating a spreadsheet, you may well decide to change the design part of the way through. If this is the case, you are likely to need to add rows or columns within the sheet, possibly between existing columns or rows of data. Excel provides a facility to do this without upsetting the existing formulae within the sheet.

Excel has a maximum of 65,536 rows and 256 columns. Even though this number is fixed, you can add rows and columns anywhere within the sheet. Adding a row or column does not actually change the total number of rows or columns: all that happens is the last row or column is removed from the sheet. The only time you cannot add a row or column is if the last row or column contains data. In this case Excel will display a dialog box informing you that the last row or column is not empty. To insert a new column, click on the column heading of the column to the right of where you want the new column to appear. Select the Insert menu and select Columns. The new column will be inserted to the left of (before) the column you first selected.

To insert a number of columns, click and drag across the column headings of a range of columns (the same number of columns as you want to insert). Access the

FAR LEFT: Excel can help you with your basic calculations.
BELOW: It is quick and simple to change the design of a spreadsheet.

Insert menu and select Columns. Excel will insert the required number of columns before (to the left of) the selected columns.

Inserting rows follows much the same procedure. Click on the row heading directly below where you want to insert a row. Select the Insert menu and select Rows. A row will be inserted above the selected row.

To insert multiple rows, click and drag across a range of row headings. Access the Insert menu and select Rows. Excel will insert the required number of rows directly above the selected rows.

When you add rows or columns, Excel automatically amends all subsequent row or column headings. For example, if you insert a column before column D, the new column will become column D, the original column D will become column E and so on. Even though the column and row headings may have changed, you do not need to adjust any formulae. Excel will automatically amend the row or column reference of any formula affected by the change.

➡ *Deleting Data and Lines*

ADDING COMMENTS

If you are designing a worksheet for someone else to use, it can be helpful to add comments to certain areas of the worksheet that may need explanation.

You may also find that you appreciate comments you have added when you return to make changes to a sheet containing complex formulae.

To add a comment to a cell, first select the cell and then access the Insert menu and select the Comment option. The keyboard shortcut to insert a comment is Shift+F2. Excel will insert a comment box that points to the current cell. By default, the box will contain your name and the cursor will be positioned for you to enter further information. Type your comment and then click anywhere in the sheet to hide the completed comment. Cells that have a comment attached can be identified by a small red triangle in the top right corner. When you move the mouse over a cell containing a comment, the comment will be displayed.

If you want to change or delete a comment, select the cell containing the comment, right click the mouse and select either the Edit Comment or the Delete Comment option from the shortcut menu.

➠ *Collaboration*

RIGHT: The AppleWorks software combines several facilities in one application.

APPLE WORKS ON THE MACINTOSH

AppleWorks (formerly known as Claris Works) is a fully integrated suite of products, with six core areas of functionality. AppleWorks 6.2, the latest version of Macintosh software, combines the capabilities of a word processor, database, spreadsheet, page layout, painting and presentations into one application. It is an ideal application with which to create dynamic business letters, newsletters and reports.

Macintosh products have a reputation for being simple and intuitive to use, and AppleWorks is no exception. Rather than focus on the functions available in individual modules, the idea is that, as you work in a window, you can draw on the most appropriate tools for the task in hand. Easily identifiable icons placed around the window represent the tools that you will need, making it easy for you to access the facilities that you need, when you need them. For example, if you have used other Macintosh or Windows-based products, you may recognize some of the drawing and painting tools which appear in the middle section of the Tools window.

Each of the core modules provides the tools necessary to perform particular types of tasks. For example, using the word-processing capability, you can type and edit text, make use of over 50 professional-quality fonts and styles to enhance text appearance, spell-check, use a thesaurus, find and replace text and perform a mail merge. Using the

spreadsheet capability, you can carry out many of the functions typically found in a dedicated spreadsheet program like Excel. For example, you can create formulae, copy and paste data, insert rows and columns, format data and print. AppleWorks also provides a range of built-in functions including statistical, financial, logical and text functions. Spreadsheet data can be represented in one of many available chart types and customized using a range of formatting options. For example, you can add colour, 3-D effects and labels to charts.

If, at any time, you need to use the range of options found in Word or Excel, AppleWorks provides you with the ability to import files from Word 2001 and Excel 2001 or earlier, and save AppleWorks files in a format which can be read by Word or Excel.

While the spreadsheet module may not provide the level of functionality found in a dedicated spreadsheet program like Microsoft Excel, and the word-processing capability may be less than that found in Microsoft Word, the beauty of AppleWorks is that you have all the tools in one product to create exciting and interesting documents. The power of AppleWorks lies in its ability to integrate information from the core modules into one document, giving you the opportunity to produce documents with a high visual or auditory impact.

Seamless integration with Apple QuickTime digital technology means that you can produce documents, which include images, digital photographs, sounds and movies as well as text and tables. Although it would be possible to create documents with equal visual appeal using a range of other products (such as those found in the Microsoft Office suite), it would be difficult to find a single product which matches AppleWorks in terms of its integration, versatility and power, and provides an all-in-one solution. Combining information into one document couldn't be easier. To add spreadsheets, charts, text, tables, images, movies and sounds, simply drag and drop.

AppleWorks can make use of the extensive range of image file formats supported by QuickTime. They include JPEG, PNG, GIF, TIFF and BMP formats. It also supports many types of sound files including MP3, MIDI, MPEG-1, AIFF and Law and video file formats, including AVI, Macromedia Flash and QuickTime Movie.

The presentation environment can be used to create multimedia slides quickly using QuickTime movies and iMovies. Presentations can be created from a selection of templates or designed from scratch. You can add titles, images, music and video to your slides, sort them into order using drag and drop, prepare and print speaker notes and apply a range of slide transitions. There are 25 slide transitions available. You can also choose to set auto-advance options or have the presentation run continuously.

AppleWorks 6.2 comes with 30 built-in templates and 100 clip art images, but if you have an Internet connection you will be able to access more than 150 professionally designed templates which are available via the Internet. Among other things, templates can be used as a basis for creating newsletters, business cards and party invitations. More than 25,000 clip art images and high-quality photographs can also be downloaded from the Internet Clip Art Storehouse directly into AppleWorks.

To run AppleWorks, you will need an Apple computer with a PowerPC processor, a Mac OS 8.1 or later, 24Mb of RAM and QuickTime 4.1.2 or later. To access the extensive range of templates and clip art on the Internet, you will need an Internet connection.

Additional benefits can be achieved using AppleWorks with Mac OS X. For example, the advanced Quartz graphics system allows you to save a document as a PDF file, which can then be read and printed by anyone with Adobe Acrobat Reader.

➡ *Excel on the Macintosh*

ABOVE: AppleWorks can use a variety of formats including video files.

AUTOMATIC TEXT

Excel comes with a built-in feature to help you enter text into your worksheet. The AutoComplete feature 'remembers' what you have typed before and will automatically complete an entry for you if it thinks you are repeating a previous entry. This has the benefit of reducing typing and ensuring that entries are formed and spelled consistently.

As you type, AutoComplete will search through your previous entries for a match. As soon as it finds a match for the first few letters it will finish the typing for you. As an example, take a worksheet where you are entering customer

ABOVE: Backing up your workbook can be helpful in the event of a disaster.

invoices. Each time you enter a new name, Excel will store it, and the next time you start to type that name, it will magically appear in the cell. If you are typing something else, just keep going – the suggestion will vanish as soon as a difference comes up.

This is a brilliant facility if you are entering repetitive information but it can be very off-putting if most of your text entries are unique. The trick is to leave it on when it is useful but turn it off when distracting. To turn AutoComplete off, access the Tools menu and select the Options option. Click on the Edit tab and click on the tick from the Enable AutoComplete for cell values box, leaving the box blank.

➠ *Words in Excel*

AVERAGES

Finding the mean. To calculate an average, you need at least two values. Excel will sum the values you select and divide the result by the number of values selected. This will provide the arithmetic mean, often referred to as the average. As with most common operations, Excel provides a function to do this for you.

The simplest way to find the average of a group of numbers is to select the cells containing the numbers and look at the AutoCalculate feature displayed on the Status bar at the bottom of the screen. By default, the sum will be displayed, but if you are mainly working with averages it may be useful to change this. Point to the summed value on the status bar and click the right mouse button. Select Average from the list of options.

To store the average value in your sheet, use the AVERAGE() function. Select the cell you want the result to appear in and click on the Paste Function button on the Standard toolbar. Alternatively, select the Function option from the Insert menu. The Paste Function dialog box will be displayed. Select the Statistical option and then select Average from the list that appears to the right of the box. Click on OK to display the Average dialog box.

If you want to find the average of a range of adjacent cells you will only need to enter information into the Number 1 text box. If you know the cell addresses of the range, you can type the information into the box; for example, B3:B12. If you are unsure, click on the spreadsheet symbol to the right of the text box. This will take you back to the sheet and you can highlight the required range of cells. Once highlighted either press the Enter key or click on the Restore dialog box symbol that will have appeared on your sheet. Click OK to complete the function.

To calculate the average of non-adjacent cells, access the Average dialog box in the same way and enter the values or cell addresses of each independent argument in a separate Number text box. For example to find the average of the values held in cells C6, D11 and F9, enter C6 in text box Number 1, D11 in Number 2 and F9 in Number 3. If you are unsure of the cell addresses, highlight the required cells on the spreadsheet as before.

➥ *Functions*

BACKING UP FILES

In addition to saving your files on a regular basis, it is a good idea to have a backup copy of important files. In the event of something disastrous happening to your workbook or computer, you can restore the backup copy.

To back up an individual workbook, click the File menu and select Save As. The Save As dialog box will be displayed. Click the arrow to the right of the Tools option and select General Options. In the Save Options dialog box, check the Always create backup box. When you save a file, Excel will automatically save a copy of the workbook at the stage it was before you saved the changes.

The backup version will be saved with the name backup of filename in the same directory as the current file. If you want to revert to the previous version of the file, open the backup as you would any other file.

In addition to backing up individual workbooks, it is important to make a regular backup of all files. If files are currently stored on a hard disk or network, create a tape or disk backup and store it safely in a separate location.

To create a floppy disk backup, put a disk in the drive, and select '3 1/2 Floppy (A:)' from the drop-down list at the top of the resulting dialog box. Keep this disk physically separate from your computer for maximum security, and back up regularly.

➥ *Opening and Closing*

BRACKETS

Using brackets with Excel. Round brackets ( ), square brackets [ ] and curly brackets { } all play important roles when working with Excel. The round

brackets, also known as parentheses, are used extensively within formulae and functions. The square brackets are used when performing links to external workbooks to identify the external workbook name. Curly brackets are used to identify an array formula.

Let's first consider the use of parentheses with Excel. When performing calculations, Excel has certain rules that determine exactly how it works out the result. Whether you enter a simple or an extremely complex formula or function, Excel will always follow the same rules. The series of operations will be carried out from left to right giving some operators precedence over others. For instance, Excel will carry out multiplication and division operations before any addition or subtraction, irrespective of order. For example, take the formula =C9-F15/10. Reading from left to right, you may assume this formula will first subtract the content of cell F15 from the content of C9 and then divide the result by 10. In fact, Excel will consider division first and will divide the content of F15 by 10 and then subtract the result from the content of C9. To force Excel to do what you want, you can use parentheses (). These take precedence over all the other operators. By typing the formula as =(C9-F15)/10, Excel will subtract the contents of the two cells and then divide the result by 10.

Parentheses are also used to enclose the arguments of a function. Functions are Excel's built-in formulae and are designed to carry out the most common calculations. All functions start with an equal sign (=), followed by the function name. The function name is followed by the arguments enclosed within parentheses. The arguments of a function provide the information that Excel needs to calculate a result.

Parentheses also play an important part when functions and formulae are nested within one another. For example, take the following formula:

$$=MAX(AVERAGE(SUM(Jan),SUM(Feb),SUM(Mar)),$$
$$AVERAGE(SUM(Apr),SUM(May),SUM(June)))$$

This formula may look complex but if you break it down it is quite straightforward. The trick is to do as Excel does and work from the inside out. Excel will sum the values in the range called Jan then sum for Feb and then Mar. It will calculate the average of the three results. The same process will then be carried out to find the average for Apr, May and June. Lastly, Excel will use these two results to calculate the maximum for the two quarters. When working with long formulae you must be very careful to ensure you have the same number of opening brackets as closing brackets, a common cause of error.

Square brackets are used with external links. When creating a formula you may need to include a value in a cell or range of cells which is stored in another workbook. To do this you need to create a link from the source workbook to the destination workbook. In order to create a link both workbooks need to be open. A simple link formula to a cell in another workbook will look something like this:

$$='C:\Finances\[HeadOffice.xls]Sheet2'\$C\$4$$

The location of the destination is enclosed within single quotes ('). The first part of the location is the path, in the above case a subdirectory called Finances held on the C drive. This is followed by the name of the destination workbook enclosed within square brackets [ ], in this case HeadOffice.xls. The final part of the location is the Sheet name, in this case Sheet2.

To recap, Excel identifies the name of the destination workbook by the fact that it is enclosed by square brackets.

Curly brackets are used to identify an array formula. A formula can create a single result or it can create several results. A formula that returns several results is known as an array formula. The reason for using array formulae is to save time because you only need to enter one formula. With a single result formula you select a cell, enter the formula and press the Enter key to confirm. With an array formula, you select a range of cells, enter the formula and then press Ctrl+Shift+Enter to confirm. This combination of keys tells Excel that you want to enter the formula into each of the cells in the range. Excel will automatically put the curly brackets around the whole formula – you do not need to enter them manually. If you look at the completed entry on the Formula bar you can see the curly brackets around the formula.

➡ *Functions, Using Cells on other Pages*

CHANGING COLUMN AND ROW SIZE

Resizing columns and rows. When you create a new workbook you will find the rows and columns are set to the default width. As you enter information into your sheet the columns and rows will not automatically resize. Excel provides several tools to help you do this yourself.

The default column width is just over eight characters wide if the default font is set, or over 64 pixels. If you enter something that doesn't fit, Excel will either not display the whole entry, display a number as an exponential value or display the error message #####. If the cell to the right is empty, text will be allowed to run over, but as soon as you enter data in the next cell you will 'cover up' the end of your data.

The easiest way to change the column width is to use the mouse. Point to the right-hand side of the column heading, at the top of the worksheet, and drag the boundary to the right to increase the width, and to the left to make the column smaller.

You can also adjust the column to an exact width, or change a number of columns to be the same width. To do this, click and hold down the mouse button on the first column heading. Then drag the mouse across the rest of the column headings to include all the columns you want to resize. From the Format menu, select Width from the Column options. Type in the required column width in characters and click the OK button to confirm.

Excel is more intuitive when it comes to row height. It will automatically adjust the row height to the size of the font being used. You can also manually change row height in much the same way as a column.

To change the height of a single row, point to the lower boundary of a row heading and drag the boundary up or down. To be more exact or to change several rows, highlight the required rows, access the Format menu and select Height from the Cells options. Type in the required height and click the OK button to confirm.

If your prime concern is to save space, you can let Excel Autofit your sheet. By doing this Excel will find the best fit. To do this, double-click on the right-hand boundary of a column heading or double-click on the lower boundary of a row heading.

➡ *Number Formats (Other), Words in Excel*

CHARTS

Excel comes with an impressive gallery of pre-designed charts to which you can add your own custom-built charts. Although you can create a simple chart in a matter of seconds, producing more complex charts can require in-depth knowledge of the myriad of chart options.

Before spending time creating your own challenging designs, consider using one of Excel's custom-built charts. Custom charts are based on the 14 standard chart types but are customized in such a way that they are suitable for a particular audience or for use with specific equipment. For example, Pie Explosion is a template for a 3-D exploded pie chart which has been specially formatted for on-screen presentations. Before you apply a custom design to your data, preview the effect that it will have.

If you do spend a lot of time fine-tuning the way your charts look, why not save your chart as a user-defined custom chart? Select the chart, click on the Chart menu

ABOVE: There are a number of pre-designed charts available on Excel.
RIGHT: Data can be used to create a 3-D Area chart.

and select Chart Type. Click the Custom Types tab and select User-defined. Click the Add button. Enter a name and description for the newly defined custom chart. From now on, when the User-defined box is checked, your chart will appear in the list.

Excel typically stores custom charts in Program Files\Microsoft Office\Office\1033. In-built custom charts are stored in X18galry.xls. When you create your first user-defined custom chart, Excel will create a file called Xlusrgal.xls which will also be saved in the 1033 folder. You can open these files and click on each sheet tab to view the chart and its settings.

If you are happy with the design of a standard or custom chart, you can set it to be the default chart type for all future charts. Select the chart and click the Chart menu followed by the Chart Type option. Click the Set as default chart button. Verify that you want to set this chart type as the default. From now on, if you create a chart by pressing F11, the chart type will be based on this default.

Many of the more difficult aspects of charting involve getting your head around complex options associated with features like 3-D. When you have created a 3-D chart, click the Chart menu followed by the 3-D View option. The 3-D View dialog box will be displayed. The value entered into the perspective box determines the depth of the chart and can be set as anything from 0 to 100 degrees. Make sure that the right angles box is not checked and use the arrows above the box to increase or decrease the perspective by 5 degrees each time. You can preview any changes made before you apply them to the chart.

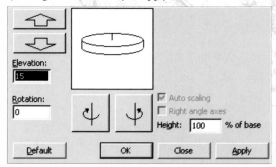

Elevation can be set to anything between -90 and + 90 degrees, where +90 degrees will produce a bird's-eye view of the chart (looking down from above) and -90 will produce a view from underneath. The chart can also be rotated up to 360 degrees, unless it is a bar chart (which can only be rotated up to 44 degrees).

If you create a 3-D Area chart, check to make sure that all data series are visible. It is easy for data series containing low values to become obscured by data series containing higher values. If this happens, you will need to change the series order. To do this, select the data series and right-click the mouse button. Select Format Data Series from the pop-up menu. Click the Series Order tab. In the Series Order box, select the series that you want to move and change the order in which it is displayed by clicking the Move Up and Move Down buttons.

A chart is dynamically linked to the source range in the worksheet from which it was created. Changes to the contents of linked cells will be reflected in the chart and changes to some elements of a chart will be reflected back in the worksheet. For example, if you are presenting a chart showing the financial results for the current year

and you want to identify financial targets for the coming year, you can do this by dragging the data point of the relevant series to a higher point. This new target will appear in the linked worksheet. If your chart is based on results created from formulae and you drag a data series to a new point, you will be prompted to use Goal Seek to indicate those cells which might need adjusting in order to achieve your new goal.

If you want to plot additional data on a chart sheet simply select the range on the worksheet and copy and paste it into the chart sheet. If the chart is embedded in a worksheet rather than in a separate sheet, select the chart and the source range will be highlighted. Drag the mouse to extend the source range and the additional data will be plotted on the chart. If you want to include data which is not adjacent to the current source range, select and drag the data into the chart.

➟ *Cutting and Pasting, Goal Seek*

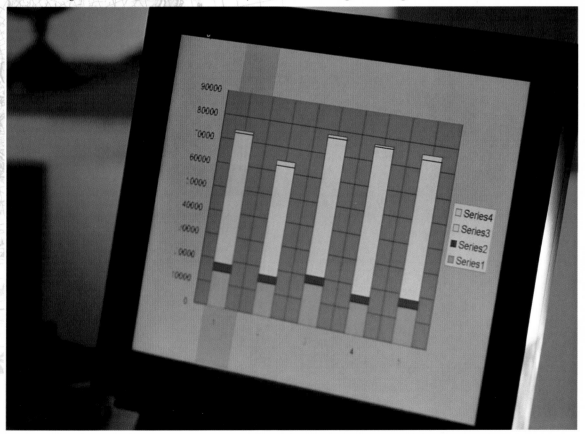

COLLABORATION

Collaboration involves teamwork, partnership and co-operation. Office 2000 comes with exciting new functionality that makes collaborating with other users via a network, Intranet or the Internet as easy as working from a stand-alone PC.

You can collaborate with other users simply by sharing workbooks via a network or via e-mail, or you can make use of some of the more powerful capabilities provided by MS Office Server Extensions (OSE). OSE can be installed as part of the Office installation process and will allow you to collaborate on web-based documents, take part in group discussions, receive e-mail notification of changes to web pages and 'meet' other users on the Internet.

Multiple users can access and edit a workbook at the same time, via a network, and see the changes made by

ABOVE: On-line collaborations can be extended to group discussions.
ABOVE RIGHT: Collaboration involves teamwork, partnership and co-operation.

other users. To share a workbook, get it to the stage where you are happy for other people to contribute to it, click the Tools menu and choose the Share Workbook option. Click the Editing tab and check the Allow changes by more than one user at the same time box. Save the workbook to an area of the network from which the other users can access and modify it. The word 'Shared' appears in the title bar.

There are limitations to what you can do in a workbook once it is shared. For instance, you cannot insert objects, hyperlinks or charts. For a comprehensive list of unavailable features, access Help. If you think you are likely to want to use some of these features, use them before making the workbook shared.

Use the options in the Advanced page of the Shared Workbook dialog box to determine how changes will be tracked and updated and how conflicts should be resolved. If you want to be able to review and merge changes at a later stage, make sure that the Keep change history option is selected.

If users cannot access a shared workbook over a network, you can prepare individual copies of a file for them to work on and then merge them into one workbook. To do this, set a workbook to be shared and choose to keep a change history. Make the required number of copies of the workbook, saving each copy with a new name. Create a workbook to contain the amalgamated results, click the Tools menu and then the Merge Workbooks option. The Select Files to Merge Into Current Workbook dialog box will be displayed. Select the files to be merged and then review the highlighted changes.

Online collaboration can involve accessing documents via the Web, taking part in group discussions and 'meeting' other users on the Internet.

make changes to the document without affecting the collaborative discussion. Using the Collaboration toolbar, users can view, search or filter discussions by author, date or time. Discussions will print on a separate page from the document.

If you would like to receive notification of changes to a web document or to a threaded discussion, click the Subscribe button on the Discussion toolbar. The Document Subscription dialog box will be displayed. Choose to be notified of file or folder changes. In the When box, specify what you would like to be notified of and the frequency with which you should be notified.

The ability to 'meet' in real-time on an Intranet or the Internet is provided through Microsoft NetMeeting. Click the Tools menu, select Online Collaboration followed by Meet Now. As long as the people you invite to join you have NetMeeting installed, you can share applications, documents, text messages, and even work on a whiteboard.

The host will begin the meeting by inviting participants to attend. During the meeting, participants will see a copy of the host screen: workbook, mouse and keyboard movements on their screen. Should it be appropriate, the host can hand control, for part of the meeting, to a participant. To take part, you will need to specify a server and provide identification information. To end a call, click the End Meeting button on the Online Meeting toolbar.

➡ **Emailing Spreadsheets, Hyperlinks, Tracking Changes, Web Pages from Excel**

To take part in a discussion, you will need to make sure that you specify an OSE-extended web server to act as the Discussion server. You can then view discussion items by opening a shared document in Excel or opening a document in a web browser. From within Excel, click the Tools menu and select Online Collaboration followed by Web Discussions. You will be prompted to enter the name of the Discussion server.

Discussion items will appear in the Discussion pane but if there are no items, only the Discussion toolbar will be displayed at the bottom of the screen. To begin a discussion, click the Insert Discussion About the Workbook button on the Discussion toolbar. Enter the discussion subject, text and any hyperlinks. You can add and view specific discussion items located within documents or general discussion items located in the discussion pane.

Discussion items are stored in a database, separate from the shared document. This means that you can

COLOUR, PATTERNS AND BORDERS

A worksheet is like a piece of paper which has been divided into columns and rows. Columns, rows and individual cells are clearly shown on screen

demarcated by gridlines, and this makes it easy for you to work your way around the worksheet. You can apply a range of formatting options to customize the way cell borders are displayed, so making your worksheet appear more professional.

ABOVE: Customize your worksheet using colours and patterns.

Make a cell, or range of cells, active by slecting them. Click the Border button on the Formatting toolbar, or right-click the mouse and choose Format Cells. You can also click the Format menu and choose Cells followed by the Border tab. There are three preset border options: None will remove a border, Outline will apply a solid border outline with automatic colour (usually black) and Inside will control the gridlines around and between a group of cells. A single cell cannot have an inside border. The Border box will allow you to preview the results of your selected option. You can click the areas of the preview diagram, or the buttons around the diagram, to add or remove diagonal, vertical and horizontal lines.

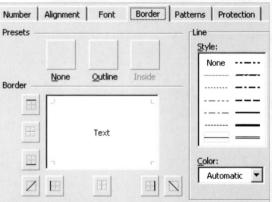

The selected border style can be applied by clicking the presets, preview diagram or the buttons above.

There are rules governing how borders are applied. All cells share a boundary with other cells. For example, the right-hand edge of cell E3 is the left-hand edge of cell F3. If a different border style is applied to the same boundary, the most recently applied border will take precedence. Similarly, a selected range of cells will be treated as a single cell. If you apply a double line style and create a left border, it will only appear as the left border of the first selected cell. To overcome this, click the Inside button in the Border dialog box.

With the Border tab selected, the right-hand section of the Format Cells dialog box displays a set of line styles and colours. Each Excel workbook has an associated colour palette which consists of 56 colours. These colours can be applied to the worksheet or to fills and lines in a chart. To set border areas to a different colour you must first choose one of the colours available from the Colour drop-down list. The colour won't take effect until you apply your choice by adding or removing lines using one of the techniques described previously. You can set a different line style by choosing one of 14 line styles available from the Line Styles box and adding border lines.

To fill a cell with a colour, select the Fill Colour button on the Formatting toolbar or select the Patterns tab from the Format Cells dialog box. Choose a pattern from the Patterns list and a colour from below the pattern to set the colour of the black lines or dots in the pattern. Choose a colour from the Cell Shading box to set a background colour. Text colour can be set through the Font tab.

the new and old colour displayed. If you are happy with your choice, click OK. To reset the palette to the default, Click Reset. Features which have been previously formatted with a modified colour will now be updated with the new colour.

Background patterns created in applications such as Microsoft Paint can be attached to an entire sheet. To do this, select only one sheet, click the Format menu and select the Sheet option. Click the Background option. Using the Sheet Background dialog box, locate a graphics file and click the Insert button. The graphic will be inserted and repeated until it fills the sheet. A background pattern will not print or save with a worksheet but it will be displayed if you choose to create a web page from a workbook.

The procedure for applying colours, patterns and line styles to most types of chart is simple. Double- click the area of the chart to change and then use the Patterns tab to set borders. There is also a range of fill effects available which includes gradients (shaded colours), textures and patterns. The procedure for applying similar attributes to a surface chart is slightly different. You need to make sure that the chart has a legend visible by clicking the Chart menu and selecting Chart Options. Click the Legend tab and then make sure that the Show Legend box is checked. Once the legend is visible, click to select it and then click the legend key for the surface level that you want to change. Access the Format menu and select the Selected Legend Entry option followed by the Patterns tab. Select options as required.

You can change the colours available in the workbook palette by selecting Options from the Tools menu and then the Colour tab. The idea is to replace one of the colours, not to add extra colours to the palette. Click a colour in the Standard palette and then the Modify button. Choose a colour from 127 standard colours and 15 shades of grey. To the right of the palette you will see

➡ *Formatting Case Study, Words in Excel*

COMPARE COSTS

Have you tried to work out which gas and electricity supplier has the best deal? Or which telephone company can offer you the most for your money? Here is a spreadsheet to help compare the costs of a particular service. In the example shown here, electricity costs have been compared from three different suppliers with calculations for standing charges and costs per kilowatt-hour to create a sample quarterly bill. The figures displayed are not reflective of what is on offer from these suppliers, but you can enter the relevant values and Excel will calculate a sample quarterly bill.

1. Open Excel. Using a new workbook, select cell A3 and enter the title Standing charge per year. Select cell A4 and enter the title Cost per kilowatt-hour. Enter the names of the suppliers in cells B1, C1, D1 etc. The width of some columns may need increasing. To do this, position the mouse pointer in between two column letters and wait for it to change to a cross with two horizontal arrows. Hold down the left mouse button and move to the right. The column to the left will be widened. Release the left button to stop widening this column.

2. Calculate an example quarterly bill (enter a title in cell A7). This will help to compare the costs from each supplier. Starting with the first supplier in column B, select the cell that will represent the standing charge for a quarterly bill (B9 in this example). Press the = sign to start a calculation, then use the mouse to select the cell displaying the standing charge per year value (B3). Press the division symbol on the keyboard (/), type the number 4, then press Return. You have now calculated a quarterly standing charge for the supplier in column B.

3. Enter a value in cell B10 for the number of kilowatt-hours used. This must be the same for all suppliers. Now select the cell to represent the cost of kilowatt-hours used (B11 in this example). Press the = sign to start the calculation, use the mouse to choose the cell for the number of kilowatt-hours used (B10), press the asterisk (*) symbol (for multiplication), then choose the cell with the cost per kilowatt-hour for this supplier (B4). Press Return on the keyboard to complete the calculation.

ABOVE: You can establish who is offering the best deal with a spreadsheet.

4. Calculate the total quarterly bill (standing charge + cost of kilowatt-hours used). Select the cell where this calculation will be displayed (B13 in this example). Press the = sign to start the calculation. Select the cell with the calculation for the quarterly standing charge (B9), press the plus (+) symbol, then select the cell for the cost of kilowatt-hours used (B11) and press Return.

5. With one quarterly bill calculated, you can copy these calculations into the columns for the other suppliers. To do this, select the cells in column B from the quarterly standing charge calculation to the total quarterly bill (B9 to B13) by holding down the left mouse button and moving down these cells. With the cells selected (apart from cell B9 they will all be highlighted in black), position the mouse pointer at the bottom right corner of the selected cells, over a small black square. When the mouse pointer changes to a thick black cross, hold down the left button and move across the screen into column D. Release the left button and your calculations will have been copied. You may find that the values for number of kilowatt-hours used will have changed through copying, so you will have to select each cell in turn and enter the same value.

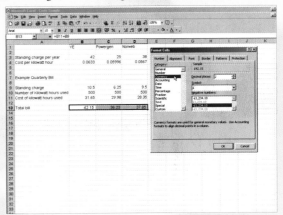

6. Test your calculations. Enter easily checked figures for standing charges and cost per kilowatt-hour, then make sure the total quarterly bill is correct. If it is incorrect, select each cell where a calculation has been created and look at the formula bar (above the column headings) to make sure the cell references in the calculation are correct. If you cannot find any problems, but the calculations are incorrect, return to step 2 and recreate the calculations.

7. You may want to display the total bill figures with pound symbols. Use the mouse to select these cells, then click on the Format menu and choose Cells. From the dialog box that appears, ensure the Number tab is selected, then choose Currency from the list on the left. Make sure that under Symbol, the pound sign is displayed (click on the drop-down triangle and change it if not) with two decimal places. Click on OK to close this dialog box and change the cells you selected.

8. Save your workbook by clicking on the File menu and choosing Save. From the dialog box that appears, select a location to save your file and enter a name for it. Click on Save. You can now use this workbook to enter cost information from an electricity supplier. If a standing charge or cost per kilowatt-hour changes, just change the relevant values in rows 3 and 4, and Excel will automatically recalculate a sample quarterly bill for you.

➧ *Price Comparison*

	A	B	C	D
		YE	Powergen	Norweb
1				
2				
3	Standing charge per year	42	25	38
4	Cost per kilowatt hour	0.0633	0.05996	0.0567
5				
6				
7	Example Quarterly Bill			
8				
9	Standing charge	10.5	6.25	9.5
10	Number of Kilowatt hours used	500	500	500
11	Cost of kilowatt hours used	31.65	29.98	28.35
12				
13	Total bill	£42.15	£36.23	£37.85
14				
15				
16				
17				
18				

CONVERT TO OTHER CURRENCIES

Thinking of a holiday abroad, or speculating on the currency markets? Here is a spreadsheet that automatically converts your British pounds to other currencies and vice versa. It can be used for any currencies, but you will need to refer to a list of the current exchange rates for accurate figures.

ABOVE: *Excel can convert money to other currencies for planning holidays.*

1. Starting with a new workbook in Excel, select cell A1 and type the words. Enter an amount in £. Enter an amount in cell B1– this will be used later to convert to other currencies. Move down the screen to cell A4 and

enter the title Currency. In cell B4, enter the title Exchange Rates to the £. In cell C4, add the title Converted value. Under the Currency heading (A4), enter a list of currencies you wish to convert, followed by their exchange rates in column B. For all major currencies this should be more than one as £1 is worth more than one of any other major currency unit. If your conversion rate is less than one, for example 0.61, enter =1/0.61 as the rate, and Excel will recalculate it for you.

2. You may need to increase the width of some of the columns in your spreadsheet. To do this, position the mouse pointer in between two column headings (the letters in grey, just above the grid of the spreadsheet) and wait for it to change to a cross with two horizontal arrows. Then hold down the left mouse button and move to the right. The column to the left will be widened. To reduce the width, move to the left. Release the left button to stop widening this column.

3. Select cell B1 (the amount to convert). Click on the Insert menu, choose Name and select Define from the sub-menu. A Define Name dialog box will appear. Type the word Sterling under the Names in Workbook section (at the top) and click on OK. You have named cell B1 Sterling. This name can be used to calculate the currency conversions in the next step.

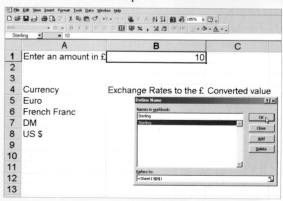

4. Select cell C5 (the first converted value for your currency table). We are going to create a calculation to convert the amount in B1 to whatever currency is listed using the exchange rate in B5. Press the = symbol to start the calculation. Type Sterling, press the asterisk (*) for multiplication, then use the mouse to select cell B5. Press Return to complete the calculation and make sure it is correct. Change the amount in B1 and the exchange rate in B5 to make sure the calculation automatically recalculates.

5. When you are satisfied the calculation in C5 is working properly, copy this cell to the other ones below it. To do this, first select cell C5. Position the mouse pointer over the bottom right corner of the cell (over the small black square) and wait for it to change to a thin black cross. When this happens, hold down the left button and move down the spreadsheet to copy the calculation into the cells below. Release the left button to stop copying.

6. Test your calculations by changing the amount in cell B1 and the various exchange rates. Use figures that are easy to check. Save your Excel file by clicking on the File menu and choosing Save. A Save As dialog box will appear. Enter a name for your Excel file and choose a location on your computer to store it. Click on the Save button and you will return to your spreadsheet. Save your file regularly. However, when you return to the File menu and choose Save, this dialog box will not appear, but the file will be saved.

7. Aside from converting British pounds to other currencies, you can also convert other currencies to British pounds. Select cell E4 and enter the title Amount in other currency. Move to cell F4 and enter the title Amount in £. Select cell F5, press the = symbol to start a calculation, select cell E5 (it will be empty), press the / symbol, then select cell B5 (the exchange rate) and press Return to complete the calculation.

8. Copy your calculation down column F (refer to the instructions in step 5 for copying) for the other currencies. Enter different amounts in column E under the heading Amount in other currency. Make sure the amount in British pounds is correct by entering easy-to-check figures. In the future, whenever exchange rates change, you can enter the new rates in the appropriate cells of your spreadsheet. Excel will automatically recalculate the currency conversions.

9. Add some colour to your spreadsheet. Select cell A4 (the Currency heading). Hold down the Shift key, then position the mouse pointer over the bottom right corner of your table (in column F) and click once. Your entire table will be selected (excluding the entries in A1 and B1. Click on the Format menu and choose AutoFormat. From the AutoFormat dialog box that appears, select a style of table you like, then click on OK. You will need to select a cell outside your table to see the colours applied. If you do not like the style of table, repeat this step, selecting the cells, and return to the AutoFormat dialog box.

➡ **Currency Data**

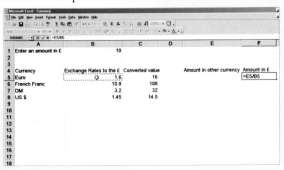

CREATE A CROSSWORD

Excel is not just useful for creating cash flow forecasts, balance sheets and other accounting procedures: it can also be used to create forms, invoices, floor plans and puzzles. The following two pages show you how to create a crossword. It may help to plan your crossword on paper before reading through the following steps.

1. Open Excel and a new workbook. Decide upon how many squares wide and tall your crossword will be. You will need to adjust the height and width of the cells you are going to use for your crossword, so select all the cells you want to use for your crossword table by holding down the left button and moving across them. Click on the Format menu, choose Row and select Height from the sub-menu. Enter the number 33 in the box that appears and click on OK. Return to the Format menu, select Column and choose Width from the sub-menu. Enter the number 5 and click on OK.

2. We're now going to remove the gridlines from all the cells, then add them to the crossword table in the next step. Click on the Tools menu and choose Options. From the dialog box that opens, make sure the View tab is selected and look for a tick box labelled Gridlines. Select the tick mark next to it to remove it, then click on OK. You will return to your spreadsheet where the gridlines will have been removed.

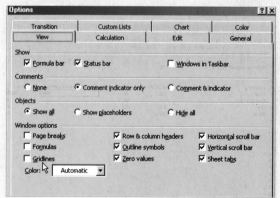

RIGHT: Excel can be used to create puzzles as well as worksheets.

3. Select the cells you want to use for your crossword table, then click on the Format menu and choose Cells. From the dialog box that opens, select the Border tab. Select a line style from the right. If you want to choose a different colour than black for your crossword table, click on the drop-down triangle to the right of Automatic and choose a colour. Finally, click on Outline and Inside to add lines to your crossword table, then click on OK to close this dialog box. Your crossword table will now have a grid.

4. Decide which cells of your crossword table need to be coloured in black. Select one of the cells to colour in, then click on the drop-down triangle to the right of the Fill Colour toolbar button (looks like a bucket, top right of the screen). If you cannot see the button, choose cells from the Format menu, click on the Patterns tab, then choose your colour. Select a suitable fill colour, such as black. The selected cell will now be coloured in. You can now select other cells in your crossword table and click on the bucket symbol for Fill colour to instantly colour them. To make it easier, choose multiple cells by holding down the Ctrl key as you select – you can then fill them in one go.

5. Enter all of the numbers for the down and across clues in your crossword. These numbers will probably look too big and in the wrong position in each square. When you have finished entering all the numbers, select them all by holding down the Ctrl key and typing 'A', selecting everything. Then click on the Format menu and choose Cells. From the dialog box that opens, select Font and add a tick mark to Superscript. Click on the Alignment tab and choose Top from the drop-down list under Vertical. Choose Left (indent) from the drop-down list under Horizontal. Click on OK.

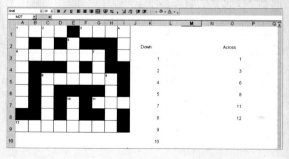

6. Enter the Down and Across numbers and corresponding clues for your crossword. You may want to display these to the right of or below your crossword table (depending on how it will be printed). Enter the numbers in separate cells and type each clue in one cell. The text for a clue will probably be wider than its cell, but this will not affect it on screen or when it is printed.

7. Save your crossword by clicking on the File menu and choosing Save. From the dialog box that appears, enter a name for your Excel file and choose a location on your computer to store it. Click on the Save button to close this dialog box and return to your crossword.

8. If you want to print your crossword, first click on the File menu and choose Print Preview. The screen will show you how your crossword will be printed. If you want to make any changes to the way it will be printed, click on the Setup button and select the different tabs to change the paper from landscape to portrait or to increase the size of the crossword. Click on OK to return to the print preview screen and see the changes you have made. When you are ready to print, click on the Print button at the top of the screen. A dialog box will open. Click on OK and wait for your printer to print out your crossword.

9. You may want to transfer your crossword to another program, especially if it is to be included in a newsletter which is being created in a publishing program, for example. To do this, select all of the cells for your crossword and the list of clues. Click on the Edit menu and choose Copy. Open the program and file you want to transfer the crossword to. You will need to paste the crossword in place. Most programs have an Edit menu with an option called paste. If not, hold down the Ctrl key and press V.

➡ *Colour, Patterns and Borders*

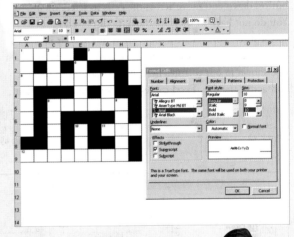

CREATE A SIMPLE CHART

Creating a chart in Excel can take just a couple of seconds, provided the data you want to use for it has already been entered into a spreadsheet. The following two pages show you how to create a chart using the spreadsheet created in the How-to guide for dividing up your bills.

1. Make sure the data you want to use for your chart is open in Excel. Using the mouse, select the headings and data you want to include in the chart (hold the left button down and move across the cells to select them). You do not have to select all the data displayed in a spreadsheet. For a chart to be created in Excel, it is best to make sure you have a properly organized table like the one shown in our pictures here, with headings to the left and across the top. Excel can easily understand the layout

of such data and produce a chart for you. Once you have selected your data, just press F11 on the keyboard and a chart will appear.

2. After creating your chart, you may notice your data has disappeared. The chart is displayed on a separate sheet (look at the sheet tabs at the bottom of the screen). You can modify this chart if you wish. For example, click on the Chart menu and choose Chart Type for a dialog box of different chart styles. Select a chart type from the list on the left, select a sub-type from the right, then preview your chart by clicking on the button labelled Press and Hold to View Sample. Click on OK to close the dialog box and change your chart to the one selected.

3. If you want to change the look of anything inside your chart (a bar, the gridlines, the plot area), position the

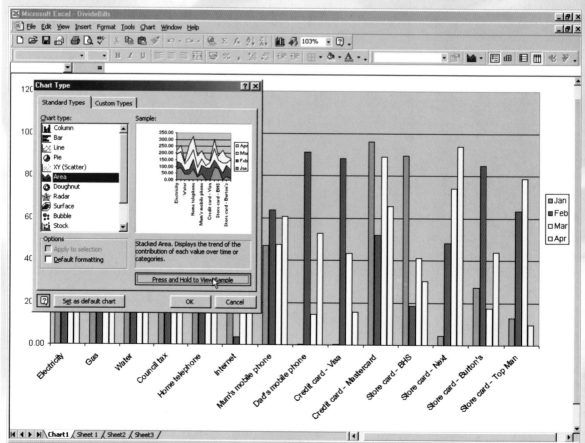

mouse pointer over the item you wish to change, then double-click. A Format dialog box will open, allowing you to make a number of changes. Click on OK to close the dialog box and apply the changes or Cancel to close the dialog box.

4. Return to the data selected in step 1 (click on the sheet tab at the bottom of the screen). Aside from creating a chart on a separate sheet, you can also create a chart and display it next to your data. To do this, select a section of your table starting at the top left corner (less data makes it easier to see the chart). Click on the Chart Wizard toolbar button (looks like a chart) or click on the Insert menu and choose Chart. From the Chart Wizard dialog box that appears, choose a type of chart you would like to produce (same dialog box as outlined in step 2), then click on Next.

5. Step 2 of the Chart Wizard dialog box allows you to display your data in rows or columns. To see which one is best, click on the Rows option, then the Columns option, and look at the preview screen for your chart. Click on Next to go to step 3 of the Chart Wizard. Here you can enter titles for the chart, add gridlines, a legend (key for the colours used), labels and more. Click on the different tabs along the top of the dialog box and choose the different options. A preview of your chart will show you what your chart will look like.

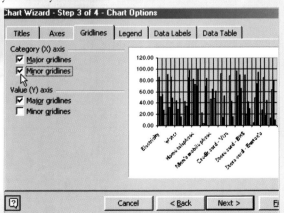

6. Click on Next when you have finished with step 3 of the Chart Wizard dialog box. The final step asks you if you want to display the chart on a new sheet or as an

object in the current sheet. Choose the latter option and click on Finish. Your chart will appear alongside your data. You can move the chart to a different position by hovering the mouse pointer in a white space inside it, then holding down the left button and moving the mouse. You can also increase or reduce the width and height of the chart. Make sure the chart is selected, then position the mouse pointer over one of the black squares around it. When the mouse changes to a double-headed arrow, hold down the left button and move the mouse pointer to resize the chart. Release the left button to stop resizing.

7. To return to your data, select a cell inside your spreadsheet. The chart will be deselected. If you need to return to your chart and edit it, click inside it. If you want to delete it, press Delete on the keyboard after selecting it.

8. If you want to create a chart using different sections of data (March and July's figures, for example), first make sure you select the column of titles for the chart (in column A in our example). Then hold down the Ctrl key and select the additional blocks of cells to be included in your chart. By holding down the Ctrl key, separate blocks of cells can be selected, but if you make a mistake, start again to avoid confusing Excel. When you have selected your cells, repeat the steps for creating a chart.

➡ *Charts*

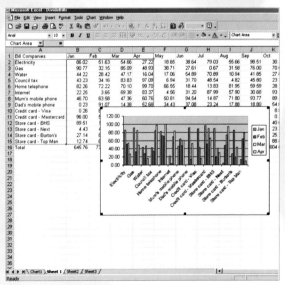

CURRENCY DATA

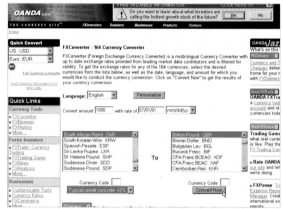

Several web sites offer exchange rates, including *www.FT.com*. The BBC offers this data in a particularly friendly fashion, at: *news.bbc.co.uk/hi/english /business/market_data/default.stm* (or follow links from the BBC News homepage at *news.bbc.co.uk*. Click on 'Business' at the list of sections on the left-hand side, then 'Market Data' in the grey box that then appears in the same place on the new page).

The BBC page shows the exchange rates between the pound, euro, US dollar and yen. Bear in mind that these are the rates paid by currency dealers exchanging millions – as a tourist, you will get less of the currency you are

ABOVE: There are web sites with currency conversion information.

buying. For rates within Europe, click on the words 'Euro Rates'; for others, click on 'World Currencies'. Rates are given for both the pound and the US dollar. 'Tourist Rates' shows Thomas Cook's prices for 28 currencies.

It might also be useful to get hold of historic exchange rates, or those for more obscure currencies. A site holding a huge amount of data is *www.oanda.com/convert/classic*. This US site holds data on 164 currencies, along with several precious metals, from the start of 1990. As a result, it's a good choice for more complicated work.

Let's say, for your accounts, you wanted to check how much your UK credit card should have charged you for a purchase of 1,000 South African rand, on 1 July 2000. Type the amount into the box following the words 'Convert amount', then change the date. This normally uses the US format of month, day, year, but you can change this using the drop-down menu on the right of this line. If you stick to the American format, you would type '07/01/01'.

Currencies are listed by country name: scroll down to 'South African Rand' and click on it so it is highlighted. The pound is listed as 'British Pound' in the box on the right, or save time by typing 'GBP' into the 'Currency Code' box under the right-hand list.

Under this section, there is a pull-down menu set to 'Interbank Rate'. Click on this and choose 'Typical credit card rate: +2%'. Several UK banks charge more, but this will give you a good idea.

Click on the grey 'Convert Now' button at the bottom-right of this form. The results tell you that, on Sunday July 1 2001, 1,000 rand will have cost you

£89.548. Helpfully, you also get the 'reverse' calculation (that £1,000 on a South African credit card would have cost 11,618 rand), in case you mixed up the order of the currencies.

➠ *Convert to other Currencies*

CURRENCY FORMATS

Displaying monetary values. One of the most common formats for numeric values is the currency format. This automatically inserts a £ sign in front of the number, commas to separate thousands and two decimal places. Sterling is normally the default currency format but it can be changed if required.

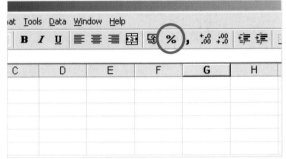

When entering a monetary value, just enter the raw number: it is much quicker to get Excel to format the cell for you. Type the number and click on the Tick button to enter it in the cell. If you want to format an existing number, just click on its cell. Then click on the Currency button on the Formatting toolbar (as illustrated above). If the Formatting toolbar is not displayed, right-click on the current toolbar, deselect it and select Formatting instead. Excel will automatically format the number for currency. For example, the number 1234.567 will display as £1,234.57.

To choose a different format, access the Format menu and select the Cells option. Alternatively, click the right mouse button and select Format Cells. Click the Number tab and select Currency from the list of formats.

There are three available options displayed to the right of the dialog box:

1. The Decimal Places option enables you to define the number of decimal places you want to display-normally this will be 2.

2. The Symbol option enables you to choose the currency symbol you require. You can use different symbols on the same sheet – but be aware that Excel will not convert different currencies automatically. In other words £100 added to $100 will come to 200 – Excel won't recognize that it's adding incompatible units.

3. The Negative Numbers option provides several different ways to display negative numbers. Some display in red to show up more easily on your spreadsheet.

When you have made your selection, click the OK button to confirm.

If you find the values appear as hash characters (######), Excel is letting you know that the column is not wide enough to display the number. You can either increase the column width manually or double-click on the right-hand side of the column heading to use the Auto Fit feature which automatically adjusts the column to the optimum width.

The Accountancy format also displays the currency symbol, commas to separate thousands and allows you to select the required number of decimal places. The main difference between the Currency and Accountancy formats involves the alignment of the currency symbol. With the Currency format the £ will be displayed

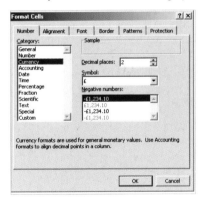

adjacent to the first digit whereas with Accountancy the £ symbols will be aligned, one under another. This may result in a gap between the symbol and first digit.

➠ *Changing Column and Row Size, Currency Data, Formatting, The Euro*

CUTTING AND PASTING

Excel is part of the Microsoft Office Suite of applications. The applications are integrated in such a way that it is easy to move between them and combine information from multiple applications into one or more documents. Documents which contain information from more than one source are sometimes referred to as compound documents.

Several techniques are employed to transfer or copy data into another application.

The first and simplest method of transferring data is via the clipboard. The Office clipboard is a temporary storage area, shared by Office programs, and designed to hold up to 12 pieces of information in memory at any one time. The idea is to place items in the clipboard using the Cut or Copy commands and then switch to another area of the same document, another document in the same application or another application entirely, and paste the contents. Information will be held on the clipboard until you close all Office applications.

To view the clipboard and its contents, click the View menu, select the Toolbars option and then Clipboard. If the clipboard is not available, it is likely that the application does not allow you to copy, paste or view multiple items.

With the clipboard open, you can copy an item into the clipboard by selecting the item in the worksheet and clicking the Copy button in the Clipboard toolbar. To paste an individual item into the current document, click any visible item in the clipboard. To paste the entire contents of the clipboard, Click the Paste All button. If you select the Paste command from the Edit menu, Excel will insert the most recently pasted clipboard item. If you have not pasted any items from the clipboard, Excel will insert the last clipboard item in the document.

When you paste an item into another application, the receiving application will make a judgement as to what type of data is being pasted and paste it in such a way that it can be usefully edited. For example, Excel worksheet data and Access database records will be pasted into Word as tables. Conversely, a Word table will be pasted into separate columns of an Excel worksheet.

To control the way in which data is pasted, click the Edit menu and select the Paste Special command. The Paste Special dialog box will be displayed. Choices include pasting the data with its original formatting, pasting data without formatting and pasting data as HTML code.

The main limitation of using the Paste command is that there is no connection between the original (source) document and the document into which it was pasted (the destination document).

If you want to maintain links between the source and destination file, or be able to make enhancements using the functionality of the application in which an object was created, you will need to make use of Object Linking and Embedding (OLE) technologies.

You can create a link to an Excel file from within another application (known as a remote reference). Although you will be able to see the linked information in the destination file, the destination file only stores a shortcut to the file location. The source of the information will remain stored with the source file. The advantages of creating links are twofold: changes made to the source file will be updated in all linked destination files and the size of the destination file will not be significantly increased because the data is stored elsewhere. For example, you can insert a link to an Excel chart into a Word document. The data from which the chart was created will remain in the original Excel workbook.

To create a link, click the Insert menu followed by Object. Select the Create from File tab and click the Link to File button. Alternatively, copy the information and use the Paste Special command. Choose Microsoft Excel Worksheet Object in the As box and click the Paste Link button.

You can edit an object by double-clicking. The application, in which the object was created, will open. If you make changes to the source data, the object will be updated in the destination file. If you move the source file, the link will be broken.

As an alternative to linking, you can choose to physically embed a copy of the data in the destination file. The embedded object will have no link to the original source and will not be updated if changes to the source file are made. However, provided that you have a program installed which can give you the functionality to make changes to the object, you can double-click the object to edit it.

BELOW: Documents created in Excel can be pasted into other Office applications.

A file containing the embedded object can be transferred to another location entirely and there is no need to maintain or update links. The main disadvantage of embedding is that the size of the destination file will be increased.

To embed an object, click the Insert menu, select the Object option and then the Create from File tab. Alternatively, in the Paste Special dialog box, click the Paste button.

➧ *Keeping Cells Still, Toolbars, Using Cells on other Pages*

CUTTING AND PASTING WITHIN EXCEL

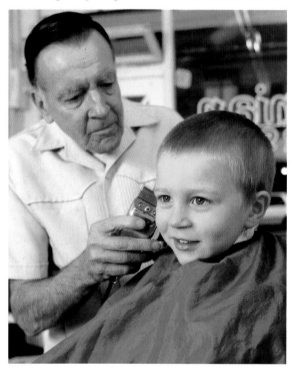

Moving the contents of cells. When designing a worksheet from scratch or making changes to an existing worksheet it is useful to be able to move things around. Excel provides buttons on the Standard toolbar for cutting and pasting the contents of cells. You can use these buttons in the confidence that Excel will automatically redefine any formulas or functions that are affected.

If you cut a value or formula from a cell and paste it into a different cell, you are in fact moving the content of that cell. The data is cut from the cell and held in the Windows clipboard until it is pasted back into another cell. You can also choose to Copy cells, which leaves the originals in place.

To cut the contents from a cell, select the cell and click on the Cut button ✂ on the Standard toolbar. Alternatively, select the cell, click the right mouse button and select the option from the shortcut menu or from the Edit menu. The cut cell will be displayed with a moving dashed line around it, known as a marquee. Once the cut button has been clicked the Paste button changes from grey to black 📋 making it active . Select the cell where you want to move to and click the Paste button. Care should be taken as the Paste command will automatically overwrite any data already in the destination range without giving a warning.

As an alternative to the clipboard, you can use the mouse to drag and drop cell contents. To do this, select the cell or cells you want to move. Move the mouse pointer to the cell frame so an arrow appears, hold down the left mouse button and drag the frame to the new position. To confirm, release the mouse button. To Copy rather than Cut, hold down the Ctrl key so a plus sign appears just by the arrow.

When you move a cell content, Excel will also transfer any formatting that is applied to that cell. If moving a cell formula, the cell references are changed automatically to be relative to their new destination. In the following example, numbers are typed into column B, formatted for currency and totalled using the SUM function. The table is then moved to column D. The formatting moves with the numbers and the function now references column D.

➡ *Cutting and Pasting outside Excel, Keeping Cells Still*

DATABASE FUNCTIONS

Excel provides a range of functions that can be used to analyze data that forms part of a list or database. To use these functions, data needs to be entered so that Excel recognizes it as a list or database. Do not leave any blank rows or columns within your database or list and make sure there is at least one empty row or column between the last data row/column and the rest of your worksheet.

The database functions, known collectively as the Dfunctions, all have the same three arguments, Dfunction(database,field,criteria).

The database argument identifies the range of cells that form your database or list. In general, a database is a series of related information that can be stored in consecutive rows and columns. Each row holds one record and the columns represent the fields. The first row of a database will usually contain the field names.

FAR LEFT: Unlike hair, information cut from Excel can always be pasted back.
BELOW LEFT: Excel users can analyze data using a variety of functions.

The field argument identifies the column that is to be used by the function. The argument can either be the name of the field (as entered in the first row of the table) or a number representing the position of the column within the database. For example, if the Bonus field is to be used within the function which is the sixth column, the argument can be entered as "Bonus", the field name within double quotes, or as 6, the column number. The criteria argument identifies the range of cells containing the conditions for the function. The criteria range usually contains a copy of the column headings (field names) as the first row, with the conditions used by the function detailed in the rows below. The criteria range must contain at least one column heading (field name) with at least one cell below that field name. If you want to include all the records within the database simply leave the row(s) below the criteria range headings blank. It is a good idea to place your criteria range to the side or above your database. If you enter it below you may well have to keep moving it as you add extra records.

Several of the example functions include two data rows within the criteria range. This specifies an OR condition. The condition in the first OR second row must be met. If two or more conditions are included within the same row, this represents an AND condition. The first AND second condition must be met.

➡ *Functions, Paste Function Button*

DATA PROTECTION LAW AND YOU

The UK, along with the rest of the European Union, has tough laws controlling the protection of data. If you use Excel (or any other software) to store information about people – say, customers of a business or members of a society – you may need to register with the Information Commissioner and comply with the Data Protection Act of 1998.

If you're maintaining a Christmas list or address book for personal use, then you shouldn't worry, but if you run a business or organization that keeps customer records, you should register. You could be liable for a fine of several thousand pounds if you don't, as well as a demand that you stop processing data.

The law says you should collect and use personal data only for a set use, process this data lawfully and fairly, and delete the data when it is no longer useful for your stated purposes. You must also make efforts to keep your data secure. This is partly a case of employing computer security, such as encrypting data and using passwords. But it is also important to train other users of the data (such as staff) in the protection of personal data. For example, someone phoning up and claiming to be a data subject should not be taken at face value: their identity should be checked by calling them back at a previously given phone number, or by asking them to supply other pieces of personal data to check who they are.

To see why this is necessary, imagine you run a small hotel and use Excel to keep registration data. One of your staff takes a call from someone saying they are a guest's secretary, and could you pass on details of his bill? If your employee helpfully reels off the details – double room occupancy, room-service meals for two – you might just be providing the evidence for a divorce case. Regardless of the morality of your guest, they could then have a case against you for releasing their personal data.

Aside from requiring you to keep personal data secure, data protection law also gives various rights to 'data subjects', the technical name for those on whom data is held. Firstly, the data subjects can demand to see the data you hold on them: this is known as a 'subject access

RIGHT: The law is strictly enforced on issues of data protection.

request'. You must provide this data, with very few exceptions. You have 40 days to comply and can charge a fee of up to £10. Apart from providing a copy of the data, you must say why it is held and how it is used. (It is particularly important, however, that you check the data subject is who they say they are.) The data subject can demand that inaccurate data is changed, and you must comply.

You must also comply with a request to delete any data held for marketing purposes. This is a particularly bad area in which to make mistakes, as they are very obvious. Most people don't like junk mail and will be particularly annoyed if you send them marketing information when they have asked you not to. What's more, since the 1998 Data Protection Act came into force, it's also illegal. You need to tell data subjects that you hold information about them. If the data is general, this can often be covered in a general statement on your web site on how you use data – most big organizations, especially those with big online operations, will have examples on their sites.

But if any of the data you hold is of a 'sensitive' nature, such as concerning

health or religion, you also need to ask for permission before processing. This is likely to apply to employee data such as sick days taken) – many companies include a clause giving permission for data-processing in their terms and conditions of employment.

The best advice is to talk to the Information Commissioner's Office. This organization will help you find out if you need to register, and what you need to do to comply with the law. It has so far been more interested in helping organizations comply than in prosecuting those who do not. When the office receives a complaint, its first response is usually to attempt to solve the problem through arbitration. Bear in mind that most organizations receive very few subject access requests. They are mainly aimed at financial institutions such as credit agencies, banks and building societies. And if you do get asked, simply remember that personal data is seen as belonging to the person it describes. If you comply with that person's wishes, you can't go too far wrong.

And there are advantages: even if you have to do some work to comply with these laws, you can also use them yourself. If you want to be removed from a mailing list or see data held on you anywhere in Europe, you have that right.

The Information Commissioner's Office can be contacted at *www.dataprotection.gov.uk* or on 01625 545700. Note that this article is not a definitive statement of the law: for this, individuals and organizations should consult a competent solicitor.

ABOVE: Data concerning health is 'sensitive' and should be handled with care.

DATE AND TIME FORMATS

Displaying the date and time. When entering a date or time into your worksheet you can type it using any one of the accepted Excel formats. Alternatively, you can enter it in its simplest form and then select a preferred format. Excel also provides a handy tool that will produce a whole series of dates if you type in the start date.

RIGHT: Date and time functions have come a long way since the days of the Aztecs.

However you type a date in Excel it will be stored as a number. To be precise it will be stored as the number of days that have lapsed between 1st January 1900 and the date you have entered. It does this so that it can perform calculations based on dates. For example, if you have entered the date an employee started with your company in one cell and the current date in another cell, Excel will be able to calculate the amount of time the employee has worked for you simply by subtracting one value from the other. This resulting value will be displayed in days but there are Excel functions available to convert this number to weeks, months or years.

The simplest way to enter a date is as mm/dd/yy. To change the format, access the Format menu and select the Cells option. Alternatively, click the right mouse button and select Format Cells. Click the Number tab and select Date from the list of formats. The range of available formats is displayed to the right of the dialog box. Make your selection and click the OK button.

Displaying a time calls for a similar process. Type the time in the simplest format, hh:mm. To change the format, select Cells from the Format menu and click the Number tab. Select Time from the list of formats. The range of available formats is displayed to the right of the dialog box. Make your selection and click the OK button. Again, Excel stores the time as a number so that it can calculate the duration between time values.

On occasion, you may need to enter dates as a series. For example, you may want to produce a worksheet that contains data for every day of the month. Rather than typing an entry for every day of the month as column headings, just type the first day of the month. Highlight this cell and approximately 30 blank cells to the right. Select the Edit menu and select Fill. Select Series and make sure the Day button is checked. Click on the OK button. Instantly you should have an entire month's worth of dates.

➠ *Number Formats (Other)*

DATE AND TIME FUNCTIONS

Date and time functions enable you to work with date and time values in your worksheet displaying full or part information. They also provide tools for analyzing and calculating date and time values.

One of the most useful functions is DATE(year,month,day), here 'year' represents a number from 1900 to 9999, 'month' represents a number corresponding to the month of the year (1 to 12) and 'day' represents a number corresponding to the day of the month (1 to 31).

Excel stores the date as a serial number. The serial number normally represents the number of days that have lapsed between 1 January 1900 and the date you have entered, although the software can also make 1904 its starting point – this is the default for Mac users. To find the serial number for the current date and time, use the NOW() function. To display just the current date, use TODAY(). These functions return the serial number of the current date and time based on your computer's internal clock.

The serial number as it stands is not particularly meaningful, so Excel formats the number to represent a date. There are also a number of functions available to display elements of the date and time, such as the month, year, hour or minute.

	A	B	C	D	E	F
1		Current date:	December 19, 2001			
2		Current Time:	12:00:51 PM			
3						
4		Function	Returns			
5						
6		=NOW()	19/12/2001 12:00			
7		=TODAY()	19/12/2001			
8		=MONTH(NOW())	12			
9		=DAY(NOW())	19			
10		=YEAR(NOW())	2001			
11		=HOUR(NOW())	12			
12		=MINUTE(NOW())	0			
13		=SECOND(NOW())	51			
14		=WEEKDAY(NOW())	4			
15		=VLOOKUP(WEEKDAY(NOW()),B17:C23,2)	Wednesday			
16						
17			1 Sunday			
18			2 Monday	<-- Lookup Table B17:C23		
19			3 Tuesday			
20			4 Wednesday			
21			5 Thursday			
22			6 Friday			
23			7 Saturday			
24						

In these examples, the functions take the value generated by the NOW function and display the appropriate part of the date or time. The WEEKDAY function normally displays the day of the week as a number between 1 and 7 with 1 representing Sunday through to 7 as Saturday. (There are other options available.) To display the actual day of the week, you will need to create a lookup table to store the numbers and the corresponding days of the week. The WEEKDAY function can then be incorporated within the VLOOKUP function to display the actual day.

Excel stores dates as serial numbers so that it can perform calculations based on dates and times. For instance, you may want to find the number of days between two dates or the number of days lapsed since a given date. To calculate the number of days until Christmas, you can enter a function that takes the date for Christmas day, converts it to a serial number and subtracts the current date as a serial number. The function =DATE(2002,12,25)-TODAY() will return an integer value representing the number of days between the two dates.

➡ *Date and Time Formats, Functions, Paste Function Button*

DELETING DATA AND LINES

Removing cells and cell content. When deleting in Excel, it is important to differentiate between deleting the data within a cell and the cell itself. The deletion of data does not change the structure of the sheet, whereas removing cells alters the order of cells and can have repercussions.

To remove the content of a cell or group of cells, select the cells and press the Delete key on the keyboard. Using the Delete key removes the content of the cell but does not remove any formatting that has been applied to the cell. For example, if the cell has been formatted for Currency and Bold, these formats will remain and be applied to any data subsequently entered in that cell.

If you want more control when removing cell content, access the Edit menu and select the Clear option. A sub-menu is displayed providing four options:

- The All option will clear everything from the cell including values, formula and formatting.
- The Formats options will clear all formatting assigned to the cell but will leave all values and formula.
- The Contents option has the same effect as pressing the Delete key. The contents will be cleared but the formatting will remain.
- The Comments option will clear the comment associated with the cell (if there is one) but will have no effect on data or formatting.

To clear the cell, click on the most appropriate option. Excel will carry out the deletion without warning, so make sure you are not deleting information that is referenced elsewhere in your worksheet. If you make a mistake you can use the Undo option from the Edit menu, or use the keyboard shortcut, Ctrl+Z.

If you want to clear only part of an entry within a cell, double-click on the cell and use the Delete key to remove the part you no longer need from the Formula bar. To confirm, either click on the Tick button or press the Enter key.

ABOVE RIGHT: Deleting a part of your work may alter its appearance.
FAR RIGHT: When deleting data it is important not to throw anything away by mistake.

Deleting a cell rather than the contents of the cell is slightly more tricky. You have to remember that deleting one or more cells will alter the entire structure of the table.

To delete one or more cells, select the cell or range of cells, access the Edit menu and select the Delete option. The Delete dialog box is displayed, providing four options. By selecting an option, you are telling Excel how to close the gap that will be created once the cells have been removed.

- The Shift cells left option button will drag the cell located to the right of the empty cell into the place of the empty cell. All adjacent cells will move with it. In other words, the gap will be closed by the cells to the right of the empty cell moving to the left.
- The Shift cells up button will move all the cells below the empty cell up one.
- The Entire row option will remove the row containing the selected cell. If more than one cell in a column is selected, several rows will be removed. The rows below will move up to close the space.
- The Entire column option will remove the column containing the selected cell. If more than one cell in a row is selected, several columns will be removed. The columns to the right will move across to the left to close the gap.

menu. The Delete dialog box does not appear because Excel assumes that you want to delete the selected row or column. You can also use this method for deleting multiple columns or rows, by selecting a range of columns or rows before selecting the Delete option from the Edit menu.

You must take care with all these commands because Excel will not warn you if you are likely to delete values or formulae that are referenced in other, remaining cells. For example, if you remove a row you must be sure that the values or formulae held within the cells in that row are not used for calculations elsewhere in the sheet. Remember, if you make a mistake you can use the keyboard shortcut, Ctrl+Z, to undo the deletion.

When Excel shifts cells upwards or to the left, it automatically adapts any formula that is affected by the change. Let's take the case where you have a row of numbers that are totalled using the SUM function, for example =SUM(A5:F5). The formula references the row number as row 5. If the row above is removed, the current row, row 5, will become row 4, replacing the deleted row 4. The formula will automatically be changed to read =SUM(A4:F4).

➡ *Cutting and Pasting Within Excel, Undo*

Another way to remove a column or row is to select the entire row or column by clicking on the column or row heading. Select the Delete option from the Edit

DIVIDE UP YOUR BILLS

If you are sharing a flat or a house, you can resolve the disputes over who has paid what with an Excel spreadsheet. The following instructions show how to list what has been spent by two people (for bills and household items), then work out who has spent the most and how much is owed to this person to break even.

1. Using a new workbook in Excel, select cell A1 and enter the word Item. Enter the names of the two people sharing the costs in cells B1 and C1. Now enter the different items each person has bought (down column A) and the cost in column B or C (depending on who has paid for it). You may need to increase the width of column A. To do this, position the mouse pointer in between the column headings A and B and wait for it to change to a cross with two horizontal arrows. Hold down the left mouse button and move to the right to stretch column A. Release the left button to stop widening this column.

ABOVE: Whatever your occupation, you will need to work out the best way to pay your bills.

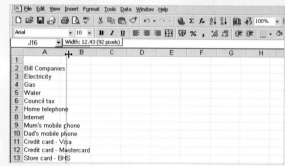

2. Select cells B2 to C16 by positioning the mouse pointer inside B2, holding down the left button, then moving down to C16. When the cells have been selected release the left button. Click on the Format menu and choose Cells. From the dialog box that appears, make sure the Number tab is selected. Choose Currency from the Category list and make sure the number of decimal places is set to 2. Make sure the £ sign is displayed under symbol (click on the drop-down triangle and choose it from the list if not). Click on OK to close this dialog box and return to your spreadsheet. Any numbers in the selected cells will now be displayed with a £ sign and two decimal places.

3. Select cell A15 and enter the title Total Spent. To create a total calculation for the first person, select cell B15 and click on the AutoSum toolbar button (looks like a Greek S symbol). The words =SUM() will appear on the screen. Use the mouse to select all of the cells from B2 to B14, then press Return on the keyboard. Repeat this step for creating a total calculation for the second person (in column C) in cell C15. Save your spreadsheet by clicking on the File menu and choosing Save. A Save As dialog box will appear. Enter a name for your Excel file and choose a location to save it in. Click on Save to return to your spreadsheet.

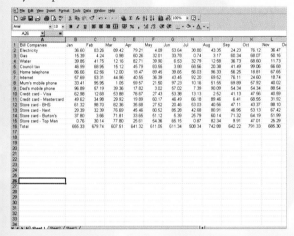

4. Test the total calculations created in step 3. Select cells B2 to B14, then look at the bottom of the screen (in the grey section) for the words Sum= followed by a total figure. This should be the same as the total figure in cell B15. If it's not, repeat step 3 for creating the SUM calculation. If a different word is displayed here (e.g. Average), right click on it and choose Sum from the menu that appears.

5. Select cell A16 and enter the title Money owed. We are now going to work out if the person in column B has spent more than the person in column C and how much is owed to him/her. Select cell B16 and click on the Paste Function toolbar button (has the letters fx on it). From the Paste Function dialog box that appears, select Logical from the Function category list on the left. Select IF from the Function name list on the right. Click on OK and proceed to the next step.

6. A grey box will appear at the top left of the screen with the word IF in the left corner. You can move this box to another part of the screen by positioning the mouse pointer inside it, holding down the left button, then moving the mouse. Release the left button to stop moving the box. Click inside the white rectangle next to Logical_test. Type B15>C15. This will be a check to see if the person in column B has spent more than the person in column C.

7. Click inside the white rectangle next to Value_if_true. We are going to create a calculation to work out how much money will be owed to the person in column B if he/she has spent the most. Type the calculation (B15-C15)/2. This will work out the difference between what each person has spent and halve the amount to calculate how much money is owed. Click inside the white rectangle next to Value_if_false and enter the number 0. Click on OK to complete this calculation and return to your spreadsheet.

8. Select cell C16 and repeat steps 6 and 7 entering C15>B15 for the Logical_test, (C15-B15)/2 for the Value_if_true and zero for Value_if_false. Click on OK to complete the calculation. Test the calculations created by entering different amounts spent to ensure one person has spent more than the other. Excel will automatically calculate how much each person has spent and how much is owed to the person who has spent the most.

➡ *SUMming up*

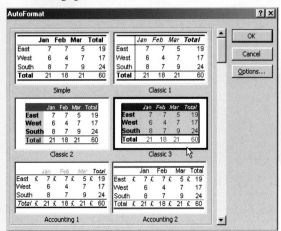

DO I NEED TO UPGRADE EXCEL?

Horses for courses. Whether you should upgrade your current version of Excel depends very much on what you use Excel for. Every new release brings more

ABOVE: The older versions of Excel provide enough facilities for most users.
RIGHT: Upgrading your version of Excel could be a costly option.

functionality and sophistication, often with the requirement for more memory and disk space. The question is: do you need and will you use the new features, and is it worth the additional cost of upgrading the Excel software and possibly your PC?

A new, enhanced version of the Microsoft Office suite, incorporating Microsoft Excel, is usually released every two years. Since 1995 there have been four releases of Excel: Excel 95, Excel 97, Excel 2000, and most recently, Excel 2002.

Upgrading can be an expensive exercise. Not only will you need to pay the cost of upgrading the Excel program, you may also find you need to upgrade your PC to ensure it meets the minimum specification for the new release of Excel. With each successive release, more disk space is required to store the program and in many cases a faster machine is needed to maintain the current level of performance. You may find your existing specification is adequate to run a new version, or you may be able to achieve the specification relatively cheaply by adding more memory or increasing the disk size. If you get to the point where you need to purchase a new computer to run a new release, you will have to weigh up the benefits very carefully.

In general, it is advisable not to lag too far behind the most recent release. If your version of Excel is more than two releases before the current one, you may find it difficult to get help and support. Microsoft usually only supports the two previous versions of software and it will stop providing bug fixes and product enhancements for earlier versions.

You may also encounter difficulties if you need to deal with files created by users who have a more up-to-date version of the software. Although Excel files are upward-compatible, this is not always the case if files are saved and used with an earlier version of Excel. For example, if you create a file using Excel 97 and forward it to someone with Excel 2000, all functionality will be maintained. However, if a file is created using Excel 2000, incorporating some of the new features supported by that version, these features will be lost when opened in the earlier version of the product. This can become a serious issue for large organizations where there may be several releases of Excel in use. By not keeping in step and maintaining a standard within the organization, functionality may be lost as files are transferred to different machines.

Excel 97 provides the majority of the features and functions available with the later versions and remains an adequate release for most users of Excel.

The latest two versions of Excel, 2000 and 2002, have been enhanced in line with developments in web integration and collaboration.

Excel 2000 was introduced at a time when organizations were starting to make information widely available to employees online. This trend led Microsoft to develop Excel 2000 to incorporate a variety of new features, designed to help users collaborate and share information via the Web and to perform more extensive analysis on their data. By enabling users to easily create and share web documents, Excel content is universally viewable by anyone with a browser. Users can create documents in Excel 2000, save them as HTML and yet still re-open and enhance them using Excel. The process of publishing an Excel spreadsheet to the Web has been simplified.

Office XP was launched in late 2001 to provide more effective use of the Web and Office together. Excel 2002 (sometimes referred to as Excel 9) forms part of Office XP and is an important upgrade for Internet collaboration. This latest release of Excel concentrates on enhancements to the way it handles web-based data and also includes more general enhancements such as improved facilities for editing, checking and auditing formulae.

So, to recap, if you are an independent user of Excel you will probably find Excel 97 is more than adequate for your needs. If you are sharing files with others, either across an Intranet or the Web, you will probably benefit from the enhancements available with the later versions. In general, before you upgrade it is worth doing your homework. Find out what new features are available with the product and make sure your PC can run the software at an acceptable level of performance. It can be extremely frustrating if you upgrade and find that Excel runs much more slowly than before and all the new features are irrelevant for your purposes. If your PC can cope with the specifications for the upgrade (or it is time for a new machine anyway!) and you think you will use the new features, then it is definitely worth upgrading. You can then be assured of receiving support and enhancements and will have no problems sharing files with other users.

➧ *Collaboration*

DO YOUR MATHS HOMEWORK

You can use Excel to work out a variety of mathematical calculations, from averages to standard deviation. The following two pages cover trigonometry and how to calculate the sine, cosine and tangent of an angle.

1. Using a new workbook in Excel, select cell A1 and enter the word Angle. In cells B1 to E1 enter the headings, Radians, Sin, Cos, Tan. You may want to increase the width of some of the columns. To do this, position the mouse pointer in between the column headings (the letters in grey) and wait for it to change to a cross with two horizontal arrows. Hold down the left mouse button and move to the right to stretch the column on the left. Release the left button to stop widening the column.

2. Select cell A2 (under the Angle heading) and enter the value 45. To calculate the sine, cosine or tangent of an angle, we need first to convert the angle to radians. Select cell B2 and click on the Paste Function toolbar button

(has the letters fx on it). A Paste Function dialog box will appear. Select Math and Trig from the list on the left. Scroll down the list on the right (alphabetically sorted) to the word Radians and select it. Click on OK.

3. A large grey box will appear at the top left of the spreadsheet. Position the mouse pointer inside the grey box, hold down the left button and move the box further down the screen, so you can see rows 1 and 2 of your spreadsheet. Click inside the white rectangle labelled Angle (in the grey box), then select cell A2. Click on OK to close the grey box and complete the calculation for converting degrees to radians.

4. Select cell C2 for calculating the sine of the angle. Click on the Paste Function toolbar button (fx symbol). From the dialog box that appears, make sure Math and Trig is selected on the left, then scroll down to find SIN on the right. Select it, then click on OK. A grey box similar to the one in step 3 will appear. Move it out of the way of rows 1 and 2, click inside a white rectangle labelled Number, then select cell B2 (the Radians calculation). Click on OK to complete the calculation and display the sine of the angle in cell A2.

5. To calculate the cosine of the angle in A2, select cell D2 and repeat step 4, choosing the word COS from the list on the right in the Paste Function dialog box. To calculate the tangent of the angle in cell A2, repeat the same procedures, but choose the word TAN from the list in the Paste Function dialog box. For both calculations, always select the radians value in cell B2.

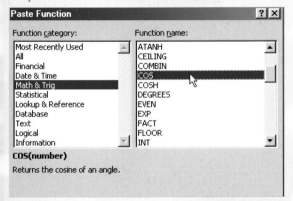

6. Save your Excel file by clicking on the File menu and choosing Save. From the Save As dialog box that appears, enter a name for your file, choose a location on your computer to store it, then click on Save. To regularly save your Excel file, either return to the File menu and choose Save or click on the Save toolbar button (looks like a brown floppy disk, top left of the screen).

7. Test your trigonometry calculations by changing the angle in cell A2. After entering a new value (press Return to enter it), the calculation for radians, sine, cosine and tangent should all automatically change. To make sure all the trig-functions are working properly, an angle of 45 returns a sine, a cosine of 0.707107 and a tangent of 1.

LEFT: You can use Excel to help with your homework.

8. If you need to find the sine, cosine and tangent of an angle to a specific number of decimal places, select cells C2 to E2 by holding down the left button and moving across them. Then select the Format menu and choose Cells. From the dialog box that appears, make sure the grey Number tab is selected at the top left, then select Number from the Category list on the left. Look at the right side of the dialog box for the label Decimal places. Click on the small up or down arrows to adjust the number of decimal places you need to display. Click on OK to close this dialog box and return to your spreadsheet.

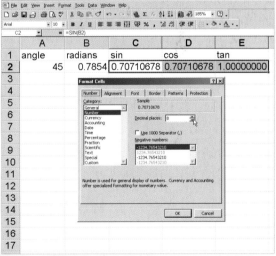

9. Add some colour to your table of trigonometry calculations. Position the mouse pointer inside cell A1, hold down the left button, then move down and across to cell E2. All of the cells in this range will be selected. Release the left button, then click on the Format menu and choose AutoFormat. A dialog box will appear with a list of formats, which can be applied to your table. Select any of the table formats listed (you can scroll down to see more). Click on OK to close this dialog box and add the formatting to your own table. You will need to select a cell outside the table to see the colouring.

➡ *Get Help with Maths Homework, Mathematical and Trigonometrical Functions*

DRAWING AND GRAPHICS

Build an impressive worksheet by making use of drawing and graphics objects. Excel comes with a range of options for inserting and customizing lines, shapes, text and clip art.

Display the drawing toolbar by selecting the Drawing button on the Standard toolbar or by clicking the View menu and selecting the Toolbars option followed by Drawing. To insert a drawing object, simply click the tool that you want to use, click on the worksheet and drag the mouse until you have an object the size and shape that you

want. If you want to insert more than one object at a time, double-click on the tool in the toolbar to keep it selected.

It is often difficult to drag an object in proportion. This can be achieved by holding down the Shift key while dragging. Hold down the Shift key while using the rectangle tool to create a square and while using the oval tool to create a circle. Lines or arrows will be drawn perfectly straight. Use the Shift key with AutoShapes and they will conform to a pre-set height to width ratio. The Alt key also performs a useful function. Hold the Alt key down while drawing, and an object will automatically be aligned to the nearest gridlines.

If you want to alter the size and shape of an object or apply formatting options to enhance its appearance, first select the object. Handles will appear around the object border. To alter the size, position the mouse over one of the handles. The mouse pointer will change to a double-headed arrow. You can then drag to increase or decrease the boundary. To move an object, point the mouse into the selected object. The mouse will change to a set of crosshairs. Click and drag to reposition.

You can select multiple objects by holding down the Shift key as you click each one in turn. You can also click the Select Objects pointer on the toolbar and then click and drag an area of the worksheet containing the objects to be selected. To do this, point into the worksheet above and to the left of the first object to be selected. A dotted rectangle appears. Hold the mouse down and drag below and to the right of the last object. All selected objects will display handles and changes made will be applied to all. You may also find it easier to make changes to several objects at the same time if you group them together. Select Group from the Draw menu and the selected objects will be treated as one object. You will now see one set of handles around

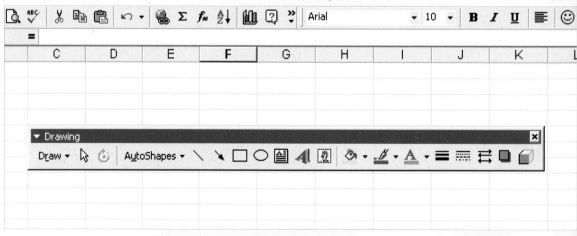

all of the objects. You can make changes to them as one object and then ungroup them again if you wish.

When several objects are placed on a worksheet they are set down in layers, with the most recently created object in front. To change the order, select the object and click the Draw menu on the Drawing toolbar. Select Order. You can choose to send the object backwards or forwards one step at a time or straight to the back or front of a stack of objects.

As you can see from the toolbar, there are many different types of objects which can be used to enhance a worksheet or chart. Text boxes offer a particularly useful way to insert text such as titles, captions, labels or notes. Text boxes are not tied to a particular cell and can be moved around. Select the Text Box icon from the Drawing toolbar. Click anywhere on the worksheet and drag the required shape and size. Don't worry if the dimensions are incorrect. Just type and the text box will expand to fit.

The AutoShapes menu invites you to choose from a set of pre-drawn shapes. Among the AutoShapes you will find a variety of stars and banners, callouts, flowchart shapes and arrows. You can create an AutoShape of your own dimensions or click on the worksheet, and Excel will insert an AutoShape with predefined measurements.

To add text to an AutoShape, draw and select the shape and then right-click. Choose Add Text from the pop-up menu. The insertion point will appear in the centre of the shape. Begin typing. Callout AutoShapes are text boxes with a pointer area.

FAR LEFT: Spreadsheets can be made more impressive with the use of graphics. BELOW: Paintings can be scanned and saved as objects which can be inserted into Excel documents.

When you draw a callout, the text insertion point will automatically appear inside the shape. To change text position, select the shape, select AutoShape or Text Box from the Format menu, and experiment with the options available under the Alignment tab.

WordArt is a tool given to produce some cleverly defined text formats. In the WordArt gallery you will see sample text. Choose a style and in the Edit WordArt Text dialog box enter the text to be formatted. If you click a piece of WordArt, the WordArt toolbar will be displayed. Through this toolbar you can control colour, size, shape, letter height, spacing and rotation.

To format any object, double-click the object and select options from the Format Object dialog box.

➠ *Colour, Patterns and Borders, Fonts, Inserting Graphics and Clips, Text Positioning*

E-MAILING SPREADSHEETS

Until recently, sending a copy of a workbook to a friend, colleague or client could be a fairly time-intensive task. It typically involved making a copy available on a network or copying a file to floppy disk and posting it. E-mail (electronic mail) has made it possible for documents to be distributed in just a few keystrokes.

You can e-mail an entire workbook, individual worksheets, charts and pivot tables. You can choose to send an individual copy or distribute to a group. There are two ways to send an Excel file. The first is to open your e-mail application, create the main body of the e-mail, attach an Excel file and send. The second option is to create an attachment from within Excel.

Select the File menu and then the Send option. If you want to send a workbook in its entirety, choose the Mail Recipient (as Attachment) option. Excel will launch your e-mail application and attach the current workbook. All that remains is for you to address the mail. Rather than attach an entire workbook you can send just the current sheet or a selection

from it, a chart or a pivot table or similar. To do this, select the first Mail Recipient option. This will allow you to insert the contents of the current worksheet into the body of a message (you can also do this by clicking the e-mail button on the standard toolbar). To be able to send Excel data in this way you will need to have specified Microsoft Outlook 2000 or 2002 as your e-mail program. This can be specified in the Programs tab under Internet Options in the Windows Control Panel. To be able to view Excel data which forms the body of a message in the correct format, you will need to have Outlook 98, Outlook 2002 or a web browser that can read documents in HTML format.

ABOVE: Entire workbooks can be sent across the globe via email.

Documents can be sent for review and the review process tracked by choosing the Mail Recipients (for Review) option. Excel will create a review request form and a set of review tools. You can create a routing list which will dictate the order in which recipients receive data and each person along the route will receive the attachment in turn. This is useful where a document needs processing in a particular order, for example, a sales order might go to the sales department, then purchasing and finally to accounts.

➡ *Tracking Changes, Web Pages from Excel*

EPOC SHEET

Epoc is the operating system used by Psion handheld computers, as well as some mobile phones. It includes a spreadsheet called Sheet, which is reasonably compatible with Microsoft Excel. In general, you can use Epoc Sheet as you would use Excel.

It is usually possible to transfer Excel files from a PC to a Psion, in a similar way that Microsoft Word files can be transferred into Epoc Word. One of the few changes made when a spreadsheet is transferred is that Sheet does not support the pages within Excel – if you transfer a multi-page Excel file into Epoc Sheet, the data from the different pages will be joined together.

Another tip is that a Psion's monochrome screen shows Excel entries that use colour in a variety of shades of grey. So if you plan to transfer a file across, you might want to avoid using light colours – it will make the files difficult to read. In Epoc Sheet, you don't have the option of different text colours but you can choose different shades of grey for text and for a cell's background – choose from black, dark grey, light grey or white. These are altered by highlighting the cells you want to affect, clicking on the menu icon printed at the top-left of the screen, then choosing either 'Font' or 'Shading' from the 'Format' menu.

Transferring files back from Epoc Sheet to Microsoft Excel usually works, although the formatting may go awry, in terms of column width, colours or fonts. The data itself should be fine when transferred.

ABOVE: No more complicated calculations, Epoc Sheet can solve almost any numerical problem.

Otherwise, Sheet is very similar to Excel. You can perform most of the basic tasks you do in Excel. In terms of graphing, it is probably easier to use than Excel.

If you want to produce a graph from part of an Epoc Sheet spreadsheet, simply highlight your choice (say, for a row of data) then touch the on-screen 'Graph' button, which will usually appear on the right-hand side of the screen. The program will then produce a bar graph of the data.

The bar at the top of the screen lets you alter the design. Touching the '3D' option gives depth to the graph, and the graph symbol just to the left of this lets you alter the kind of graph you see – bars, pie charts and line graphs are possibilities. You may want to click on 'Label type' and choose 'Label' to see the values producing the graph. Touching the 'Sheet' button takes you back to the main spreadsheet. Compared with the graphing wizard in Excel, this facility is basic but very simple to use.

ERRORS – SORTING THEM OUT

Preventing and correcting errors. It is easy to assume that your worksheet is providing accurate information but blind faith can be dangerous! When working with large or complex worksheets, it is difficult to be certain that results are correct. Excel provides a number of tools that help you prevent errors happening, and when they do, identify the error and put it right.

The number one rule is to try to ensure that errors do not occur in the first place. The majority of errors are due to inaccurate typing or simple mistakes when entering cell references.

Typing errors The easiest way to check for typing errors is to use the spellchecker. To run the spellcheck program, access the Tools menu and select the Spelling

ABOVE: Some errors cannot be corrected without extensive telephone support.

option. Alternatively, click the ABC button on the toolbar or press F7. Excel will also automatically correct your mistakes for you. The AutoCorrect feature replaces common typing errors with the correct version and provides the opportunity for you to add your 'favourite typos' to its memory. To take a look at the automatic corrections that are already there or to add some more, access the Tools menu and select the AutoCorrect option. You will find that most of the obvious typos are included, but it may be useful to add words that are specific to you.

Preventing incorrect entries Errors can also occur if your worksheet is misused. For example, if someone is unfamiliar with your worksheet, they could easily enter data in a cell that contains a formula. In most cases this will result in an error message, so the problem will be identified. To prevent it happening in the first place, ensure that all cells containing formulae or other information that should not be overwritten are protected. To do this you will need to unlock the cells that can be changed and then protect the entire worksheet. Highlight the cells to be unlocked, access the Format menu and select the Cells option. Click on the Protection tab and remove the check from the Locked check box. Then protect the sheet by accessing the Tools menu and selecting the Protection, Protect Sheet options.

It is not so easy to identify a mistake if the user simply enters a wrong value. For example, they may enter a value that is out of range, a percentage over 100 or a tax code that does not exist. The examples are endless. These may all cause an error that Excel does not flag. Prevention is better than cure, so make sure that only valid data is entered in the first place. To validate an entry, access the Data menu and select the Validation option. The Data Validation dialog box provides three different ways to prevent wrong entries. The Settings options allow you to specify what type of data can be entered into the cell and, if numeric, the range of numbers that are valid. The Input Message option provides the facility to display a message when a cell is selected. This message can provide advice about entering data in the correct format. The third option, Error Alert, allows you to enter an appropriate error message if incorrect data is entered. You can use any combination of these options when validating an entry.

The Auditing feature Excel will indicate an error by displaying an error message in the cell rather than the expected result. You can identify an error message quite easily: it will always start with a hash character (#). One

of the most easily identified error messages is a series of hashes (####), which indicates that the column is not wide enough to display the content. If you get an error message and are unsure of the cause, the Excel auditing feature can be used to trace the problem. The Excel tools

BELOW LEFT: The Protection tab serves as an emergency service for your spreadsheet.

designed to help you trace errors can be found on the Auditing toolbar. To display the toolbar, access the Tools menu and select the Auditing, Show Auditing Toolbar options. The toolbar provides an option to find all the cells that are referred to by the formula entered in the selected cell (Trace Precedents) and an option to find all the cells that have a dependency on the formula in the selected cell (Trace Dependents). The Trace Error option can be used to trace an error back one step at a time. Each time you click the button it will move back one step.

Circular references One of the most common causes of an error is due to a formula including a reference to itself. This is known as a circular reference. The following example shows the SUM function trying to sum cells B3 to B8 when the formula itself is in B8. This causes a circular reference.

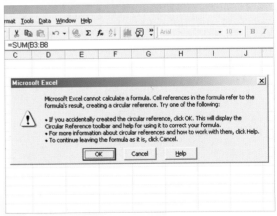

Excel recognizes the error and displays a help dialog box. If you click OK, further help information is displayed. When you leave Help, the Circular Reference toolbar appears, allowing you to jump to any cell within the circular reference. The toolbar also contains the Trace Precedents and Trace Dependents auditing buttons.

➡ *Brackets, Locked and Hidden cells*

EURO, THE

Euro conversion and display. Recent releases of Excel (Excel 2000 and later releases) provide a new Euro Currency Tools add-in program. The add-in provides a formatting tool to display the Euro currency symbol and a function to convert the currencies of countries which are part of the European Union (EU) to the Euro.

Before you can include the Euro in your worksheet, you will need to load the Euro add-in. To do this, access the Tools menu and select the Add-Ins option. The Add-Ins dialog box is displayed. Check the Euro Currency Tools check-box. If the Euro tool is not listed, you will need to install the add-in program before you can load it. During the Microsoft Office setup, add-ins are saved in the folder … Program Files\Microsoft Office\Office Library. Use the Browse button to locate the Eurotool.xla file from within this subdirectory. Select the file from the list and click the OK button. As soon as you close the Add-Ins dialog box, the Euro button will be available from the formatting toolbar.

To format a cell or number of cells to display the Euro symbol (¤), select the cells and click on the Euro button

on the Formatting toolbar. By default, the Euro symbol will be displayed in front of the number with two decimal places. Alternatively, select the cells and access the Format menu. Select the Cells option and click on the Numbers tab. Select Currency from the list of options and locate the Euro symbol from the Symbol drop-down menu. You can change the number of decimal places displayed and choose to display negative numbers in red. Once you have made your choices, click on the OK button.

Excel will also recognize the Euro symbol and automatically format the cell for Currency if you type the Euro symbol either before or after the figure. You can leave a space between the symbol and the number or type the symbol adjacent to the number. To type a Euro symbol on a US or UK keyboard, type Alt+0128 on the numeric pad (the number pad to the right of the keyboard).

The EUROCONVERT function enables you to convert values between the Euro and other European

Union national currencies. It also provides a facility to convert a number from the currency of one EU member to another by using the Euro as an intermediary. This is known as triangulation.

The syntax for the EUROCONVERT function is as follows:

EUROCONVERT(number,source,target,full_precision, triangulation_precision)

The **number** argument refers to the currency value you want to convert or a reference to the cell containing the value.

The **source** argument refers to a three-letter string corresponding to the ISO code for the currency you want to convert from. Alternatively, the source argument could be a reference to a cell containing this code. The ISO codes can be found by accessing the Office Assistant and searching for Euro. Select help on the Euroconvert topic to find a full list of ISO codes.

The **target** argument refers to a three-letter string corresponding to the ISO code for the currency you want to convert to. Alternatively, the target argument could be a reference to a cell containing this code.

The **full_precision** argument needs to be a logical value, either TRUE or FALSE, specifying how to round the resulting value. Your choice of true or false depends on whether you want Excel to adopt the currency-specific rounding rules or not. If you enter FALSE, Excel will use the currency-specific rounding rules to determine the number of decimal places used to calculate the currency's conversion. If you enter TRUE, Excel will ignore the currency-specific rounding rules and use the six-significant-digit conversion factor with no follow-up rounding. If you omit this argument, Excel will assume a FALSE entry and adopt the currency-specific rounding rules. The currency-specific rounding rules for each EU currency can be found by accessing the Office Assistant and typing Euro as the search text. Select the Euroconvert help topic.

The **triangulation_precision** argument is used if you are converting between the currencies of two different EU countries rather than to or from the Euro. In this case, Excel converts the source currency to the Euro and then converts the Euro to the target currency. If you omit this argument Excel will not round the intermediate Euro value. If you want to round the intermediate Euro value, enter a digit equal to or greater than 3 to specify the number of significant digits to be used for the intermediate Euro value. For Excel 2000 to recognize Euro values, your operating system must support the Euro sign. Microsoft Windows 2000 Professional and Windows 98 provide this facility. If you are working with Windows 95 or Windows NT Workstation 4.0, you will need to download the support.

If you have a version of Excel earlier than Excel 2000, you can still work with the Euro by accessing the available tools from the Microsoft Office Euro web site.

➡ *Currency Formats, Financial Functions, Paste Function Button*

EXCEL ON THE MACINTOSH

Although the Apple Macintosh computer has its own unique operating system, Microsoft has developed Excel to work in much the same way as it does on a Windows platform. Excel for Windows and Excel for the Macintosh (Mac) share a common interface and functionality, making it easier for companies to support both platforms.

The following illustrates Excel file formats:

Windows	Macintosh
4.0	4.0
5.0	5.0
95	98
97	2001
2000	Excel X
2002	

LEFT: The Mac is a powerful numbers machine and its version of Excel has some unique features, like List Manager.

Excel 2001 is the current version for the Mac OS 8.1 to 9.2. Excel X is the latest version for the Mac OS X. In much the same way that recent versions of Excel for Windows automate repetitive tasks, integrate with the World Wide Web and provide powerful collaboration facilities, so too do Excel 98, Excel 2001 and Excel X for the Macintosh.

File compatibility is an important issue for many Microsoft clients. Recent surveys show that many Mac users also use a PC and regularly share files with users of Windows-based applications. A key feature of Office 2001 and Office v. X is their high degree of compatibility with Office 97, Office 2000 and Office XP.

Although compatibility with Windows-based products is important, Microsoft has also developed many new 'First for the Mac' features which are designed to take advantage of innovative Mac technologies. For example,

Excel X uses the power of Quartz 2-D Drawing Technology to create transparent charts.

One of the features unique to Excel for the Mac is List Manager, which helps users convert cells into manageable lists and then sort, filter, format and print. A floating tool palette provides the tools to help you manage your list. Useful commands include the Total Row command which you can use to add a row to the end of a list and then perform a calculation on the information in the column. Excel helps to manage large lists by fixing list headers at the top of a screen while you scroll or print.

Another unique feature is the FileMaker Pro Import Wizard, which will allow you to import data from the popular Mac database, FileMaker Pro. You can import data by dragging a file from the Finder into Excel and then use the Import Wizard to choose the records to import.

Excel 2001 also includes a calculator to enable new spreadsheet users to understand and work with cell formulae.

➡ *Importing Data, Versions of Excel*

EXPLAINING THE SCREEN

What can you see? If you have worked with other spreadsheet programs, many elements of the screen will be familiar. If there are elements you are not sure of, the Excel What's This help facility will quickly provide an answer. To use this help facility, access the Help menu and select the What's This option. A question mark appears. Drag the question mark to the element of the screen you want help on and Excel will provide a concise and informative description.

1. Title Bar The title bar appears at the top of all Microsoft applications. It displays the name of the application and current workbook on the left-hand side and holds control buttons to make changes to the window on the right-hand side.

2. Minimize Button The minimize button on the title bar will reduce the Excel window and display it as a button on the Windows task bar. The minimize button on the menu bar will minimize the current workbook.

3. Maximize Button The maximize button on the title bar will restore the Excel window to full size if not currently full size. The maximize button on the menu bar will maximize the workbook window. If you click on a maximize button when the window is full size, the window size will be reduced (but not minimized).

4. Close Button The close button on the title bar will close Excel. The close button on the menu bar will close the current workbook. Clicking either close button will

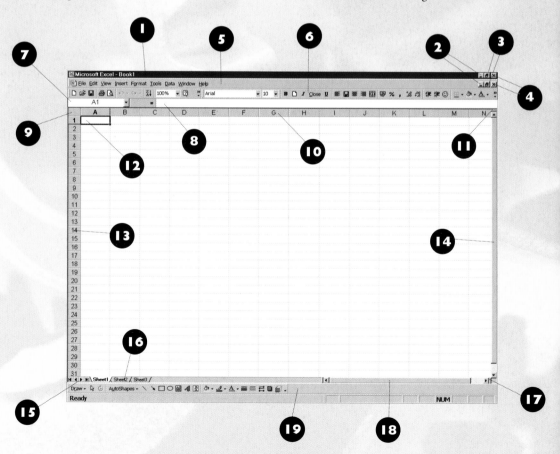

prompt Excel to ask you whether you want to save the changed workbook(s).

5. Menu Bar The menu bar provides a selection of options for creating and maintaining your workbook. By clicking on a menu name (File, Edit etc.), Excel provides a list of further related sub-options.

6. Toolbar Excel provides a full range of toolbars, each containing a number of related buttons. These buttons provide a shortcut to commonly used options. A different toolbar can be selected by right-clicking on the current toolbar.

7. Name Box The name box will display the cell address or name of the currently selected cell or range of cells. The drop- down box provides a list of all the named cells within the worksheet.

8. Formula Bar The formula bar acts as a holding place of information that is being entered into a worksheet or changed. As soon as you press the Enter key or click the tick box to the left of the formula bar, the information is entered into the worksheet and the formula bar is cleared.

9. Select All Button When you click on the select all button, the entire worksheet is selected.

10. Column Headings There are 256 columns in a worksheet labelled A through to IV. The column heading displays the label A through to Z, then AA to AZ, BA to BZ and so on through to IA to IV. By clicking on a column heading, the entire column will be selected.

11. Horizontal Split Box This split box can be used to split or divide the window horizontally so that you can view two areas of the worksheet at the same time. Drag the split box down the vertical scroll bar to the position where you want the window split.

12. Active Cell Indicator There are 16,777,216 cells within each worksheet. A dark border identifies the selected cell. This is known as the active cell indicator.

13. Row headings There are 65,536 rows within each worksheet. The row heading displays the label 1 through to 65,536. If you click on the row heading, the entire row will be selected.

14. Vertical Scroll Bar The vertical scroll bar allows you to scroll up and down through the rows of the worksheet.

15. Tab Scroll Buttons The tab scroll buttons are used to scroll the sheet tabs when some of the sheet tabs are not visible. If you click the right mouse button on the tabs, a menu of sheets will appear.

16. Sheet Tabs The sheet tabs display the names of the worksheets that make up the current workbook. By default, each new workbook contains three sheets named Sheet 1 to 3. A workbook can contain an unlimited number of sheets. To make a sheet active, click on the sheet tab.

17. Vertical Split Box This split box can be used to split or divide the window vertically so that you can view two areas of the worksheet at the same time. Drag the split box across the horizontal scroll bar to the position where you want the window split.

18. Horizontal Scroll Bar The horizontal scroll bar allows you to scroll left and right through the columns of the worksheet.

19. Status Bar The left-hand side of the status bar displays the current command or operation and the right-hand side displays the status of the Num Lock, Caps Lock and Scroll Lock keys. If you do not want the status bar displayed, access the View menu and uncheck the status bar option.

➠ *Help with Help*

EXPORTING DATA

There are many ways in which you can transfer Excel data to another application. The process of exporting, however, typically involves converting Excel data into a format which can be translated by another application.

Perhaps the simplest form of exporting is to save an Excel workbook with a file format compatible with a previous version of Excel or another application. In the Save As dialog box, choose the format from the Save as type list. The many options include saving as a web page

ABOVE: To export data from Excel, the file is usually saved in a different format.

format, as text or as a Lotus 1-2-3 file. Although you should be able to open the file in an application that supports the chosen format, you may find that some features have not been successfully converted.

Where exporting data is a frequent operation between applications, you may find that there is a more formal conversion process. Transferring data between Excel and Access is one example of this. It is quite common for users to set up simple databases in Excel but quickly find that the database has become unmanageable. Similarly, users may find that they want to perform some of the more sophisticated functions that come with a dedicated database program.

Excel's database capabilities are limited to working with one data table at a time. If you need to query or consolidate data which is stored in disparate worksheets or workbooks, you may be better off taking the information into Microsoft Access. Access is a relational database. It allows you to create relationships between tables and draw related information from a group of tables to perform consolidated queries or reports.

To prepare Excel data for exporting, make sure that there are no blank rows or columns. Each individual row of data will become a record in Access and column headings will be taken as field names. Select the cells you need to transfer and include the column headings. Give the range a name by entering the name in the Name box and save and close the file.

Switch to Microsoft Access and open the database into which the range should be imported. Click on the File menu and choose Get External Data followed by Import.

The Import dialog box will be displayed. Select Microsoft Excel from the Files of type box. Use the Look in list to find and select the file you want to import and click the Import button.

The Import Spreadsheet Wizard will be displayed. You can choose to see a list of all worksheets in the workbook file or named ranges. If you have previously named the range, select the range from the list. Click Next. If you check the First Row Contains

Column Headings box, Access will use these headings as field names in its table.

The next step is to choose to store the data in a new or existing table. You then have the opportunity to choose which fields to import and to name and index them. Access will then offer to set a primary key for the table. A primary key is a means of identifying each unique record. Finally, all that remains is to give the table a name in the Import to Table box.

With both Excel and Access open at the same time, you can drag and drop an Excel list into the Tables group of the Access database window.

If you have installed the AccessLinks add-in program, you can also take the route of converting Excel data into an Access database by clicking the Data menu and choosing the Convert to MS Access command. Click the New database option or add to an existing database. Once converted, changes made in Access will not be reflected in the original Excel data.

If you want to maintain a link to the Excel file, switch to the Access database and click the File menu. Choose the Get External Data option followed by Link Tables. Select Excel as the file type and then select the Excel file. Click the Link button and follow the prompts from the Link Spreadsheet Wizard. Changes made to the Access table will be updated in the Excel file.

You might also find it useful to export Excel data, such as client names and addresses, into Microsoft Outlook. Set a range name for the information to be exported. From within Outlook, click the File menu and select the Import and Export option. The Import and Export Wizard will appear. Select the Import from another program or file option and choose Microsoft Excel followed by the file to import. You will be prompted to select a destination folder. Complete the steps in the Wizard.

Excel 2000 also has the ability to export data to a web page using Extensible Markup Language (XML) format. While HTML codes are used for determining the way that a web page should look in a browser, XML is used to publish structured content to the Internet. Workbooks can be saved in XML spreadsheet format and can then be read by a variety of applications.

➡ *Cutting and Pasting, Web Pages from Excel*

FEATURES FOR THOSE WITH DISABILITIES

As a company, Microsoft is committed to developing software applications, which are accessible to everyone, including people with disabilities. Many of the Microsoft Office suite tools can be customized to give people with disabilities greater control over their working environment.

One of the first things you may want to do is to change the system options, which govern accessibility. Click the Windows Start menu and select the Settings option followed by Control Panel. Double-click Accessibility Options. Click a tab and choose your options.

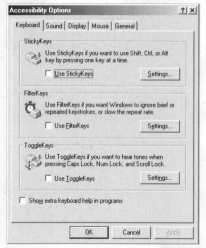

Display settings can be altered to make them more readable by the visually impaired. For example, you can change the magnification of a spreadsheet, make toolbar buttons larger, change the colour and size of text and create custom colour palettes.

By default, everything you see on the screen is set to a magnification level of 100 per cent. You can increase the 'zoom percentage' to 400 per cent which will greatly magnify cells and their content. Click the drop-down box to the right of the Zoom button on the standard toolbar. Choose a percentage from the list or type in a percentage up to 400 per cent. To enlarge the selected area to fill the window, click Selection. The size of the screen is not related to printing size. Sheets are printed at 100 per cent

ABOVE RIGHT: Most Office suite applications can be adapted to suit disabled users.

unless you change the scaling on the Page tab of the Page Setup dialog box (File menu).

You can increase the size of all toolbar buttons across the Microsoft Office suite in one go. Click the Tools menu followed by Customize, and then the Options tab. Click the Large icons check box.

You might also find it useful to create a custom toolbar containing frequently used buttons and menu commands. Click the Tools menu followed by the Customize option. In the Customize dialog box, click the Toolbars tab and click New button. A very small empty toolbar will appear in the worksheet. Click the Commands tab in the Customize dialog box, select a command and drag a button to the toolbar. To remove a button from a toolbar, drag the button off.

If you have installed a Microsoft IntelliMouse, you can move quickly around your workbook without scrolling or clicking buttons. For example, you can move quickly to the end of a document with one click of a mouse.

Click the mouse wheel to begin scrolling and move the mouse in the direction you want to scroll. You can speed up or slow down this process by dragging away from or towards the origin mark. Click any mouse button to stop AutoScrolling.

As you create column entries, Excel compiles a list of the entries. If you start to enter text in the column and it matches a pre-existing entry, Excel will complete the entry for you. You can also right-click and choose the Pick From List option.

You can change the colours in a workbook palette by clicking the Tools menu followed by Options and then the Colour tab. Select a colour in the Standard palette and click the Modify button. Choose a colour from 127 standard colours and 15 shades of grey. To the right of the palette you will see the new and old colour displayed. If you are happy with your choice, click OK. You can copy a colour palette to another workbook.

If you find help topics difficult to read, you can change text font, size and colours in the cascading style sheet of your web browser settings. For help on these settings, click Help in your browser.

If you have Internet access, visit *www.microsoft.com/enable/* for more detailed information on accessibility features available in Microsoft applications. There you will find guides, organized by disability. Each guide provides details on accessibility of Microsoft products, supporting documentation, a list of keyboard shortcuts, training resources, technical support and tips and tricks.

➡ *Mouse and Excel, Toolbars*

If you would prefer to use the wheel as a means of zooming in on a worksheet rather than scrolling, click the Tools menu and select Options followed by the General tab. Check the box labelled Zoom on roll with IntelliMouse.

You can customize IntelliMouse buttons so that they perform frequently used commands. You can even record and assign a keystroke to a button, such as Ctrl + S to save. The wheel and buttons can be set to perform different tasks in different applications. If you have difficulty in controlling mouse movements, there are many shortcut keys available.

If you find that you frequently mistype a particular word, you can make sure that it is automatically corrected for you as you type. You can do this in one of two ways. You can make changes to a misspelled word in the Spelling dialog box and then click the AutoCorrect button. Alternatively, you can click the Tools menu and select the AutoCorrect option. In the AutoCorrect dialog box, type some characters or a word in the Replace box and type the replacement text in the With box. Whenever you type these characters, Excel will replace them with the correct version.

FEATURES FOR THOSE WITH DISABILITIES
CASE STUDY

Doris is in her sixties and has discovered the joys of using a computer later in life. One day a week she goes to her local community centre where she has the opportunity to learn how to use a computer to manage her finances and send e-mails to her family. She really looks forward to her weekly sessions and meeting other learners of a similar age.

Doris has found getting to grips with using a computer a lot easier than she imagined but she often struggles to read the screen because she suffers from a degenerative eye condition. She mentions her problem to her tutor and between them they endeavour to improve her ability to read and access what is on the screen. The following illustration shows how an Excel worksheet might look to a user who has Windows standard display set as the default display mode.

Fortunately for Doris, her tutor is well informed and knows that Microsoft applications can be customized in a variety of ways to help people with disabilities. They start off by looking at the display settings located in the Windows Control Panel.

Before making changes to Windows settings, make sure that you close any open applications first. Click the Windows Start menu and select the Settings option followed by Control Panel. To view display settings, double-click the Display option icon.

Click the Settings tab. In the Desktop area drag the slider bar towards Less to decrease the resolution of the screen (measured in pixels). The higher the screen resolution, the more information you will be able to see on the screen at any one time but the consequence is that items will appear smaller. Conversely, if you set a lower screen resolution, screen elements will appear larger and less information will be displayed on the screen at any one time. Experiment by dragging the slider bar to 800 by 600 pixels. Now click the down arrow to the right of the Font size box and select Large Fonts. You may be prompted to either wait briefly while the display is refreshed or to re-start Windows in order for the settings to take effect.

Changing these settings can make an enormous difference as you can see from the following illustration.

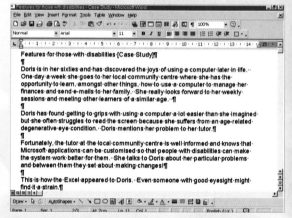

Now click on the Appearance tab. Microsoft provides a set of display schemes, which govern how each of the Windows elements will appear on the screen. Schemes vary in the colours, sizes and formats used for each screen element.

Select Windows Standard (extra large). You can see how the current settings will be displayed on the desktop before making a firm choice. Before confirming your choice, experiment with different colour schemes and levels of contrast, like that of Lilac (large), illustrated below.

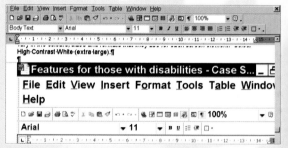

Just as you can find books published in large print in a library, you can also enlarge toolbar buttons and text on screen. From within Excel (or any Office application) you can make toolbar buttons appear larger. To do this, click the Tools menu followed by the Customize option. In the Customize dialog box, click the Options tab. Check the Large icons box in the Other section. This will increase the size of all toolbar buttons across the Microsoft Office suite in one go.

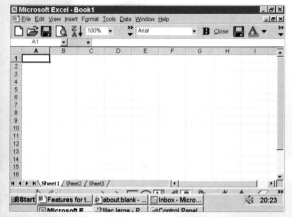

You might also find it useful to create a custom toolbar containing frequently used buttons and menu commands. Click the Tools menu followed by the Customize option. In the Customize dialog box click the Toolbars tab and click New button. In the New Toolbar dialog box, type a name for the toolbar. A small empty toolbar will appear.

For the purposes of this scenario we are going to add Zoom in and AutoCorrect. To do this, click the Commands tab in the Customize dialog box and click View in the Categories list. Click and drag the Zoom icon from the list of Commands onto the new toolbar. Next, click on the Tools command in the Categories list and drag the AutoCorrect icon to the toolbar.

To make sure that they work, select 400% as the Zoom percentage from the Zoom box on the new toolbar.

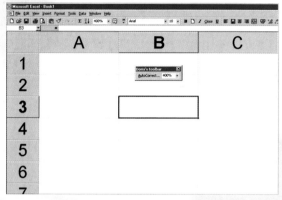

Finally, change the colours in your workbook palette by clicking the Tools menu followed by Options and then the Colour tab. Select a shade of red in the Standard palette and click the Modify button. Choose a shade of blue.

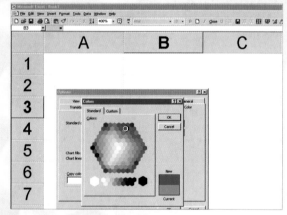

To the right of the palette you will see the new andold colour displayed. Click OK to replace red with blue. Click the Reset button to return to the default colour.

Once you have created a custom-built palette, you can copy it into other workbooks. To do this, open a workbook and click the Tools menu. Select Options followed by the Colour tab. Select the name of the workbook from the list in the Colours copy from box.

Doris is so pleased with her discoveries that she delights in showing her grandchildren, Katie and Alex, how to set up their own toolbars and colour palettes!

FILTERING A LIST

Finding specific information. As a database or list grows, it becomes tedious scrolling through the data in order to find specific information. To make life easier, Excel provides the AutoFilter feature to filter a list to display only the required records.

A list or database is simply rows of information. The first row contains descriptive labels for each column within the list. Each column contains the same type of information. For example, one column may contain names and another telephone numbers. Lists should not contain any empty rows as Excel determines the boundaries automatically and an empty row signifies the end of the list.

When Excel filters a list, it hides all the rows apart from those that meet a particular specification. This specification is often referred to as the search criteria. For example, taking a list of names and addresses, you may want to write to only those people living in Glasgow. In this case you would filter the list based on the criteria that the entry in the town field matched Glasgow.

To use AutoFilter, select a cell anywhere within the list, access the Data menu and select the Filter, AutoFilter options. Excel analyses the list and displays drop-down buttons located at the right-hand side of each cell in the first row of the list. If you click on any of these buttons a list of

possible filter criteria is displayed. Each list will contain all the different items within the column, with four additional default options and a custom option.

The All option displays all the items in the column. This option is used to remove or cancel any previous filtering on that column.

The Top 10 option has a rather misleading name. It does not necessarily filter out all but the top 10 records in the list. You can determine exactly how many records you want to include and these can be either the top or bottom (highest or lowest) values in the list. When you select the Top 10 option the Top 10 AutoFilter dialog box is displayed.

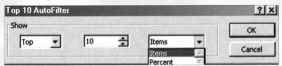

You can select either top or bottom and the number of values you want to display. You can also choose a filter based on Item or Percent. For example, you may choose to filter the top five records or the top 5% of records.

The Blanks option filters the list to only display records with a blank entry in the selected column. The NonBlanks option only shows those records with a non-blank entry in the selected column. These two options are only available if the list contains blank fields within the column.

The default AutoFilters allow simple selections with the facility to define AND links across several columns. A filter including an AND link requires the record to meet both the first and second criteria in order to be included. Taking as an example a list containing client details; name, address, sales figures etc., an AND filter can be used to find the 10 clients with the highest sales figures who are also based in London. To do this, click on the drop-down button at the top of the Town column and select the London entry. Then click on the drop-down button at the top of the Sales column and select the Top 10 option. As you are only interested in the top 10 items

LEFT: You can find specific information by filtering a list.

you can accept the defaults in the dialog box. This will result in a filter that only includes the records for the top 10 clients based in London.

The Custom option provides more flexibility when defining the filter.

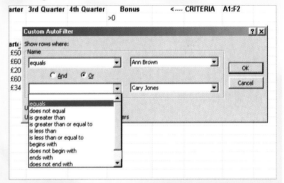

The Custom option allows you to define AND filters for the same column. This can be extremely useful when you want to find records within a specific numeric range. For example, you can filter on the Sales column to find all Sales that are greater than £10,000 and less than £15,000. To do this, click on the drop-down button at the top of the Sales column and select the Custom option. In the first box select 'is greater than' and the second box type 10,000. Make sure the And button is checked. In the boxes below, select 'is less than' in the first box and type 15,000 in the second. Click the OK button to confirm.

The Custom option also enables you to define OR filters across two columns. Records are only included if they meet the first criteria or the second criteria. In the above example, the Custom option is used to find records where the name is either Ann Brown or Cary Jones.

Wildcards can be used to filter entries that only match part of the search criteria. For example, if you type the criteria *Crotan* for the Company column you will find Crotan Ltd, Crotan plc, The Crotan Group etc.

In most cases AutoFilter is more than adequate to enable you to locate specific records but on occasion it may have limitations. For example, you can only filter on one or two criteria for the same column. If you want to find all records where the town is London, Leeds or Manchester you will need to use a more advanced filtering technique as demonstrated in the following case study.

FILTERING A LIST CASE STUDY

As lists of information grow, it becomes increasingly difficult to locate specific records. By filtering the list you can remove from view all but the information you require. This case study considers the benefits of both the Excel AutoFilter and Advanced Filter features.

This scenario considers a training and development company that holds sales details as an Excel list (see Order a List Case Study). A number of staff will benefit from learning how to filter the list to provide different views of the data. A training session has been designed to show, by example, how the Excel filtering features can make life easier whatever their requirement.

The four Account Managers use the list on a daily basis and often sort the information to make it easier to locate a specific record. This serves the purpose but can still involve scanning a number of records. By setting up a filter, they can easily locate one or more records based on a given criteria. The first example creates a filter to locate all of Jane's sales records for the customer, ChemLake Ltd.

To generate this filter, position the cell pointer within the list, access the Data menu and select the Filter, AutoFilter options. Excel analyses the list and displays drop-down buttons located at the right-hand side of each cell in the first row of the list. To only display Jane's records, click on the button to the right of the Account Manager column heading.

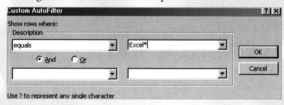

Each item within the list is displayed. Click on Jane and only Jane's sales records are displayed. To filter the list further, click on the button to the right of the Client column heading and click on ChemLake Ltd from the list

of clients. All the sales records for Jane that refer to courses booked by ChemLake Ltd are displayed.

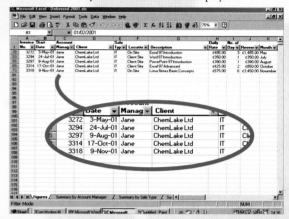

If Jane needs to narrow down the search further, to only locate Excel courses, she will need to filter the Description column. By clicking on the drop-down button on the Description column heading, a list of courses will be displayed. Jane wants to list all Excel courses, not just Introduction or Advanced. To define this filter she will need to use the Custom option. To do this, click on the drop-down button to the right of the Description column heading and select the Custom option.

To ensure all Excel courses are included, the * wildcard is used to represent any series of characters. As long as the entry starts with the word Excel it will be included within the filter. If you are not sure whether the description is Introduction to Excel or Excel Introduction, it is advisable to also precede the criteria by a *.

The Sales Director often requires specific detailed information. Her latest request is for a summary of all the new technology courses that have been run during the past year. The filter needs to find all records for Dreamweaver, FrontPage, Director or PhotoShop courses, regardless of level. This filter requires more than two OR conditions on the same column of data. The Excel AutoFilter feature cannot do this.

This is where the Excel Advanced Filter comes into play. It is not difficult to use, just more time-consuming to set up. Before you can use the Advanced Filtering feature you need to set up a criteria range. The criteria range must contain at least two rows with the first row being a copy of at least some of the column headings of your list. The row or rows below the headings contain your search criteria.

You can enter the criteria range anywhere within the spreadsheet but it is advisable not to put it on any row occupied by the list. This is because Excel hides some of the rows when filtering records and you may find that your criteria range disappears! The best position for the criteria range is either above or below your list, although if putting it below, leave room for additional records that may be added to the list.

To create the filter, copy the column headings (fieldnames) from the list to a new location. In this case it could be below the list as no more records will be added for this year. You do not need to include all the fieldnames in the criteria range but it does no harm to do so. In order to find all Dreamweaver, FrontPage, PhotoShop and Director courses, type these four entries in separate rows underneath the Description column. As you want to find all courses regardless of whether they are advanced, introductory etc., use the * wildcard both before and after the course name to find all variations.

To activate the filter, access the Data menu and select the Filter, Advanced Filter options. Ensure that the List range contains all the rows in your list. The Criteria range needs to include the copied headings and the four rows below

containing the search criteria. Click the OK button to filter the list based on your criteria. To re-display all the records, run the advanced filter again but remove the criteria from the criteria range.

ABOVE: Filtering a list in Excel locates your records for you and saves you time wading through a mountain of paperwork.

FINANCIAL DATA

If you want financial data to use in a spreadsheet, the web is the best place to look. Several web sites provide up-to-date information for a large number of shares and funds, and may also do some of the calculations for you.

One of the best is run by the *Financial Times* newspaper, at *www.ft.com*. If you want the price of a share or a fund in any of seven countries, including the UK and the US, just type its name into the box on the left-hand side marked 'Share prices and Portfolio' and choose the country from the drop-down list. For example, if you hold shares in the BT Group, floated on the London Stock Exchange, you could type BT into the box, choose UK from the list, and click on the brown 'Go' button. The result is a list of UK companies which the search engine matches to BT – BT Group is, unsurprisingly, the first on the list. Make a note of its code – 'UK:BTA' – which you can type into the box in the future, leading you directly to the share price in question. Unit trust funds are also listed – just search on the full name of the fund.

However you get there, the result is a page offering you detailed information about the share, including a graph (which can be rescaled by clicking on the 'interactive charting' link underneath), what the price has done recently, company news, and of course, the price itself. This can be entered into an appropriately set-up spreadsheet to calculate the value of your

ABOVE: To use the Financial Times *web sites you need a username and password.*

shareholding (basically, by multiplying by the number of shares you own).

If you don't mind the company knowing something about your shareholdings, you can cut out some of this work by setting up a portfolio at FT.com – you are supposed to enter a name and postcode to access this service. You set one up by clicking on the 'Manage my stocks and track companies' link, just below the search box for individual shares and funds. The *Financial Times* group of web sites uses a single log-in system, called FT Passport. If you've previously used any of its services, that's the username and password you need now. If not, click on 'register for an FT passport' first.

Once you're in, you have to set up your portfolio. Let's say you own 300 BT Group London shares. You can choose the currency your portfolio is calculated in from the drop-down list marked 'Portfolio Currency' (the default is UK sterling). To add the first entry, type in 'UK:BTA', the symbol for BT Group UK shares. There's a link for looking up symbols if you don't already know them. Click on 'Add' when you have entered the symbol correctly.

positions. When you've finished, click on the brown 'Finish' box at the bottom left.

Your portfolio is then available online. Each item can be adjusted by clicking on the double arrow symbol at the left of the item's line, and the system automatically calculates how much money you've made or lost. You can then enter this number directly into a spreadsheet used to calculate your overall wealth, rather than do the calculations within your own software. FT.com also allows you to set up multiple portfolios, and has a range of graphing tools.

If you decide to get into trading shares and funds, the Web can be useful in two further ways. Firstly, buying and selling are often cheaper online. There are plenty of suitable web sites – research several to get an idea of prices. A directory such as Yahoo will provide you with a list.

Secondly, you can get advice and ideas on shares and funds from other investors. The Motley Fool web sites (*www.fool.co.uk*, or *www.fool.com* for the US site) include tutorials in investing, plus message boards with the thoughts of experienced online traders. In the UK, *www.hemscott.net* provides data on individual companies.

It is worth adding a couple of caveats: don't gamble money on shares that you can't afford to lose, and talk to a financial adviser if you need any guidance. What you see online may well be trying to sell you something unsuitable. Be warned.

➡ *Manage your Savings, Manage your Shares*

A line of data will then appear representing your BT shares. The first box shows the date of purchase – the system assumes you've just bought the shares, but you can change the purchase date. The next box, headed 'POSITION Type', has 'Long' as its default. With normal investments, leave this box alone. (The other option, 'Short', means you owe someone the shares, a more complex financial position.)

In the next group of boxes, you need to fill in the number of shares you own and the trade price (how much you paid for them per share, in pence). For the purposes of working out the value of your shares, you can ignore the commission box.

You can continue to build up the portfolio, by entering more shares and funds as above, and also cash

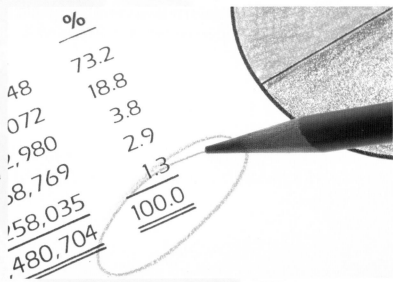

FINANCIAL FUNCTIONS

Financial functions are designed to perform common business calculations often related to borrowing or saving money. In general, this group of functions has a number of common arguments.

- **fv** – the future value of an investment after all the payments have been made.
- **nper** – the total number of payments or periods that make up an investment or loan.
- **pmt** – the payment that is made each period to either an investment or a loan.
- **pv** – the present value of the investment or loan at the beginning of the investment.
- **rate** – the interest rate or discount rate for a loan or investment.
- **type** – payment type, entered as 1 for the beginning of the month, 0 (or omit) for the end of month.

BELOW: You can create a theoretical budget for a long-term project or loan payments.

As a working example, assume you need to borrow £10,000 to build a conservatory. You know you want to pay back the money on a monthly basis over 10 years and that the current interest rate is six per cent. Will the monthly repayments be too high for your budget?

The PMT function can be used to calculate the payment for a loan based on constant payments and interest rate. The function is entered as PMT (rate, nper, pv,fv,type), where the first three arguments are compulsory and the last two optional.

The function can either be entered manually or you can use the Paste Function dialog box to enter each argument separately. With the repayment example, the current yearly interest rate is six per cent, but as you are going to pay off the loan on a monthly basis this needs to be entered as six per cent/12. Note that this could also be entered as 0.06/12 (but not 6/12, as this would mean charging a 600% interest rate!). The number of payments you will make over the 10 year period will be 12 per year (10*12). The present value of the loan or the amount you intend to borrow is £10,000.

In this case, the future value argument can be omitted as you do not require a cash balance at the end of the

period. Assuming that you are repaying the loan at the end of each month, the type argument can either be entered as 0 or omitted, as 0 is the default value.

	A	B	C	D	E	F	G	H
1	**Repayment Model**							
2								
3	Loan Amount	£10,000						
4	Interest Rate	6%						
5	Term	10						
6								
7	Monthly repayment	-£111.02		<-- =PMT(B4/12,B5*12,B3)				
8								
9								
10	**Loan Model**							
11								
12	Monthly repayment	-111.02						
13	Interest rate	6%						
14	Term	10						
15								
16	Loan	£10,000		<-- =PV(B13/12,B14*12,B12)				
17								

The present value function PV(rate,nper,pmt,fv,type) works in a similar way but returns the total amount that a series of future payments is worth now. This function will prove useful if you want to determine how much you can borrow based on a set term, the current interest rate and an affordable monthly repayment.

➡ *Functions, Paste Function Button*

FIND AND REPLACE

Locating and changing values. As a worksheet grows and becomes more complex, it is sometimes difficult to pinpoint certain data or text. Excel provides a command that enables you to search for specific information throughout the whole worksheet. Taking this a step further, you can also find and replace one or more occurrences of specific information with something else.

The Find command compares the contents of every cell in the worksheet with the search text you have entered. Each time a match is found, the search is paused and the cell containing the match is displayed. When you find what you are looking for, you can stop the search or carry on until all matches are found.

To use the Find command, either access the Edit menu and select the Find option, or use the keyboard shortcut Ctrl+F. Use the Find What text box to enter the text you want to find. The Search drop-down list allows you to specify whether you want Excel to search by rows or columns. The choice you make will depend on how your sheet is constructed.

RIGHT: The Find and Replace feature helps users search for specific details.

The Look in drop-down list provides three options. The Values option will find values (numbers or text) and the result of any formulae. The Formulae option will also locate values but it will find the actual formulae rather than the result of the formulae. Use the Comments option if you only want to search for comments. Select the Match case check box for a case-sensitive search. Select the Find entire cells check box if you want to find cells that contain your search text and nothing else.

Start the search by positioning your cell pointer in the top left-hand cell of the sheet or the point from where you want to start searching. Click on the Find Next button and keep clicking this button until you find the match you want. If you decide you want to replace the entry you can click the Replace button and this will take you to the Replace dialog box. Complete or interrupt the search by clicking the Close button.

To replace the contents of cells, access the Edit menu and select the Replace option. The Replace dialog box provides similar options to the Find dialog box except you also need to enter an expression in the Replace with text box. When Excel finds a match for your search entry, you can choose to replace the entry with the contents of the Replace with box, replace all subsequent matches or find the next match. Click the Close button to interrupt or complete the command.

➡ *Undo*

FIND MISSING ADDRESS DATA

If you've set up Excel as an address book, it becomes particularly obvious when something is missing from an entry. Fortunately, the Web can often be used to fill in the gaps.

In the UK, one of most common missing items is a postcode. Without it, your letters are likely to take longer to reach their destination, as automated postal sorting equipment will not work. Royal Mail, which encourages customers to use postcodes to speed up sorting, has put the postcodes of the UK's 27 million addresses online.

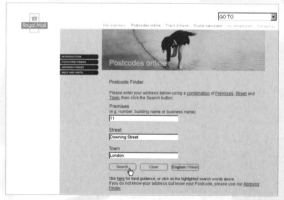

To search, start at *www.royalmail.com/paf*. (You might also find the 'Postal calculator' useful at some point.) Then click on the underlined words 'Postcode Finder' in the second paragraph of text. On the page that appears, you need to type in the name or number of the premises in the first box, the street in the second, and the town in the third. So, if you wanted the postcode for the chancellor of the exchequer – perhaps after working out how to run the economy with your spreadsheet – you would enter '11', 'Downing Street' and 'London' in the three boxes respectively, and then click on 'Search'.

The Royal Mail system will come back with the full official address, in this case:

> Chancellor Of The Exchequer
> 11 Downing Street
> LONDON
> SW1A 2AB'.

The web site allows you to search for postcodes with incomplete information. It will work with just a street name (entering 'Downing Street' alone produces 19 possible locations, from Ashton-under-Lyme to Smethwick), or with any two of the three pieces of information. It also works with English and Welsh. If you're unsure of a spelling, you can enter part of the name, followed immediately by an asterisk, although this means

coming up with more possibilities. If you use '11', 'Down*' as the street name and 'Lond*' as the town, you get 21 possibilities, with the Chancellor's address top of the list.

The site has a reverse function, too. If you know someone's postcode, but aren't sure of their full address, you can enter just the postcode. If you do this alone, you will get the exact address if it is for an organization that receives a lot of post: 'SW1A2AB' will produce 11 Downing Street. If you enter a residential postcode, you will probably get about a dozen or so addresses on one street – you will need the premises number or name to make the address precise.

For UK phone numbers, BT provides an online directory enquiries service. It can be accessed through the BT home page, at *www.bt.com*. The link is listed as 'Directory Enquiries', in the blue box at the top right of the screen. The service allows you to search for 10 numbers each day for free, and more if you register.

You need to enter at least a partial name and area to start a search. The system will accept the first four letters of a name, followed by an asterisk, so you could search for someone in Birmingham with 'birm*'. You can also

enter a person's initial and street address for either businesses or individuals, to narrow the search. If several phone numbers fit your search you will receive a list of possibilities. If so, click on 'Go' next to the one that fits. The system will then provide the person or business name, address, postcode and phone number, from within and outside the UK.

A useful extra function is offered through the link marked 'See map details' from this answer page. Clicking on this takes you to a street map showing where this person or business lives. Of course, none of this will work for ex-directory numbers.

The Yellow Pages site, at *www.yell.com* (run by BT), has UK and US editions. This provides similar facilities to BT's directory enquiries for businesses only, except that it lets you search on business type as well as name. It also has a mapping facility, which is very useful if you want to find a service near where you live or work. It will also search to find businesses in a small area, such as that covered by a postcode zone (like W1, or the West End of central London). The US version of yell.com works in pretty much the same way, except that the location can also be qualified by state.

To find US zip codes, go to *www.usps.gov*, the site for the US Postal Service, and click on the 'Find Zip Codes' link. This will give you the full nine-digit zip code for an address. To find the basic four-digit codes for a town, or to find a town from a zip code, click on the link at the bottom of the page marked 'City/State/ZIP Code Associations page'.

There are several web sites allowing searches for US residential phone numbers, but *www.whowhere.lycos.com/Phone* is a pretty good option. As with BT, this provides a link to a map when you find the person you're looking for.

➥ *Manage an Address Book*

ABOVE: The Web makes it possible to locate people all over the world.
LEFT: Locating people in a large city can be made easier using an address book.
FAR LEFT: Addresses can be found on the Internet at www.royalmail.com.

FONTS

A font is the name given to the complete set of characters in a typeface. Two of the most commonly used fonts are Arial and Times New Roman. A font will govern the appearance and style of the character set, including the appearance of lower- and upper-case letters, small capitals, numbers, fractions, symbols and punctuation. In the following paragraph you will see some examples of fonts.

This 1st **SENTENCE** has been **typed** using the font named ARIAL and shows how upper case, small capitals, numbers and "punctuation" appear.

Although this 2nd SENTENCE has been created using the same size of font, it has been created using the TIMES NEW ROMAN font and so has a unique appearance.

This sentence illustrates the Comic Sans MS font, which is often used to create more casual pieces of communication.

The final sentence uses Edwardian Script.

Excel comes with a set of ready-made fonts that are provided through Microsoft Windows and will help you to improve the presentation of your worksheet.

Presentation can be as important as the information itself, especially if you need to report on your findings or publish your work on the Internet. Select the cells which need to be enhanced and access a list of installed fonts by clicking the Font buttons on the Format toolbar. Alternatively, click the Format menu and select the Cells option followed by the Font tab. If you only want to apply or change the format of a few characters in a cell, select the characters in the formula bar and then apply the format.

You will notice that many fonts listed are preceded by the letter 'T'. This means that they are True Type fonts. True Type fonts print in exactly the same way as they are displayed on the screen. A message appears to this effect in the box at the bottom of the Format Cells dialog box. If you are going to present or publish your work, however, you should be aware that fonts available on your computer may not be available on others. You would be wise to view your document on another machine before making extensive changes.

Each font is available in a range of sizes. Character heights are typically measured in points, with 72 points being equal to one inch in height. The height is measured as the distance between the highest and lowest point of the set of characters. If you want to create text which is

ABOVE: Fonts are a set of characters with a particular appearance.
RIGHT: Each font is available in different sizes and styles.

can apply a colour from the colour palette or apply a range of special effects such as strikethrough, superscript or subscript. As you select each option, the Preview box will give you a glimpse of how your text might look.

There might be an occasion when you can't see all the information in a cell and you want to shrink the font size so that all your characters are visible. Select the range of cells and from the Format Cells dialog box select the Alignment tab. In the area of the dialog box dedicated to Text control, check the Shrink to fit box.

You can work with fonts to enhance the presentation of charts, in much the same way that you can improve the look of a worksheet. Double-click the area of the chart to display the Format dialog box and click the Font tab. Alternatively, select the area of the chart which contains the text that you want to format and select the Format menu. There will be an option to format the text in the area of the chart that you currently have selected. To change the text for the entire chart, you will need to select the chart area. You can do this by clicking the mouse in the area beyond the plot area. The words Chart Area will appear in the Name Box.

As you will have gathered from this section, improving the appearance of your charts and worksheets couldn't be easier. You simply select the area to be changed, select the Format menu followed by the option which indicates the area you have chosen to format, and make your choice from a range of options in the Format dialog box.

➠ *Words in Excel, Formatting Case Study*

approximately 0.5 inch in height you will need to select a font size of 36 points. If you want text to be approximately 0.25inch in height, select 18 points as the size.

If you find a font that you particularly like, you can set it to be the default font for all future worksheets. Select the Tools menu followed by Options. The Options dialog box will appear. Select the General tab and select a Standard font and Size. The standard font will take effect the next time that you load Excel and create a new worksheet. It will not affect worksheets created and saved prior to setting the default.

Additional text attributes can be applied through the Formatting toolbar and Format Cells dialog box. You can underline characters or make them bold or italicized. You

FORMATTING CASE STUDY

Simon Parker, the owner of a small mobile catering business, has been asked by a potential buyer to produce a report giving a breakdown of daily income and expenses. Should the buyer decide to go ahead with the purchase, he wants to be able to see at a glance which products are most profitable and which he should discontinue. Simon prepares the worksheet; for details on how he did this, see the Outlines Case Study on page 142. The worksheet has been designed to include all the relevant information. Formulae have been entered to calculate the total cost of making each roll, the profit per roll, the daily profit per roll and the total daily profit. The total daily profit looks very healthy but Simon knows that in order to make a good impression on the buyer, the presentation of the worksheet may be just as important as the information that it contains.

All figures, apart from the number of sandwiches sold each day, need to be displayed as currency. To do this, click in cell C3, hold the Shift key down and click in cell J8, to select all cells between. Click the Format menu and select the Cells option. In the Format Cells dialog box, click the Number tab and select Currency from the Category list. Set the number of decimal places to 2. Click the Format Painter tool on the Standard toolbar and select cells C10 through to J10 to extend the currency format. Apply currency format to all other relevant cells. Click the Format Painter tool a second time to de-select it.

Excel comes with a set of ready-made fonts, which can help to improve the presentation of your worksheet. A font is the name given to the set of characters in a typeface. Fonts govern the appearance and style of the character set, including how lower and uppercase letters, small capitals, numbers, fractions, symbols and punctuation are displayed. To apply different fonts to

your worksheet, first select the cells to be enhanced and then click the Format menu followed by the Cells option and then the Font tab. Alternatively, choose a font from the Font list on the Formatting toolbar. If you only want

RIGHT: Excel can help you produce reports for your business.

to apply or change the format of a few characters in a cell, select the characters in the formula bar and then apply the format.

To make the worksheet heading more distinctive, select cell D1. Click the down arrow to the right of the Font box. You will see a list of fonts displayed in their unique style. Select Broadway (or similar). From the Font Size box, select 24 points.

To format the headings for the sandwich fillings, select cells B2 through to J2. Select Bangle (or similar) from the Font box and 12 points as the size. Click the bold button. Widen columns as necessary. To access a wider range of formatting options, click the Format menu followed by the Cells option. In the Format Cells dialog box, click the Font tab. Click the down arrow to the right of the colour box and choose Blue from the colour palette. Double-click the Format Painter tool and "paint" this format to all text entries in column A. Extend the width of column A to include the widest text entry. Save the file as Formatting.xls.

Select all figures relating to rolls, except for the total daily profit for rolls, and apply Sky Blue as the colour.

Select the total daily profit for rolls figure and apply the colour Indigo. Use the Format Painter tool to apply the same colours to the relevant cells in other sections.

Extend the height of row 1 by dragging the line between row 1 and 2 down. Click the Alignment tab in the Format Cells dialog box and select Center from the Horizontal box. Now select cells B2 through to J2. Click the Alignment tab and choose Center from the Horizontal box and Center from the Vertical box. Some options may result in you having to adjust column widths or reduce font size, in order to accommodate the style of text.

Select cells B2 through to J2 (sandwich fillings) and click the Format menu followed by Row and then AutoFit. This will adjust the row height to the minimum needed to display the height of the tallest cell. To adjust column widths to the minimum necessary to display the contents of the selected cells, click the Format menu followed by Column and then AutoFit Selection. If you change the content of a cell at a later stage, you may need to repeat this process.

To place a box around a selected area (for example cells A2 through to J11), select the Border tab from the Format Cells dialog box. In the Presets box, click Outline and Inside. Choose a line style and select Light Blue as the colour. Click on each of the lines in the Preview diagram to apply these attributes. Format each of the remaining sections in the same style. Increase the size of the total daily profit figure to 16 points.

Your worksheet should resemble the following illustration.

FUNCTIONS

A function is a ready-made formula. Functions are provided as part of the Excel program and are designed to save you time. Rather than create your own, sometimes complicated formulae, Excel provides a range of built-in formulae known as functions, which range from simple summation to complex financial and conditional functions. Functions can also be built into your own formulae providing flexibility when calculating, verifying or changing the data on your spreadsheet.

To ensure a function provides the correct result, it is essential to follow the rules:

1. The function must start with the equal sign (=). This tells Excel that what follows is a formula that needs to be calculated.

2. The equal sign must be followed by the function name such as SUM, to total or sum the values in a range of cells.

3. The function must be followed by round brackets, known as parentheses () to enclose the function argument(s).

4. The arguments provide the information that Excel needs to work out the result of the function. The content of the argument depends on the particular function but often includes cell addresses. The argument for the SUM function is the range of cells to be summed. For example,

ABOVE: A function is a ready-made formula, designed to save the user time.
RIGHT: Using Excel can familiarize pupils with mathematical formulae.

the function =SUM(B3:B9) will produce the sum of the values stored in cells B3 through to B9: B3:B9 is the argument for this function. Some functions do not require an argument. For example, the =TODAY() function which provides the current system date.

5. If the function has more than one argument, a comma should be used to separate each argument.

6. The syntax of the function must be correct. The syntax dictates the order and the data type of the arguments within the function. An error at this stage can produce an incorrect result.

Functions can also be included within a formula or nested within another formula. Nested formulae can become very complex and it is important to consider the syntax, particularly ensuring that each opening bracket has a matching closing bracket – a common cause of error.

Working with functions can be made easier if the cell or range name is used in the formula rather than the cell address. For example, it is easier to understand the function =SUM(Expenses) rather than =SUM(C5:C17).

By default, Excel displays and prints the result of functions rather than the function itself. It is often useful to display and print the actual function or formula, especially if checking for errors or working with a sheet created by someone else. In order to print functions, they must be displayed first. To do this, select Options from the Tools menu, click on the View tab and check the Formulas check box.

➧ *Brackets, Paste Function Button*

GET HELP WITH MATHS HOMEWORK

An award-winning web site is *www.learn.co.uk*, run by the *Guardian* newspaper. It is organized to work with the UK education system of key stages, where key stage 2 is aimed at children from the ages of seven to 11, stage 3 from 11 to 14, stage 4 from 14 to 16, and AS levels, over the age of 16.

Spreadsheets are excellent for supporting the learning of several elements of mathematics, such as percentages, formulae and more complex statistical and trigonometric functions.

As an example, on the *learn.co.uk* home-page, click on the 'Mathematics' link under the 'Key stage 3' heading, then 'Percentages' on the resulting page. This takes you to the 'Lesson objectives' page – the content of the lesson can be accessed by the links on the left-hand side of the screen. The first section explains that a girl achieving a score of 90/100 in a test has a percentage of 90 per cent.

This can be shown within Excel. Type '=90/100' into a cell. It is initially converted into decimals (0.9), but you can see it as a percentage by highlighting the cell, choosing 'Cells' from the 'Format' menu at the top of the screen, then picking 'Percentage' from the 'Number' menu offered in the resulting box. This turns the content of the box to '90.00%'. As long as the equal sign appears at the front of the fraction in question, this allows pupils to play around with the function. Putting in '=2/3' would show that two-thirds in percentage terms is 66.67% (rounded to two decimal places).

Several lessons deal with brackets. From the home page, if you click on 'Mathematics – Higher' under 'Key stage 4', you can find 'Using brackets in algebra' in the 'Number and algebra' list of lessons. This gives the example of '2 x (3 + 4)', meaning that the brackets require you to add three and four, then multiply by two. Again, this can be tried in Excel by adding an = sign to the front of this formula. An asterisk is used in spreadsheets to multiply. Typing '=2*(3+4)' into a cell does indeed produce '14', with the bar at the top of the screen showing the formula. The lesson page says this formula is equivalent to 6+8 – this can be checked by typing '=6+8' into a cell.

➡ *Do your Maths Homework*

GET NUTRITIONAL INFORMATION

You can use a spreadsheet to keep track of your weight, a diet or an exercise plan. Firstly, it makes sense to check your ideal weight – being too light can cause health problems just as serious as being too heavy. Ideal weight is usually calculated using the Body Mass Index. You can work this out in Excel, or use a web site – either way, the information you need is available at *www.bbc.co.uk/health/fightingfat/bmi.shtml.*

Linked pages in the BBC site hold a lot of data about eating sensibly. The advice includes a warning to those who should not diet, especially people who have any medical conditions or pregnant women.

Often, a diet can simply involve cutting down on certain foods and alcohol, but if you want to count calories, a spreadsheet will help. There is a lot of information about diets available online: some are paid for, but some are available free. An Irish web site, *www.diet-i.com*, provides data on areas including how many calories you burn up each day, at *www.diet-i.com/weight_loss/calories.htm*. This site also has advice about weight loss.

If you intend to count calories, some of the data you require will appear on food packaging, but more is available online. Try the database at *www.caloriescount.com*. Say you want to find out how many calories are in an apple. Click on the 'Enter calculator' button, then type 'apple' into the search box. You get a number of results, starting with 'apple (raw with peel) – three inches' at 81 calories. This US site is run by a group of manufacturers of low-fat foods – note the suggestion that you might want to find the calorie value of 'low fat chips' on the search page. (And bear in mind that 'chips' in the US means 'crisps' in the UK.)

Another (usually better) way to improve your health is to do more exercise. To refer again to the BBC's health pages (*www.bbc.co.uk/health/fightingfat/active.shtml*), you should aim for 30 minutes of moderate exercise each day. This is yet another measurement you could log on a spreadsheet – it means you can make sure you average 30 minutes a day, even if you do more some days and less others.

Finally, if the idea of losing weight makes you feel depressed, the following guide to the calorie-burning capacity of certain activities may cheer you up: *www.aardvarkexpress.com/storycalorieguide.htm.*

➡ *Manage a Diet*

GOAL SEEK

Formulae are the basis of mathematical operations and typically contain a combination of cell references and numeric values. When you are constructing a formula, you usually know which cells or values to include in the calculation but not what the end result will be. However, if you do have an end goal in mind, you can use Goal Seek to work backwards through a formula and determine what values each cell needs to contain to achieve the end result.

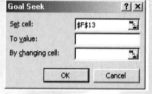

ABOVE: Spreadsheets can be used to record dietary information and exercise plans.
RIGHT: Goal Seek is a powerful tool for assessing and identifying results.

Let's take a simple example. You want to retire in five years' time and buy a holiday cottage. You enter the monthly amount that you currently save into a cell on the worksheet and in another cell you enter 60 as the number of months that are left before you retire. In a third cell, create a simple formula to calculate your current savings multiplied by 60. Given that your current level of savings can be maintained, your formula will calculate how much you will save in the next five years. But what if you know that you need to save a specific amount for your holiday cottage, say £50,000? This is where Goal Seek comes in.

Select the cell containing the formula and click the Tools menu. Select the Goal Seek option. The Goal Seek dialog box will appear. Click in the Set Cell box and collapse the dialog box. Select the cell on the worksheet that contains the formula and click to expand the dialog box again. Type the result that you want to achieve in the To value box and click in the By changing cell box and select the cell that contains the value to change. In the

previous example, it will be the cell that contains the monthly savings. Click OK. The Goal Seek Status dialog box will indicate whether or not a solution has been found. Click OK and Goal Seek will update the worksheet with the new values. Look at the value in the adjustable cell. Has it changed in line with the result that you wanted?

You do need to be aware that some problems cannot be solved. If this is the case and there is no solution, Excel will display a message in the Goal Seek Status dialog box telling you so.

On occasion, Excel may report that a solution is not available when you believe it is. If this is the case, it is worth considering a few options. First, check your logic and make sure that the formula cell does depend on the specified changing cell. If you are convinced it does, try either of the following steps.

- Try changing the current value of the By changing cell box in the Goal Seek dialog box to a value that is closer to the solution. Re-issue the command to see if a solution can now be found.

- Select the Calculations tab of the Options dialog box and try adjusting the Maximum iterations setting. If you increase the number of iterations, Excel will try more possible solutions.

Goal Seek does have a limitation in that only one cell can be adjusted at any one time. For example, it can't tell you what monthly payment you need to make and the number of months over which you need to make this payment in order to save your £50,000. If you need to change more than one variable at a time, you will need to use Solver.

The Solver tool extends the facilities of Goal Seek but it is fairly complicated to use.

Excel also provides another way to perform goal seeking through manipulating the data series in a graph. If you have created a chart based on information relating to your formula, you can change the data point on a chart and Goal Seek will find and adjust the value in the worksheet and re-plot the chart.

➡ *Functions*

HELP WITH EXCEL

There are several sites maintained by organizations, companies and individuals to provide extra help with Excel. One of the better basic ones is at *www.coe.uncc.edu/project_mosaic/PC/excel*, a site run by the University of North Carolina in the US.

The site is divided into four sections. The first, 'Frequently Asked Questions', covers 11 fairly basic queries, such as how to create a graph. (The answer can of course be found elsewhere in this book.) The answers are clear and often illustrated. The other sections, 'Getting Started in Microsoft Excel', 'Cell Formatting' and 'Creating and Editing Graphs', are similarly aimed at the learner. In each case, the answers are clear, illustrated and well laid out. This is worth looking at if you need a little extra help with the basics.

Another US university, Columbia in New York City, hosts a short introductory help page, at *www.ldeo.columbia. edu/~martins/ees/excel/ms_excel.html*. This may be helpful for Apple Mac users, as the screen shots are taken from this type of computer.

For a comprehensive range of options, try *www.mrexcel.com*. This site has loads of features – look down the line of blue buttons on the left of the home page. It has tips of the day and the week, horror stories – such as the boss who asked if someone could add a fourth dimension to a graph – challenges for those wanting to test their Excel skills, and a book list.

However, this site also has two interactive features, either of which might give you a personal response. You can email Mr Excel, who will reply to some emails through the web site like a software agony uncle. Or you can post your query on the site's message board. This has had tens of thousands of postings – and many people willing to provide answers, it seems. Please note you that are more likely to get an answer if it isn't one that can be answered easily through Excel's internal Help function, or somewhere else on this site.

Specialist help for business users can be found at *http://lacher.com*, run by an Ohio-based consulting firm. This includes help with about a dozen specific topics, such as 'Forecasting Techniques' and 'Number of Days, Months and Years Between Two Dates'. The site offers small downloads for some solutions. It also holds a bibliography.

www.xlhelp.com/Excel/help.htm is basically a list of links to more help sites. Some of these offer highly specialized help, such as for using Excel with radio telescopes or soil hydrology.

➠ *Help with Help*

ABOVE LEFT: Everybody encounters problems with spreadsheets and charts – some seem more difficult than they really are. Internet help sites are designed with users in mind and are often free of the jargon associated with experts and developers.

HELP WITH HELP

Excel provides help and assistance at a number of levels from the Office Assistant through to help from the World Wide Web. Some help is context-sensitive and will be relevant to whatever you are doing at

the time. Alternatively, if you want more information on a specific topic, Excel provides a search facility to enable you to gain detailed help on that subject.

The Office Assistant is available with all Office applications and is designed to help you work more effectively. It is intuitive and will offer help if it thinks you need it. For example, the Assistant will automatically provide help if you are using a new function for the first time. It also provides tips, step-by-step explanations and a facility to search for help on a specific topic.

In most cases the Assistant pops up of its own accord, but if you need to call for assistance, click on the Office Assistant button on the Standard toolbar. The Office Assistant button can also be found in some dialog boxes and menus.

ABOVE: The Office Assistant provides users with tips and a search facility.
RIGHT: Office on the Web can offer you support in times of trouble.

If you have a specific question, click in the Assistant window and type your question in the box. Click the Search button to locate and display any related help topics. If the Assistant cannot find any information relating to your request, a message will appear asking you to rephrase your question. Once it has found a match, click on the most appropriate help topic to display the help information.

If you spot the Assistant with a light bulb above it, Excel believes you are going the long away around your current task! Click on the Assistant to discover a hot tip on how to work more efficiently.

The default Assistant image is an animated paper clip, referred to as Clippit. There are a number of other images that you may prefer. To change the Assistant image, right-click on the Assistant and select the Choose Assistant option from the shortcut menu. The Office Assistant dialog box is displayed. Click on the Gallery tab and use the Next button to display the range of available images. Once you have selected your preferred Assistant, click OK.

If you want to change the way in which the Assistant offers help, right-click on the Assistant and select the Option category from the shortcut menu. Check or uncheck the available options to customize the Assistant to suit your requirements. You will probably find that the Respond to F1 key box is checked. If you uncheck it, the F1 key will call up Excel Help instead of the Office Assistant. You need to decide whether you prefer F1, the standard help key, to call up the Office Assistant or Excel Help. Your choice will depend on which you use the most.

The easiest way to get help on elements of the screen or the range of menus, options and toolbars is to use the Excel context-sensitive help. To do this, access the Help menu and select the What's This option (SHIFT+F1). A floating question mark will appear next to the mouse pointer. As you move the mouse the question mark will move with it. Point and click on the element to display help information.

You can also gain context-sensitive help when accessing a dialog box. Either click on the question mark on the dialog box title bar or right-click on any element within the dialog box to display the What's this option.

To determine the full extent of Excel's help facilities, access the Help menu and select the Contents and Index

option. The Microsoft Excel help dialog box will be displayed. This provides a list of contents as well as an alphabetical index. An alternative way to access this dialog box is to press the F1 key. If you find this calls up the Assistant instead, you will need to uncheck the Respond to F1 key box in the Assistant dialog box.

The Microsoft Excel help dialog box provides three tabs: Contents, Answer Wizard and Index. The Contents option provides a list of available help subjects divided into chapters and sub-chapters. Each sub-chapter provides one or more pages of information on the subject.

The Index option provides a different method for finding help on a specific topic. The topics are listed in alphabetical order and you can either scroll down to find the topic you want or, to speed up the search, start typing the first couple of letters of the topic and you will jump to the relevant place in the list.

The Answer Wizard option resembles the Office Assistant allowing you to ask simple questions.

If you cannot find the help you need using the Excel facilities, you can access additional help via the Web. To do this, access the Help menu and select the Office on the web option. You will need access to the Internet to use this option.

There are a number of options available to you including support, access to an online tutorial and the facility to download Office accessories.

➡ *Help with Excel, Microsoft's Excel Page, Shortcut Keys*

HISTORY OF SPREADSHEETS

Spreadsheets came into being soon after the world's first commercially-viable personal computer, the Apple II. Previously, if you wanted your own computer, you built it from a kit; then in 1978, you could buy an Apple II from a shop, ready to go. It cost $3,000 including a colour display, keyboard (previously an optional extra) and a floppy disk drive. This was cheap compared with the multi-user 'mainframe' computers dominant at the time, but still expensive for an individual.

But the Apple II was purchased by middle managers in businesses, so they could use VisiCalc, the first spreadsheet software. Its writer, Dan Bricklin, was a computer programmer who went to business school. There, he learnt about spreadsheets – banks of blackboards used by large companies to work out complex financial or manufacturing numbers. These boards were divided into grids, and used reference numbers akin to those used in the game battleships. Some cells were connected to others, so if, for example, a cost was increased, projected profits would decrease in tandem.

The trouble was that these connections had to be reworked individually and manually every time a number

RIGHT: Spreadsheets came into being soon after the world's first commercially viable personal computer, the Apple II.

was changed. This was time-consuming and prone to error. So Bricklin simply put it all into a computer program. It allowed business school graduates to run a spreadsheet without needing a big room of blackboards and a staff of arithmeticians. And it allowed them to change the numbers and see the effects in a fraction of a second. In short, it allowed users to play with a complex web of numbers – and therefore with the workings of a factory, a business or an entire economy.

Bricklin wrote the original demonstration of VisiCalc over a weekend, in a computer language called Basic. With a partner, Bob Frankston, he then developed it for the Apple II, because Frankston knew how to program the Apple. It took about a year, working nights on a minicomputer running software that would make it behave like an Apple II.

VisiCalc was published in October 1979, with Bricklin's company taking a royalty and a publisher making and distributing disks. It cost $100. Initial sales were poor, but eventually small businesspeople started to catch on and spread the word to middle managers in large corporations.

For these people, VisiCalc alone justified buying the Apple II. Large organizations owned computers, but staff had to book and justify time spent using the system. Managers couldn't just play with numbers on a large central computer, but they could with Apple and VisiCalc.

Other spreadsheets appeared. In one, you chose how many cells you wanted to create, rather than just being given a page full of them (as in Excel). In another, you could enter text rather than numbers or mathematical formulae (this idea did get picked up for use in Excel). But the next leap forward for spreadsheets happened at a company called Lotus. Lotus produced a spreadsheet called Lotus 1-2-3, which was designed to work with IBM's new PC. (Due to IBM's strong brand and then its willingness to allow others to use the design, the PC soon outsold the original personal computer maker Apple – and it still does.)

Bricklin produced a version of VisiCalc for the IBM PC, but it hadn't been adjusted (or 'optimized', in jargon) to work well on this new, hugely popular computer. Enter Mitch Kapor, who produced a successful add-on piece of software for VisiCalc. His work was bought up by the publisher (unlike Bricklin, who preferred to keep getting royalties), and with the proceeds, Kapor decided to set up a company called Lotus to produce a spreadsheet optimized for the IBM PC. Rather than go for individual middle managers, Lotus advertised its software, 1-2-3, direct to large corporations, organizations that had bought reliable mainframe computers from IBM for decades.

Kapor hoped to sell $4 million worth of 1-2-3 during 1983. Instead, Lotus sold $53 million that year, growing to $157 million in 1984, pulling IBM PC sales up in its wake. Lotus, which later created highly specialized software helping employees to work in groups, was eventually bought by IBM, and it remains a distinct division. IBM still sells Lotus 1-2-3. The latest version, release 9.5, costs $315, and includes the ability to enter numbers by speaking them into a microphone.

Microsoft, which produces Excel and is the world's largest software company, actually offered to buy Lotus in 1984 – and was turned down. It dominated operating system software for the IBM PC, as IBM placed Microsoft's DOS operating system on every machine before it was sold. DOS developed into Windows, and nearly all manufacturers of PCs continue to place Microsoft operating systems on PCs before sale.

The vast licence fees from DOS and Windows gave (and still gives) the firm a strong cash flow to launch other software. It launched its spreadsheet, Excel, in 1985, initially for the Apple Macintosh. By the early 1990s, Microsoft was well ahead of Lotus in sales. Excel is now part of the Microsoft Office group of programs, the most widely used application software in the world.

➡ *Lotus 1-2-3*

HYPERLINKS

A hyperlink is a link in a document which allows you to jump to a defined area of the same document, another Excel workbook, a file in another application or a page published on the World Wide Web. Hyperlinks can also be used to launch an e-mail program and insert the mail address specified in the link.

Hyperlinked text is set apart from other text in that it is depicted in a different colour or underlined. Hyperlinks can also be represented by icons or buttons.

To insert a hyperlink, select the cell which will represent the link. right-click and choose Hyperlink from the shortcut menu or click the Insert menu and select the Hyperlink option. The Insert Hyperlink dialog box will be displayed. Click one of the images displayed down the left-hand side of the dialog box to select the type of object you want to link to.

To link to an existing file or web page, click an icon to view and select from recently used files, web pages or web addresses. Alternatively, browse for a file and double-click to select. If you want a tip to appear when the mouse rests on a hyperlink, click ScreenTip and type the text.

➡ *Web Pages from Excel*

IMPORTING DATA

If you want to bring data into Excel from another application, there are a number of options open to you. The method that you choose will depend upon the type of data that you want to import (e.g. text, web page, Access database, Lotus 1-2-3 worksheet), the level of integration between the source application and Excel, and the reason for bringing the data into Excel.

At the simplest level, if you only want to transfer a small amount of data or data from an unusual source (such as a mainframe application), you can copy it into Notepad and paste it into Excel. Although this is simple, you might find that you then have to invest time in reformatting the data.

If the file type is supported by Excel, for instance a Lotus 1-2-3 workbook, you can open it directly in Excel. In the Open dialog box, select the file from the Files of Type list. Once opened, you can then save the file as an Excel workbook. If the file contains complex formulae or macros, Excel may not be able to convert them successfully.

ABOVE: Wherever you are collecting data from, you may wish to import it into Excel.

If you need to import text files, Access files or web pages, you can adopt a more formal import process.

Most applications can read text files. Importing a text file is sometimes the only way that Excel can read information that has been created in another application, such as a mainframe. Rather than re-creating mainframe database records, you might be able to save and import them into Excel as a text file.

Applications differ in the way that they store information relating to database fields. Sometimes an application will allocate a certain number of spaces for each field in the file. For example, a width of 30 characters might be allocated for an address field. If the address entered is less than 30 characters, space characters will be used to take up the remaining width. Such files are known as fixed width text files. Other applications use a more efficient method to store field information. Instead of specifying a fixed column width, a delimiter character is used to signify the end of each field. Commas, tabs, semicolons and single spaces are typically used as delimiters.

When importing a text file, Excel needs to recognize where one field ends and another begins, so that it can place related information into the same column (this is known as parsing). In other words, it needs to know either the width allocated to each column or the delimiter character. If it doesn't have this information, the text file will be imported into a single cell or column.

If you open a text file via the Open dialog box, the Text Import Wizard will be launched. If you don't want to use the Text Import Wizard, hold down the Shift key while opening the file.

The first screen of the Wizard should illustrate how the data is organized, i.e. by fixed width or delimited. You can set the first row to be imported and specify from which platform the file originated. This can be important because operating systems may use different methods to indicate the end of a row.

For delimited text files, indicate in Step 2 of the Wizard which character is used as the delimiter. If you are likely to have empty fields and you want Excel to maintain the correct data structure by creating empty cells in their place, make sure that the Treat consecutive delimiters as one box is unchecked.

If the data has been stored using the fixed column width method, Step 2 of the Wizard will prompt you to organize the data into columns by placing lines where you want column breaks. Click the Data preview area to insert column break lines. Use this method to insert blank columns. The third step is to select each column and set the format. The file will be imported into its own workbook.

Importing a text file as an external data range provides a more flexible alternative. Using this method, the imported range will reflect changes made to the source file. Click the Data menu followed by Get External Data and then Import Text File. When you have completed the steps in the Wizard, the Import Data dialog box will be displayed. Indicate where the data is to be placed.

BELOW: Just as goods can be imported into warehouses, so data can be imported into Excel.

Select any cell in the external data range and view the shortcut menu. Use the Edit Text Import option to specify import settings and the Refresh Data option to define how data will be updated.

You can import a HTML file from within Excel using the Open dialog box or you can export a web page to Excel from within your browser. Depending on the level of complexity and interactivity within the web page, you may find that some features are not imported.

You can also analyse Access data in Excel. Switch to the Access form, report etc., and click the Tools menu. Select Office Links followed by Analyze it with MS Excel. The form will be opened as a workbook.

⟹ **Web Pages from Excel, Exporting Data**

INFORMATION FUNCTIONS

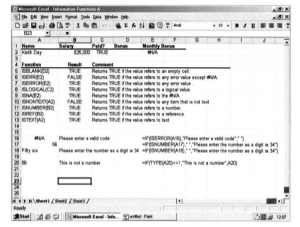 The Information functions provide status information regarding the selected value. The majority of the information functions are referred to collectively as the IS functions. They can be used to check the type of value and return TRUE or FALSE depending on the outcome. All IS functions have just one argument, the value you want to test.

In most cases, the IS functions are used within other functions as a means of testing a result. With the above examples, an IF function is used to test the content of the value in column A. The example in row 16 uses the ISERROR function to see if an error has been caused by the value entered into cell A16. If it has, a message is displayed. The following two examples use the ISNUMBER function to test whether a number has been entered. If TRUE, a blank is displayed. If FALSE, a prompt is displayed asking the user to re-enter a number.

The TYPE function returns a number representing the type of value. For example, 1 for a number and 2 for text. The example in row 20 uses the TYPE function to determine whether the content is in fact a number.

➡ *Functions, Paste Function Button*

INLANDREVENUE.GOV.UK

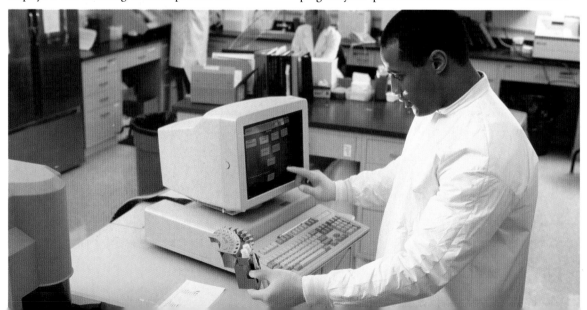 One of the most useful things you can do with spreadsheets is keep track of your tax. For those who have to fill in a tax return, or keep track of taxes for a business, it's a dull job that simply has to be done accurately, with a record of how you get to the resulting numbers.

The UK government's tax collection agency provides the data you need to do these taxes. In fact, for those filling out a self-assessment tax form without too many complications, it also provides the facility to file it online, at *www.ir-online.gov.uk* (there's a link from the Inland Revenue's home-page). However, you may still want to work out your taxes separately in a spreadsheet, so you have an approximate idea of how much you will need to keep in reserve. Even for full-time employees who have their taxes calculated automatically by their company, you may want to check your employer has got it right.

The web site provides the basic data you need to program your spreadsheet for tax calculations. There are

BELOW LEFT: Information functions allow you to assess information and test for errors, therefore are useful in a wide range of practical situations.
BELOW: Whatever your occupation, you should always keep a tax record.

links from the right-hand side of the home page covering several industries that have special tax arrangements, such as construction. However, the data that affects almost everyone is available from the 'Rates and Allowances' link (scroll down to the section marked 'Facts and Figures'), or at *www.inlandrevenue.gov.uk/rates*. If you click on the first link, 'Income tax', you get the key information: allowances (the amount of annual income you are allowed to receive tax-free) and the bands of income and percentages of income tax charged in each.

Almost everyone is affected by National Insurance, which is covered by the second link. This is more complicated because it is calculated per week. Unlike income tax, it is currently payable only on a band of earnings: if you earn more than a certain amount, you don't pay any extra (the current numbers are on the site).

For the self-employed, it's even more complicated. This group pays Class 2 contributions – a minimal £2 a week, except for certain professions – but also Class 4 contributions on a band of profits. Again, these boundaries are listed on the site.

Income tax and National Insurance will cover the bulk of most people's taxes. However, data is also listed for other areas, such as savings (taxed slightly differently from other income) and stamp duty (tax on trading property and shares).

If you want more help (and goodness knows, most people do), you could try looking through the Revenue's leaflets designed to help explain the tax system, at *www.inlandrevenue.gov.uk/leaflets*.

➠ *Work Out your Taxes*

INSERTING GRAPHICS AND CLIPS

There are many ways to improve the look and feel of a worksheet. Excel has an in-built gallery of pictures, photographs, clip art and sounds which can

easily be inserted into a worksheet to emphasize key points. Graphics which have been created using another application can also be used.

Individual media files, including pictures, sounds and animations, are known as clips. To insert a clip from the Excel clip art gallery, click the Insert menu, select Picture and then Clip Art.

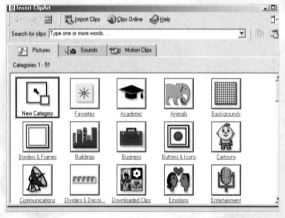

ABOVE: Inserting graphics can make a spreadsheet look impressive.
ABOVE RIGHT: To access the Microsoft Design Gallery Live site, select the Clips Online icon.

The Insert Clip Art dialog box will be displayed. Across the top of the dialog box you will find tabs which relate to the types of media clips available, such as Pictures, Sounds and Motion Clips. Select a tab and then choose a clip from one of the categories displayed. If you are not sure which category will contain suitable pictures, type a key word in the Search for clips box and press the Enter key. Click on a clip and a pop-up menu will appear. Choose whether to insert into a worksheet, preview, add to the favourites folder, or find clips which are similar in artistic style, colour or shape.

If you want to use clips which are stored on a CD-ROM, hard drive or network, select the Import Clips icon at the top of the dialog box. From the Add clip to Clip Gallery dialog box, you can opt to copy or move the additional clips into the clip gallery so that they are available for future use.

If you have a connection to the World Wide Web via an online service and modem, plus a browser which can display frames and JavaScript (such as Microsoft Internet Explorer 4.0), you can access a web site which has been created specially for clip gallery users. To access

the Microsoft Design Gallery Live site, select the Clips Online icon. Type a subject in the Search for box. You can limit the search to specific categories from the Search in box and to particular types of media in the Results should be box. A selection of clips will appear. Click once on a clip to preview it and again to have it downloaded into the clip gallery. From then on in, the clip will be available in the Downloaded Clips category.

Corporate photographs, logos or even sound bites can help draw attention to key information within a worksheet. Excel allows you to import a range of graphics files which have been created using other applications. The following graphics are all supported: Windows Bitmap files (.bmp), Windows Metafiles (.wmf), files with a Graphics Interchange Format (.gif), Enhanced Metafiles (.emf), Joint Photographic Experts Group (.jpg) and Portable Network Graphics (.png). Note that some of the graphic filters required to import the above formats are only available if you have installed Microsoft Office.

To insert a picture, select the Insert menu and then the Picture option. You can choose to insert Clip Art, a picture stored in another file, AutoShapes, an Organization Chart, WordArt, or pictures created using a scanner or digital camera. To insert a picture created in another application, select the From File option. The Insert Picture dialog box will be displayed. Navigate through your filing system until you find a picture to insert, then click on the picture and then on the Insert button.

To change or enhance a picture, click on it. The Picture toolbar will be displayed. If it is not displayed, select the Format menu followed by the Picture option. The toolbar consists of special picture formatting tools which help you to control the image, brightness and contrast, colour and line styles. There is also a crop tool which can be used to remove parts of the picture that you

don't want to be displayed. If you don't like the changes you have made, select the Reset Picture button. When a picture is selected, some of the options on the Drawing toolbar also become available. However, you may have to ungroup a picture so that it becomes a drawing object, before you can use some of the drawing tools and options.

If you have a TWAIN- compatible scanner or camera connected to your PC, you will be able to transfer electronic images from the device into an Office application. Microsoft Office 2000 supports TWAIN 1.7. You can insert a scanned photograph or a photograph taken with a digital camera directly into Excel. To do this, place a picture in your scanner or capture the image on camera and click the Insert menu followed by Picture. Choose the From Scanner or Camera option. The Insert Picture from Scanner or Camera dialog box will be displayed. If you have more than one device connected, select the device. If you are using a scanner and are happy with the default or pre-defined settings for scanned images, click Insert. If the Insert button is unavailable, or you need to change the scanned image settings or insert an image from a camera, select Custom Insert. Follow on-screen instructions to complete the Insert.

➠ *Drawing and Graphics*

JARGON BUSTING

 What does it mean? Jargon is rife in the computer world and Excel has its fair share of special terms, some common to other applications and some peculiar to itself. Understanding the special terms used by Excel can make it much easier to discover the full power of this sophisticated product. Here are just a few examples of Excel's special language.

Absolute Cell Reference With an absolute cell reference, row and column references do not change when you copy the formula to another cell. You can spot an absolute cell reference by the dollar signs before the row and column reference. For example: $B$3.

Add-In An optional program that comes with Excel, providing extra commands or features. Before you can use an add-in, you need to install it on your computer and then load it in Excel.

Assistant The Office Assistant is available with all Microsoft Office applications and provides help and tips relevant to the current task.

ABOVE: The Office Assistant can provide information relevant to the current task.

Automatic Function Designed to accelerate the entering and formatting of data. There are some functions that are common to most Office applications, such as AutoCorrect (automatically corrects spelling mistakes). Other functions are more applicable to Excel, such as AutoCalculate (displays statistical information regarding the currently selected cells).

Cell A cell is created where a worksheet row and column meet. The resulting cell is where you enter your data. Cells can contain text, numbers or formulae.

Cell Frame The cell frame is the border around the cell. You can tell when a cell is selected as the cell frame becomes a thick black line.

Cell Reference Each cell within a worksheet can be identified by a unique reference. The reference is determined by the intersection of a vertical column and a horizontal row. For example, the cell created by the intersection of column C and row 5 is referenced as cell C5.

Clipboard The contents of cells are stored in the clipboard when they have been cut from their original location and are waiting to be pasted into a new location.

Dialogue Box (Spelt as the Americanized 'Dialog Box' in Excel) is displayed where there are multiple choices available. Sometimes if you select an option from a menu, a dialogue box is displayed providing a number of further options. Once you have made your selections you close the dialogue box by clicking the OK button.

Format You format a worksheet to improve and enhance the way it looks. This can include using colour, borders, shading, currency and percentage symbols and page numbers.

Formula Used to calculate results from the data stored in a worksheet. The use of formulae is what makes an

BELOW: The Wizard facility takes you through some operations step by step.

electronic spreadsheet so powerful. When data changes, the formulae automatically recalculate everything.

Function Provided as part of the Excel program and designed to save you time. Rather than create your own, sometimes complicated formula, Excel provides a range of built-in formulae known as functions, which range from simple summation through to complex financial and conditional functions.

Macro A macro is a recorded series of commands that you can play back at any time. Macros are usually created for operations you carry out on a regular basis.

Mixed Cell Reference With a mixed cell reference, either the row or column reference is relative and the other is absolute. The absolute part of the reference can be identified by a dollar sign before the row or column reference. For example, $B3 or B$3.

Mouse Button A personal computer mouse has two buttons referred to as the left button and the right button (sometimes there is also a centre button used to scroll quickly up or down the screen). The left mouse button is used to select a cell, menu items and options. The right mouse button activates the Excel shortcut menus. References to 'left-clicking' and 'right-clicking' means using the left and right mouse buttons.

Pane The Excel window can be divided into two or four separate areas. Each area is known as a pane. By dividing the window into panes, you can view different areas of your worksheet at the same time.

Relative Cell Reference (see Cell Reference) The default cell reference is known as a relative reference. The row and column references change when you copy a formula to another cell.

Table A connected data range within a worksheet.

Template Used as a starting point for future workbooks. A template is essentially a model on which you can base your new workbook. It can contain any or all of the components of a workbook, including data and formatting.

Toolbar Excel comes with a number of toolbars that contain buttons or icons for all the most commonly used commands. Instead of using the Excel menus to select a command you can save time by clicking on the appropriate button on the toolbar.

Wizard Part of the Excel help facility designed to lead you step by step through certain operations.

Workbook An Excel file is known as a workbook and is made up of a number of worksheets.

Worksheet A single page in an Excel workbook is known as a worksheet. A worksheet is made up of rows and columns. Where each row and column intersect a cell is formed.

➡ *Help with Help.*

KEEP A LIBRARY

 With books, CDs, music cassettes and video tapes scattered around the house, it would be useful to know where they are all located, especially if friends want to borrow them. The following two pages show you how to list your personal collection in a spreadsheet and use some of the tools in Excel for sorting, filtering and finding.

1. Starting with a new workbook in Excel, select cell A1 and enter the headings for your library (Title, Author/Singer, Format, Location, Notes). Enter each heading in a separate cell across the top of the spreadsheet. Start entering the details for your books, CDs, videos and anything else you wish to record. You may wish to stretch the width of columns to hold data. Do so by clicking on the right edge of the lettered top of each column, holding the mouse button down, and moving the mouse right. In some columns, you may notice that Excel tries to complete words for you. For example, after typing the word book in the Format column, whenever you type the letter B in this column, the word book will appear. This is called AutoComplete. Press Return to accept the entry or continue typing to overwrite it.

2. Make sure you regularly save your Excel file. Click on the File menu and choose Save. If you have not saved this file before, a Save As dialog box will appear. Enter a name for your Excel file and choose a location on your computer to store it. Click on the Save button and you will return to your spreadsheet. When you return to the File menu and choose Save, this dialog box will not appear, but the file will be saved.

3. When you have finished entering the details of your books, music collection and videos, you may want to sort the order of the listings. To do this, press Ctrl, then A, selecting the whole sheet.

4. With your list selected, click on the Data menu and choose Sort. From the Sort dialog box that appears, make sure the option for Header Row is selected near the bottom. Click on the drop-down triangle under Sort by and choose a heading from your list. Select to sort Ascending or Descending. You can choose to sort on two additional levels if you wish. Click on OK to close the dialog box, sort your list and return to your spreadsheet. You can return to the Sort dialog box and change the sort order whenever you want.

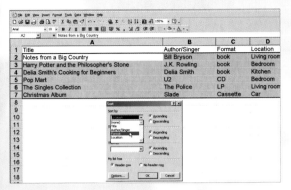

5. If you want to see all of your CDs, for example, or the contents of your collection stored in your living room, you can filter this information from your list. First, select your entire list (see step 3). Then click on the Data menu, choose Filter and select AutoFilter from the sub-menu. A series of drop-down triangles will appear next to each heading in your list. Click on the drop-down triangle next to Format and choose CD, for example. Only the CDs in your library will now be listed.

6. You can continue filtering on other headings. Whenever you filter on a heading, the drop-down triangle will be coloured in blue to tell you that you have filtered on it. To return to seeing all the records listed, click on a blue drop-down triangle and choose the All option (at the top of the list). Alternatively, click on the Data menu, select Filter and choose Show All from the sub-menu. If you want to remove the AutoFilter drop-down triangles, return to the Data menu, select Filter and click on AutoFilter.

7. If you want to find a particular book, for example, select your entire list (see step 3), click on the Data menu and choose Form (for Excel 2000 you may need to select the arrows at the bottom of the menu to expand it and see Form). From the dialog box that appears, click on the Criteria button and enter the information you are looking for in the appropriate heading (your headings should be listed). Click on the Find Next and Find Prev buttons to move through the records that match your criteria. To search for something else, click on Criteria, click on the Clear button and enter some new details to look for. To return to your spreadsheet, click on the Close button.

8. To find out how many books, CDs, tapes and other items you own, first sort your library on the Format heading (see steps 3 and 4). Then click on the Data menu and choose Subtotals. The Subtotal dialog box will appear. Click on the drop-down triangle at the top (under At each change in) and select Format. Make sure Count is listed under Use function. Add a tick mark to Format under Add subtotal to. Remove any other ticks. Click on OK to return to your spreadsheet. Click on the numbered buttons at the top left of your spreadsheet or the plus and minus symbols to see different levels of subtotals for your library. To remove the subtotals, select a cell inside your list, return to the Subtotal Dialog Box and click on the Remove All Button.

➡ *Publication Data*

LEFT: Spreadsheets can be used to catalogue your books and CDs.

KEEPING CELLS STILL

Using references. When you move or copy a cell containing a formula, Excel will automatically adjust the formula to the new location. You can control what happens to your formulae by using different types of cell references. In this way you can tell Excel to adjust formulae to their new location or to keep them still!

Each cell within a worksheet can be identified by a unique reference. The reference is determined by the intersection of a row and column. For example, the cell created by the intersection of column C and row 5 is referenced as cell C5.

When creating a formula you should always include cell references rather than values. In this way you can easily make changes to your worksheet without having to alter the formulae manually. For example, if you are creating a worksheet to calculate commissions, the current commission rate should be entered in a cell and that cell referenced in the formula to calculate commission.

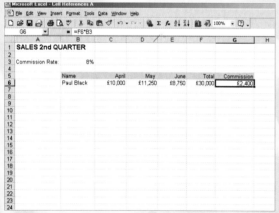

The commission rate of 8% is entered in cell B3. This value is then used to calculate the commission for Paul Black by referencing the cell address rather than the actual percentage. The formula is entered in cell G6 as =F6*B3. By doing this, you can change the commission rate in B3 at any time and the calculation in cell G6 will automatically update.

When you use a reference in a formula, there are three types of references available.

Relative: The default reference is known as a relative reference. The row and column references change when you copy the formula to another cell.

Absolute: With an absolute reference, row and column references do not change when you copy the formula to another cell.

Mixed: With a mixed reference, either the row or column reference is relative and the other is absolute.

References are relative by default. If you copy a formula containing relative addresses to another cell, Excel does not produce an exact copy. What actually happens is Excel adjusts the formula to be relative to the new location. This is best explained by example. Take a formula that adds the content of the two cells directly above. The formula is entered in cell B3 as =B1+B2. If the formula in cell B3 is then copied to cell D3, the formula will no longer read as =B1+B2 but as =D1+D2. The formula still totals the contents of the two cells above but it has changed relative to its new position.

So, why would you want to use an absolute address and copy the formula exactly as it is? Let's return to the previous commission example. If you enhance the worksheet to include figures for your other sales staff, you will need to enter several more formulae to calculate their total sales and commissions. Alternatively, you could save time by copying the formulae for Paul Black to the rest of the team.

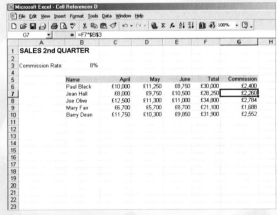

```
[X] Eile Edit View Insert Format Tools Data Window Help
D ☞ ■ 🖨 🎒 🔃 ❤ ✗ 🖻 🖺 ❤ ⋈ ▾ ⋈ ▾ 🍓 Σ ƒ* ☝↓ ☝↓ 🏛 🐼 100% ▾ ②.
  F7      ▾  = =SUM(C7:E7)
     A          B        C        D       E        F         G      H
1  SALES 2nd QUARTER
2
3  Commission Rate:     8%
4
5                Name      April      May      June    Total   Commission
6   Paul Black    £10,000   £11,250   £8,750   £30,000      £2,400
7   Jean Hall     £8,000    £9,750    £10,500  £28,250
8   Joe Olive     £12,500   £11,300   £11,000  £34,800
9   Mary Fair     £6,700    £5,700    £8,700   £21,100
10  Barry Dean    £11,750   £10,300   £9,850   £31,900
11
...
22
```

Copying the commission totals is fine. The formula is copied in a relative way. This gives the correct result for each of the other sales people. The formula to calculate the total sales for Paul Black is =SUM(C6:E6). When copied to the row below it reads =SUM(C7:E7), totalling the values for Jean Hall.

```
[X] Microsoft Excel - Cell References C
[X] Eile Edit View Insert Format Tools Data Window Help
D ☞ ■ 🖨 🎒 🔃 ❤ ✗ 🖻 🖺 ❤ ⋈ ▾ ⋈ ▾ 🍓 Σ ƒ* ☝↓ ☝↓ 🏛 🐼 100% ▾ ②.
  G7      ▾  = =F7*B4
     A          B        C        D       E        F         G      H
1  SALES 2nd QUARTER
2
3  Commission Rate:     8%
4
5                Name      April      May      June    Total   Commission
6   Paul Black    £10,000   £11,250   £8,750   £30,000      £2,400
7   Jean Hall     £8,000    £9,750    £10,500  £28,250      £0
8   Joe Olive     £12,500   £11,300   £11,000  £34,800
9   Mary Fair     £6,700    £5,700    £8,700   £21,100
10  Barry Dean    £11,750   £10,300   £9,850   £31,900
11
...
24
```

Copying the formula for Commission does not work so well. Copying the formula that calculates the commission for Paul Black, =F6*B3, to the cell below will produce the formula =F7*B4, not what you want! Again, Excel has copied the formula in a relative way. The

formula has been copied to the cell below and therefore the cell references in the formula are now one cell below what they were before. With the first reference, F7, that is what you want, the total sales for Jean Hall. However, you still want to multiply the total by the commission rate held in cell B3. This is where absolute referencing comes in. By making B3 an absolute address, it will remain as B3 wherever you copy it to.

You can enter an absolute address manually by typing a dollar sign ($) before the column and row reference ($B$3). Alternatively, you can use a handy keyboard shortcut to do it for you. To do this, enter the formula as usual but before you confirm press F4 on the top row of your keyboard. The reference will display as absolute.Going back to the commissions worksheet, if you edit the formula for Paul Black's commission to read =F6*$B$3, you can then copy it, with confidence, for the rest of the team.

```
[X] Microsoft Excel - Cell References D
[X] Eile Edit View Insert Format Tools Data Window Help
D ☞ ■ 🖨 🎒 🔃 ❤ ✗ 🖻 🖺 ❤ ⋈ ▾ ⋈ ▾ 🍓 Σ ƒ* ☝↓ ☝↓ 🏛 🐼 100% ▾ ②.
  G7      ▾  = =F7*$B$3
     A          B        C        D       E        F         G      H
1  SALES 2nd QUARTER
2
3  Commission Rate:     8%
4
5                Name      April      May      June    Total   Commission
6   Paul Black    £10,000   £11,250   £8,750   £30,000      £2,400
7   Jean Hall     £8,000    £9,750    £10,500  £28,250      £2,260
8   Joe Olive     £12,500   £11,300   £11,000  £34,800      £2,784
9   Mary Fair     £6,700    £5,700    £8,700   £21,100      £1,688
10  Barry Dean    £11,750   £10,300   £9,850   £31,900      £2,552
11
...
23
```

If you name a cell or range of cells using the Name, Define options from the Insert menu, Excel will automatically use an absolute reference for the name. In most cases this is want you will want. The third type of reference involves either the row or column being absolute. This is identified by a dollar sign ($) in front of either the row or column reference. The keyboard shortcut F4 can be used to create a mixed address. Press F4 to toggle between the different addresses.

➡ *Cutting and Pasting within Excel, Functions*

KEEP TRACK OF YOUR MILEAGE

If you need to record your business mileage for tax purposes or an expense claim, the following two pages show you how to create a spreadsheet to do this. Working on a weekly basis, Excel can calculate the number of miles covered in a trip and the total miles covered in a week. If you claim mileage (e.g. 30p per mile), there is also a section to help calculate a claim.

1. Using a new spreadsheet in Excel, select cell B1 and enter the heading, Start. In cells C1, D1 and E1, enter the headings, End, Miles, Total. Select cell A2 and enter the week you want to start recording your mileage. You may want to increase the width of some of the columns in your spreadsheet. Position the mouse pointer in between the column headings (the letters in grey) and wait for it to change to a cross with two horizontal arrows. Hold down the left mouse button and move to the right to stretch the left column. Release the left button to stop widening the column.

2. Under column A, enter the business trips you have made for the week displayed in cell A2. Enter the mileage at the start and end of the trip in the respective cells in columns B and C. Do not enter the amount of miles covered for each trip or the total miles. This will be calculated in the next step.

3. Select cell D3. This should be the cell that will represent the amount of miles covered for the first business trip listed. To calculate the amount of miles covered, press the = symbol to start a calculation, select cell C3, press the minus symbol (-), followed by cell B3 and press Return to complete the calculation. Make sure the figure in D3 is correct by changing the figures in cells B3 and C3 to amounts that are easy to work out (start figure of 1000, end figure of 2000).

4. Copy the calculation created in step 3 to the other cells in column D. First, select cell D3 and position the mouse pointer over the bottom right corner of it (over a small black square) and wait for it to change to a thin black cross. When this happens, hold down the left button and move down the screen to copy the calculations. Move down to the last business trip listed for the week, then release the left button to stop copying.

5. Save your Excel file by clicking on the File menu and choosing Save. From the Save As dialog box that appears, enter a name for your file, choose a location on your computer to store it, then click on Save.

6. Calculate a total for the amount of business miles covered in the week. Using column E, select a cell below the end of the list of business trips for the week. Click on the AutoSum toolbar button (looks like a Greek S symbol). The words =SUM() will appear on the screen. Use the mouse to select all of the cells in column D, displaying the total miles for each trip (hold down the left button and move down them to select). Press Return to complete the calculation.

7. Make sure the total miles calculation created in step 6 is correct. Using the mouse, hold down the left button and select all of the cells in column D, which display the total miles for each business trip. When you have selected them, look at the bottom of the screen in the grey section for the words Sum= and a total figure. If another word is

	A	B	C	D	E	F
1		Start	End	Miles	Total	
2	W/C 6/5/2002					
3	Meeting in Croydon	15258	15778	=C3-B3		
4	Smith Bros	15878	15998			
5	Head office	15998	16122			
6	Meeting in Liverpool	16134	16225			
7						
8						

	A	B	C	D	E	F
1		Start	End	Miles	Total	
2	W/C 6/5/2002					
3	Meeting in Croydon	15258	15778	520		
4	Smith Bros	15878	15998	120		
5	Head office	15998	16122	124		
6	Meeting in Liverpool	16134	16225	91		
7					=SUM(D3:D6)	
8						
9						
10						

here, right-click on it and choose Sum from the menu that appears. Make sure the Sum figure displayed at the bottom of the screen is the same as the one created in step 6.

8. If you claim mileage (e.g. 30p per mile), you can use Excel to calculate your claim. Underneath the SUM calculation created in step 6 (in column E), enter the amount in pounds you claim per mile (30p should be entered as 0.30). Add a suitable title for this cell in column A, such as Amount per mile. Select a cell below the amount you entered (in column E). This will display the amount to claim. Press the = symbol to start the calculation, select the cell representing total miles, press the asterisk (*) for multiplication, then select the cell representing the figure for amount per mile. Press Return to complete the calculation.

9. Make sure your mileage claim is correct by changing the amount per mile to 1 (for £1) and ensuring the amount to claim is the same as the total miles calculation. Enter the

words Total Claim in the adjacent cell in column A. Save your Excel file again. You can now use this spreadsheet each week for calculating mileage and claims. If you need to add extra rows into the business trips section, right-click on a row number for one of the business trips (far left of the screen) and choose Insert.

➡ *Travel Information*

LOCKED AND HIDDEN CELLS

Preventing changes to data. Once you have completed your worksheet, the next step is to protect the formulae. It is very easy to overwrite a formula and so it makes sense to prevent accidental changes. For added protection, you can also hide formulae so that only the results can be viewed on the worksheet.

Excel provides a handy facility to protect the sheet against unwanted entries and changes, accidental or otherwise. In order to be protected, cells must be locked and protection must be active.

LEFT: Keeping track of your mileage is useful for budgeting and expense claims.

By default, Excel locks all the cells in a worksheet, but as protection is switched off, this has no effect. If you activate protection, all cells will be locked and you will not be able to alter any data at all. In most cases you will want access to some cells, usually those containing values. Therefore, you need to unlock the cells you want access to before activating protection.

In many cases the cells you want to unlock will be in non-adjacent cells. To unlock them all in one go, select the cells by holding down the Ctrl key and clicking and dragging the mouse across the required cells or ranges of cells. Once selected, release the mouse button and the Ctrl key. The selected cells will be shaded. Access the Format menu and select the Cells option. Click on the Protection tab.

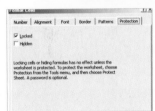

The Locked check box will contain a tick. Click on this box to remove the tick. If you also want to hide the formulae, click on the Hidden box. If hidden, the result of the formula will still appear on the sheet but the formula will not display on the Formula bar. Click on the OK button to confirm. The selected cells are now marked to be unlocked and, if selected, the formulae marked to be hidden. Remember though, you need to protect the sheet before anything happens.

To protect the sheet, access the Tools menu and select the Protection, Protect Sheet options. The Protect Sheet dialog box will be displayed. You can check or clear the boxes depending on which elements you want to protect. You can also include a password if you want to prevent another user changing your protection settings and gaining access to the locked cells. Click on the OK button to complete. You should find that you can only make changes to the cells that you unlocked.

If, at a later stage, you want to remove the protection so that you can make changes to your worksheet, access the Tools menu and select the Protection, Unprotect Sheet options.

➡ *Passwords*

LOGIC FUNCTIONS

The logic or conditional functions are used to test whether a specified condition is true or false. The IF function is widely used to return two different values depending on whether a condition is true or false, whereas the other functions within this category simply return a true or false value.

The IF function has three arguments IF(logical_test,value_if_true,value_if_false).

The logical_test argument is a value or expression that will provide a true or false result. For example, B3=0, Target>Profit.

The value_if_true argument is the value or formula that is returned if the logical_test argument is TRUE. If you omit this argument, the IF function will return TRUE (if the test is true).

The value_if_false argument is the value or formula that is returned if the logical_test argument is FALSE. If you

ABOVE: Logic functions can determine whether conditions are true or false.
RIGHT: Lookup and reference functions enable you to locate information easily.

omit the argument, the IF function will return FALSE (if the test is false).

The NOT function reverses the value of its argument. It can be used to make sure a value is not equal to a particular value. The NOT function has one argument, a value or expression that can be evaluated to TRUE or FALSE. If the value is FALSE, NOT returns TRUE; if the value is TRUE, NOT returns FALSE. For example, NOT(TRUE) equals FALSE, NOT(2+2=5) equals TRUE.

The AND function only returns TRUE if all its arguments are TRUE. If one or more of the arguments is FALSE, the function will return FALSE. The AND function can include up to 30 arguments to be tested as true or false. If the specified range contains no logical values, AND returns the #VALUE! error value. For example, AND(TRUE,2*2=4,2+4=6) equals TRUE (all arguments are true), AND(2+2=4,2+3=6) equals FALSE (one of the arguments is false), AND(1,2) equals #VALUE! (none of the arguments are logical values).

The OR function returns TRUE if any one of the arguments is TRUE. If all the arguments are FALSE, it will return FALSE. The OR function can have up to 30 conditions. If the specified range contains no logical values, OR will return the #VALUE! error value. For example, OR(2+2=4,2+3=6) equals TRUE, OR(1+1=1,2+4=5) equals FALSE, OR(1,2) equals #VALUE!.

The FALSE() and TRUE() functions return the logical value FALSE or TRUE. You can also type the word FALSE or TRUE directly into the worksheet or formula, and Microsoft Excel will interpret it as the logical value.

➠ *Functions, Paste Function Button, Statistical Functions*

LOOKUP AND REFERENCE FUNCTIONS

The lookup and reference functions provide the facility to locate a specific value from a list or find a reference for a specific cell. Probably the most commonly used functions from this category are the lookup functions.

The VLOOKUP function (vertical lookup) searches for a value in the leftmost column of a table and returns a value located within a specified column from the same row. VLOOKUP(lookup_value,table_array,col_index_num,range_lookup)

The lookup value is the value to be found in the first column of the table. It can be entered as a value, a reference or a text string. This function does not differentiate between upper and lower case, so you can type your search text in either case and a match will be found.

Table refers to the table of information to be searched. This can be referenced as either cell addresses or a range name.

Column index number refers to the column containing the information you want to return. The first column in the table is column 1. Range lookup tells Excel whether you want to find an exact match. The argument must be entered as a logical value. If true (1) or omitted, VLOOKUP will return the nearest match. If false (0), only an exact match will be found and if no exact match is available the #NA error message will be returned. If range lookup is set to true, the table must be sorted into ascending order based on the first column of the table in order for the nearest match to be established.

This example shows VLOOKUP being used to provide contact and birthday details for a specified friend. The name of the friend is entered into cell B1 and the lookup functions in the cells below provide the relevant details. They do this by extracting the information from the specified column. For instance, to find the e-mail address, the function looks for the name held in cell B1, within the table called details (B9:F20) and extracts the result from column 4 (the e-mail information). The range lookup is set to false (0) as only an exact match is required.

The HLOOKUP function (horizontal lookup) provides the same facility but searches for a value in the first row of a table rather than the first column and returns a value in a specified row.

➡ *Functions, Paste Function Button, Order a List*

	A	B	C	D	E	F
1	Name		Evie		<---- Name	
2	Phone Number		3219986		<---- =VLOOKUP(Name,Details,2,0)	
3	Fax Number		4498567		<---- =VLOOKUP(Name,Details,3,0)	
4	E-Mail		Evie@happy.com		<---- =VLOOKUP(Name,Details,4,0)	
5	Birthday		7-Oct		<---- =VLOOKUP(Name,Details,5,0)	
6						
7						
8		Name	Phone	Fax	E-Mail	Birthday
9		Mary	5673854	9854628	M@234.com	02-Oct
10		Ali	4657629	2378543	AliP@day.com	13-May
11	Details -->	Fran	9823416	6574632	FD@234.com	05-Dec
12	B9 F20	James	2198456	2288546	James@happy.com	23-Apr
13		Ray	6743298	6775439	RAT@day.com	12-Aug
14		Calli	4579844	7755339	CalliE@234.com	23-Dec
15		Joe	3344874	6579346	J&T@day.com	18-Sep
16		Evie	3219986	4498567	Evie@happy.com	07-Oct
17		Ella	9975443	4398567	ELLA@day.com	22-May
18		Hans	3322445	5895643	H@123.com	09-Dec
19		Jon	5478563	2387547	Jon@weather.com	25-Sep
20		Sam	2121341	4387579	S_Hughes@weather.com	29-Jun
21						
22						
23						
24						
25						

Sheet1 / Sheet2 / Sheet3 /

Ready

LOTUS 1-2-3

The spreadsheet that started it all. Lotus 1-2-3 is a three-in-one computer application, combining spreadsheet, graphics and data management. Produced by the Lotus Development Corporation, Lotus 1-2-3 first appeared in 1982. Its ease of use and versatility most certainly contributed to the rapid acceptance of the IBM Personal Computer within businesses worldwide. 1-2-3 is still widely used today and forms part of SmartSuite 9.7, the latest edition of an office suite of applications produced by IBM.

Users of either 1-2-3 or Excel can easily master the alternative application because the look and feel of the worksheets, the menu options and functions are all similar. If you are converting from 1-2-3 to Excel, select the Lotus 1-2-3 option from the Help menu, click the OK button and Excel will provide a demonstration on how to use the selected feature or command.

Alternatively, if you check the Instructions button before clicking on OK, Excel will paste the instructions for the task onto your worksheet so that you can view them as you complete the task.

There are differences between the applications, some minor and some more fundamental. For example, with 1-2-3, a command is selected before you specify the cell or range that the command affects. When using Excel, the cell or range is selected before a command is specified. This has the advantage that once a range is selected, several commands or actions can be executed in succession without reselecting the range.

ABOVE:RIGHT: Converting all your worksheets to fit one application makes life easier.
ABOVE: Lotus includes spreadsheets, graphics and data management facilities.

The process for creating and entering formulae in Excel is different from 1-2-3. For example, 1-2-3 formulae start with a plus sign (+), functions are preceded by an @ sign and periods (..) are used to signify cell ranges. If any of these formats are entered into an Excel worksheet they will automatically be converted to the Excel equivalent. To ensure that Excel will accept all formulae entered in 1-2-3 format, make sure that the Transition Formula Entry box is checked. To do this, access the Tools menu and select Options. Click on the Transition tab and check the Transition Formula Entry box.

Some of the navigation keys used to move around a worksheet differ between Excel and 1-2-3. For example, in Lotus 1-2-3, pressing the HOME key selects the cell in the upper-left corner of the worksheet; in Microsoft Excel, pressing the HOME key selects the first cell of the current row. You can change the navigation keys in Microsoft Excel to mirror the Lotus 1-2-3 method of moving around. To do this, access the Tools menu and select Options. Select the Transition tab and check the Transition Navigation Keys box.

Rather than working with two applications, it makes sense to convert worksheets to your preferred application. Whether converting from 1-2-3 to Excel or vice versa, it is always advisable to back up (make a copy of) the file to be converted first. Then if something goes wrong you can always revert to the original copy. It is also a good idea to print a copy of the original worksheet so that you can check accuracy and formatting after the conversion.

You can convert a 1-2-3 file to an Excel file by simply opening the file in Excel, accessing the File menu and selecting the Open option. To save the file as an Excel worksheet, access the File menu and select the Save As option. Make sure the Save As Type box is set to 'Microsoft Excel Workbook'. Alternatively, you can use the File Conversion Wizard. To do this, ensure all the files you want to convert are held in a single folder. Access the Tools menu and select the Wizard option. If File Conversion is not available from the list, you will need to install it as an Excel add-in program. Follow the instructions on the screen to specify how you want to convert the files.

When converting from 1-2-3 to Excel it is worth noting the following:

1. The majority of Lotus 1-2-3 functions have Microsoft Excel equivalents, although some Excel functions use different calculation rules; certain 1-2-3 formulae and functions may not translate correctly into Excel. Particular attention should be paid to formulae that contain character strings and functions that exist in Excel but have a different argument order. If you are converting a 1-2-3 file containing a formula not supported by Excel, Excel will replace the formula with #VALUE and include the comment "Formula failed to convert".

2. A 1-2-3 PrintGraph (*.PIC) file must be imported into Excel as a picture and cannot be converted to an Excel chart.

3. Lotus 1-2-3 sheet names will not be converted when the file is brought into Excel. Sheet names can be reassigned from within Excel by double-clicking on a sheet tab and retyping the name.

4. Excel only permits letters, numbers, underscore and backslash characters to be used for the range name. 1-2-3 also allows the use of special characters. When converting from 1-2-3 to Excel, all special characters in 1-2-3 names are automatically converted to underscores.

5. Microsoft Excel does not fully run Lotus 1-2-3 macros that have been created using versions later than Lotus 1-2-3 Release 3.0.

➡ *History of Spreadsheets*

MACROS

Recording steps to replay. A macro is a recorded series of commands that you can play back at any time. Macros are usually created for operations you carry out on a regular basis. By recording what you do, the macro saves you having to repeat working steps by replaying the recorded commands automatically at the click of a button.

The easiest way to understand Excel macros is by example. Macros are recorded and replayed in the same way regardless of whether they are composed of 10 or 100 key strokes and commands. To illustrate the concept, a simple example will be taken. A macro will be generated to enter the current time and date.

ABOVE: Macros are recorded sets of commands that can be played back.
RIGHT: Macros can make things easy for even the most inexperienced user.

To start the macro, access the Tools menu and select the Macro option. Select Record New Macro. The Record Macro dialog box is displayed.

Give the macro a meaningful and unique name (spaces are not allowed). For this example something along the lines of InsertDateTime will be appropriate. Type a description for the macro, always useful if someone else may inherit or work with your worksheet. You can also define a keyboard shortcut to make it as easy as possible to replay your macro. Finally, decide where you want to save your macro. By default, your macro will be saved in the current workbook. You also have the option to save it to a personal macro workbook, if you want to be able to use the macro in other workbooks, or to a new workbook. Click on the OK button when you have made your choice.

The Stop Recording toolbar is displayed. It contains two buttons, on the left the Stop Recording button and on the right the Relative Reference button. You need to click on the Relative Reference button whenever you want a reference to a cell to be relative to its new position. This sounds complicated, but take the example of entering the date and time. When you replay the macro, you will want the date and time inserted at the current position of the cell pointer, not where the cell pointer was when the macro was recorded.

For this example, click on the Relative Reference button and then enter the date and time into two cells, one underneath the other. Use the TODAY() function and format the top cell to display the date and the cell below the time. Change the colour of the text, shade the two cells in a complimentary colour and put a box around the cells. When you have finished, click on the Stop Recording button.

If you set a keyboard shortcut, you can simply press Ctrl plus the selected letter to run the macro. If not, access the Tools menu and select Macro, Macros. The Macro dialog box is displayed. Choose the macro from the list and click on Run to replay the macro.

The Macro dialog box also provides the facility to create a keyboard shortcut for your macro after it has been recorded. Access the Macro dialog box, select Options and enter an appropriate letter to be used with the Ctrl key to run the macro, for example Ctrl+D. Click on the OK button to confirm.

You can also edit your macro by selecting the Edit option from the Macro dialog box. Excel will open a Microsoft Visual Basic (VB) window. Macros are stored as VB code and, if you understand VB, you can make changes to the code. If VB is not your area, it is still worth a look; you will certainly be able to understand some of the steps. If you need to make changes and programming is not your thing, you are probably best off deleting the macro and starting again. There is an option in the Macro dialog box to delete the selected macro.

If you are going to use your macro frequently it may be worthwhile assigning a button to it. Before doing this, decide which of the Excel toolbars you want your button to appear on and select that toolbar so that it is displayed. To create a button, access the View menu and select the Toolbars options. Select the Customize option from the bottom of the list. The Customize dialog box will be displayed. Click on the Commands tab and scroll down the Categories box to select the Macros option. A Commands list box will appear to the right of the dialog box containing a Custom button (a smiley face). Drag the button onto the current toolbar. right-click on the new button and select Assign Macro from the shortcut menu. The Assign Macro dialog box is displayed. Choose the macro you want to assign to the button and click on OK. right-click on the button on the toolbar again and this time select Change Button Image.

Select a different image and close the Customize dialog box. The new button on the toolbar will activate your macro each time you click on it.

You can also design your own button by right-clicking on the button and selecting the Edit Button Image option.

➡ *Keeping Cells Still*

MACROS CASE STUDY

 This case study provides a practical example which shows the benefits and advantages of using macros when consolidating data.

The scenario is that of Cliff Redford who is responsible for producing the monthly accounts for a Charity. This involves consolidating information from fundraising offices. Cliff has designed the worksheet as a template so that the information received from each office is presented with an identical layout. Each month, he has been manually copying the sheets into a consolidation workbook. This is proving time-consuming so he has decided to use macros to speed up the operation.

As a starting point, Cliff is going to automate the consolidation of the summary information from each office. He has already produced a template that has been sent to each office. He is going to use this same template to create the consolidation sheet.

You can discover exactly how Cliff designed and created this template by reading the Templates Case Study entry, see page 172. To actively work through this example, create the template before continuing.

To create the consolidation workbook, access the File menu and select the New option. The Monthly Summary Report template will be found under the General tab. Click on this template and click the OK button. The blank summary report will be displayed. As this report will be used and saved on a monthly basis the consolida-

ABOVE RIGHT: Macros can help you consolidate data.

tion report will also be saved as a template. Access the File menu, select Save As, name the file Monthly Consolidation Report. Select Template from the Save As File Type drop-down list and click on the Save button. Save as a template regularly during development.

This worksheet is protected so that data can only be entered in the blue cells. Protection will need to be removed before changes can be made. To do this, access the Tools menu, select the Protection option and select Unprotect Sheet.

The next step is to create the blank sheets that will contain the information from each office. Name the current sheet Consolidation by accessing the Format menu and selecting the Sheet, Rename options. For this example, the data from five offices will be consolidated, the principal is the same regardless of the number of sheets.

Name the next five sheets Office 1 through to Office 5. If you need to insert more sheets, access the Insert menu and select the Worksheet option.

Make the Consolidation sheet active and create a formula to add the monthly revenue for the Charity shops for each of the five offices. Click on cell B6 and type =SUM('Office 1:Office 5'!B6). Copy this formula to all the other cells containing formulae, including the

totals. It will copy in a relative way so that, for example, the formula in cell B13 will read =SUM('Office 1:Office 5'!B13). Change the label in cell A1 to 'Regional Code': and type a suitable code. Save the template.

Before creating the macro you will need some test data. Create five worksheets using the Monthly Summary Report template. Enter some dummy data in each and save them as Office 1 through to Office 5. It is important to know where these files are saved. Make sure all the files are closed.

Here goes! Access the File menu, select New and choose the Monthly Consolidation Report template. To start recording the macro, access the Tools menu and select the Macro option. Select Record New Macro. Type the macro name into the dialog box (no spaces allowed), type a suitable shortcut letter, a brief description and

select This Workbook as the location to store the macro. Click the OK button. A Macro toolbar will appear containing the Stop button.

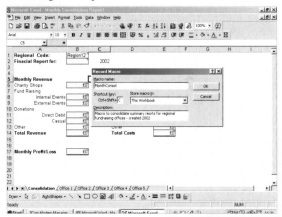

The macro is now recording. Running through the steps is tedious and needs concentration but the good thing is you only need do it once.

Click on the Office 1 sheet tab to display the blank worksheet. Position the cell pointer in cell A1. Access the File menu and select Open. Locate the worksheet called Office 1 and click the Open button. The Office 1 worksheet is displayed in the current window. Click the Select All button located at the top left of the column and row headings. The entire worksheet will be highlighted. Click the Copy button on the Standard toolbar. Access the Window menu and select the Monthly Consolidation worksheet from the bottom of the menu. This will take you back to the consolidation worksheet. Click the Paste button on the Standard toolbar. Click the Office 2 sheet tab and repeat the above steps. Repeat the same steps for the remaining sheets.

When complete, click the Consolidation sheet tab and click the Stop Recording button.

Before you can test it has worked you need to delete the data in all but the Consolidation sheet and resave the template with the macro. To do this, select Office 1 sheet, click on the Select All button and press the Delete key. Repeat for each of the other Office sheets. Now save the Monthly Consolidation template and close all open files.

To run your macro, open the template Monthly Consolidation report and simply press Ctrl + C. Save your consolidated report as a worksheet.

MANAGE A DIET

Excel's ability to create calculations is ideal for monitoring a long-term action plan such as a diet. The following two pages show you how to set up a diet spreadsheet, add up what you eat in a day according to a points system and make sure you don't exceed your daily allowance.

I. Open Excel with a new workbook. Select cell B1 and enter the title Monday (or Mon for short). Move two cells to the right (cell D1) and enter Tuesday, then continue across the screen, missing one cell and entering the day of the week. Select cell A2 and enter the title Breakfast. In cell A6 type Lunch, in A10 type Dinner, in A15 type During the Day, and finally in A20 type Total Points.

2. You may want to increase the width of some columns and reduce the width of others. Columns B, D, F, H, J, L and N will display numbers, so these columns can be

ABOVE: Dieters can monitor the food they eat with a spreadsheet.
ABOVE RIGHT: It is easier to control weight loss if you record your progress.

narrow. Each column to the left of these will display information on what you've eaten, so they will need to be wider. To increase or reduce the width of a column, position the mouse pointer in between the column letters above the grid. When the mouse changes to a cross with two horizontal arrows, hold down the left button and move to the right to increase the left column or move to the left to reduce it. Release the left button to stop changing the column's width.

3. Select cell B20. This cell will display the total number of points for a day's eating. Click on the AutoSum toolbar button (looks like a Greek S symbol). The words =SUM() will appear. Using the mouse, select all the cells from B3 to B19 by holding down the left button and moving down them. Make sure the content of cell B20 reads =SUM(B3:B19), then press Return to complete the calculation. Then copy cell B20 (press Ctrl with C) to D20, F20, H20, J20, C20 and N20.

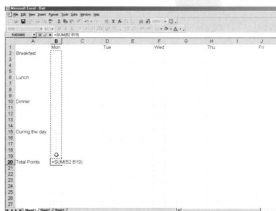

4. Click on the File menu and choose Save. A Save As dialog box will appear. Enter a name for your Excel file and choose a location on your computer to save it to. Returning to your spreadsheet, make sure the total calculations created in step 3 work properly by entering numbers for points in the different columns for the days of the week. To double-check a total calculation is correct, select all the cells that make up the calculation by holding down the left button and moving down them. Look at the bottom of the screen (in the grey section) for the words Sum= and a total figure. Make sure this figure is the same as the total figure created in step 3.

5. Select cell B20 (the total points for Monday). We are going to set up Excel to check this figure and display it in another colour if the total points exceed the daily allowance. Click on the Format menu and choose Conditional Format. From the Conditional Formatting dialog box that appears, click on the drop-down triangle to the right of the word between, and change this to greater than. Click inside the white box to the right of this and enter a number for your daily points or calories allowance.

6. With the Conditional Formatting dialog box still open, click on the Format button inside it and a Format Cells dialog box will open. Using the tabs for Font, Border and Patterns, choose a style of text and some colouring to be applied if you exceed your daily diet points allowance. You will not be able to change the font or size of the text, but you can change the colour of it, add a border and fill colour. Click on OK to return to the Conditional Formatting dialog box, then OK again to return to the spreadsheet.

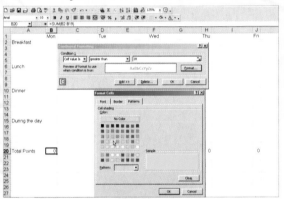

7. Test the conditional formatting set up in steps 5 and 6 by entering a sufficient number of points in column B to make sure the total points in B20 exceeds the daily points allowance. The formatting set up in step 6 should be displayed in B20 if the total exceeds the daily points or calories allowance. If this works properly, you can copy this conditional formatting to the other total figures. See step 8 for how to do this.

8. Make sure B20 is selected, then double-click on the Format Painter toolbar button (looks like a large

paintbrush). The mouse pointer will adopt a paintbrush. Click inside the total figures for the other days of the week (D20, F20, H20 etc.) and the conditional formatting will be copied into these cells. When you've finished copying, click once on the Conditional Formatting toolbar button to switch it off (or press Escape on the keyboard – top left).

9. When you use your diet spreadsheet during a week's dieting, enter what you've eaten in the appropriate columns and the respective points or calories. Excel will automatically calculate the total points for a day and alert you if you've exceeded your daily allowance.

➡ *Get Nutritional Information*

MANAGE AN ADDRESS BOOK

Excel is capable of storing long lists of information, useful for an address book, for example. The following two pages show how to create an address book and look for specific information. There is also a separate set of instructions on transferring information to and from Outlook Express.

I. Using a new workbook in Excel, select cell A1 and enter a series of titles across this row for the different headings you want in your address book (surname, first names, address, city, postcode, telephone number, e-mail address). You may want to increase the width of some of the columns in your spreadsheet. Position the mouse pointer in between the column headings (the letters in

ABOVE: Addresses and other contact information can be stored in Excel.

grey) and wait for it to change to a cross with two horizontal arrows. Hold down the left mouse button and move to the right to stretch the left column. Release the left button to stop widening the column.

2. Enter the address book information under the appropriate headings for people and businesses you know. Save your Excel file regularly by clicking on the File menu and choosing Save. When you do this for the first time, a Save As dialog box will appear. Enter a name for your Excel file and choose a location on your computer to save it. Click on the Save button to return to the spreadsheet. In the future, when you click on the File menu and choose Save, the file will automatically be saved and the dialog box will not appear.

3. When you have finished entering your address book information, you can use Excel to find particular addresses and sort addresses. To find an address, first select the entire address list including the headings in row 1 – select cell A1, scroll down to the bottom right corner of the list, hold down the Shift key on the keyboard and click inside the cell in the bottom right corner of the list to select the entire list. Click on the Data menu and choose Form. From the dialog box that appears, select the Criteria button and enter the information you are looking for under the appropriate heading. Click on the Find Next and Find Prev buttons to search for an address. To do another search, click on Criteria, then click on Clear and enter the search details. Click on Close to return to your spreadsheet.

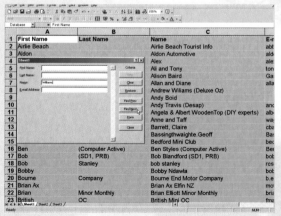

4. An alternative method of finding an address is to select cell A1, click on the Edit menu and choose Find. From the dialog box that appears, enter the details you are looking for in the Find What box. Click on the drop-down triangle to the right of Look in, and make sure the word Values is displayed. Choose whether to search by rows or columns (click on the drop-down triangle to change this option). Click on the Find Next button to begin searching. Excel will inform you if it cannot find any records matching your search criteria. Click on Close to return to your spreadsheet.

5. If you want to see a list of addresses that hold something in common (all in the same country), first select the entire address list including the headings in row 1 (see step 3 for instructions). Then click on the Data menu, choose Filter and from the sub-menu that appears, select AutoFilter. A series of drop-down triangles will appear next to each heading in your address list. Click on a drop-down triangle and a list of the contents of the information under this heading will appear. You can now click on an item on the list to filter it and only display address records containing the selected information. To return to displaying all address records, click on the drop-down triangle again and select All (at the top of the list).

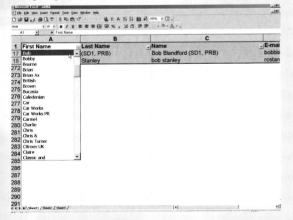

Exporting and Importing from Outlook Express

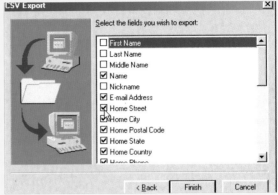

Addresses can be transferred to and from Outlook Express. To transfer addresses from Outlook Express to Excel, open Outlook Express and click on the Addresses button to open your address book. From the address book, click on the File menu and choose Export, then select Other Address Book. Another dialog box will appear. Select Text File (Comma Separated Values), then click on Export. Proceed through the dialog boxes to specify where you want to save your exported address book (click on Browse) and which categories of information you want to export.
When you have finished exporting, open Excel, click on the File menu and select Open. Change the Files of Type to Text Files, then locate your exported address book and open it.

To transfer an address book created in Excel to Outlook Express, first click on the File menu and choose Save As. From the dialog box that appears, change the Save As Type to CSV (Comma delimited), choose a location to save it and enter a name. Once the file has been saved, open Outlook Express and the address book, then click on the File menu, choose Import and select Other Address Book from the sub-menu. Select Text File (Comma Separated Values) from the dialog box that appears, then click on Import. Proceed through the steps (similar to exporting) to locate your Excel CSV file and import the address information.

➡ *Find Missing Address Data*

MANAGE A SPORTS LEAGUE

Excel is ideal for storing a sports league table for football, rugby, cricket and other sports. It can calculate points, differences and who should be at the top of the table. The following two pages show you how to create a football league table with calculations to work out games played, goal difference, points and placements.

1. With Excel open and a new worksheet on the screen, select cell A1 and enter the titles shown in our picture. Enter each title in a separate cell, making sure cell I1 contains the title Points. Next, enter the names of your

ABOVE: Spreadsheets can be used to manage sports league tables.

teams and the figures for the number of games won, drawn and lost. In columns F and G, enter the number of goals scored by the team (For) and the number scored against them (Against). You do not need to list your team in the correct order (with the team at the top of the table in row 2). This will be done for you in step 7.

2. To calculate the total number of games played, select cell B2. Click on the AutoSum toolbar button (looks like a Greek S symbol). The words =SUM() will appear on the screen. Position the mouse pointer over cell C2 (number of games won), hold down the left button and move across to cell E2 (number of games lost). The calculation in the cell should now read =SUM(C2:E2). Press Return on the keyboard to complete it and make sure it is correct.

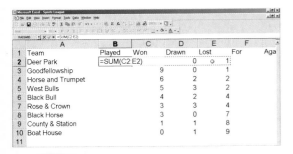

3. Select cell H2 (the goal difference for the first team listed in your league table). We are going to create a calculation to work out the goal difference. Press the = sign to start the calculation, then use the mouse to select cell F2 (goals scored by this team), press the minus (-) symbol, then select cell G2 (number of goals scored against this team). Press Return to complete the calculation and check it.

4. Calculate the points per team according to the number of games won and drawn. The example here allocates 3 points for a win and 1 point for a draw (you may want to use different figures depending on your own league rules). Select cell I2. Press the = sign to begin the calculation and press (to open a bracket. Select cell C2 (number of games won), press the asterisk (*) followed by the number 3 (3 points for a win). Press) to close the brackets followed by a plus symbol (+) and select cell D2 for the number of games drawn (no need to multiply this by a number because each draw is one point). Press Return to complete the calculation.

5. Select cell B2 (total number of games played). We are going to copy this down the table for the other teams listed. Hover the mouse pointer over the bottom right corner of the cell (over the small black square) and wait for it to change to a thin black cross. When this happens, hold down the left button and move down the screen to copy the calculation into the games played cells for the other teams listed. To stop copying, release the left button. Check the calculations are correct. Repeat this step for cells H2 (goal difference) and I2 (points).

6. Check the calculations you have created and copied for total games played, goal difference and points. Enter

easily checked figures for games won and drawn and goals scored for and against. When you are satisfied the calculations are correct, enter the correct figures and save your table by clicking on the File menu and choosing Save. From the Save As dialog box that appears, enter a name for your Excel file and choose a location on your computer to store it. Click on Save to return to your spreadsheet.

7. To work out who is at the top and bottom of the league table, select cell A1, hold down the Shift key, then click on the points for the team currently at the bottom of the list. Your entire table will be selected. Release the Shift key, click on the Data menu and choose Sort. From the Sort dialog box that appears, make sure that under the section labelled My list has, the option for Header row is selected.

8. Look at the top of the Sort dialog box. Click on the drop-down triangle under Sort by and choose Points. Make sure the option Descending is selected next to this. Move down a level in this dialog box (under Then by), click on the next drop-down

triangle and choose Goal difference. Also, make sure Descending is selected next to this. Click on OK and your table will be sorted. The team with the most points will be listed at the top. Any teams with the same points will be sorted on goal difference.

9. When updating your league table in the future, the calculations for total games played, goal difference and points will be automatically changed. The order of the table will not, so you will need to repeat steps 7 and 8.

➡ SUMming Up

	A	B	C	D	E	F	G	H
1	Team	Played	Won	Drawn	Lost	For	Against	Goal Differe
2	Deer Park	10	9	0	1	27	5	
3	Goodfellowship	10	9	0	1	21	3	
4	Horse and Trumpe	10	6	2	2	9	4	
5	West Bulls	10	5	3	2	15	4	
6	Black Bull	10	4	2	4	6	5	
7	Rose & Crown	10	3	3	4	4	8	
8	Black Horse	10	3	0	7	3	10	
9	County & Station	10	1	1	8	2	12	
10	Boat House	10	0	1	9	0	18	

MANAGE ORDERS

Excel can be used to list orders for a business and print out invoices. The following two pages show you how to list orders when they are received, print out an invoice and analyse the orders (who has ordered which products, which customers spend the most).

Customer reference and product codes have been used, but you do not have to use these, especially if your business has a small list of customers and products.

1. Using a new workbook in Excel, select cell A1 and enter a series of headings across the spreadsheet for the different categories of information you want to store concerning orders. Our example shows headings such as date, customer reference, customer name, product code, description, unit price, quantity, price, VAT and total. You may need to increase the width of some of the columns. To do this, position the mouse pointer in between the column headings (the letters in grey) and wait for it to change to a cross with two horizontal arrows. Hold down the left mouse button and move to the right to stretch the left column. Release the left button to stop widening the column.

2. Enter the details for orders received under the appropriate headings. When you have entered a customer name, for example, you will find that when you enter the first letters of the name again, Excel will try to complete it for you (press Return to accept this). Do not enter any details in the last three columns for Price, VAT and Total. This will be

covered later. Save your Excel file by clicking on the File menu and choosing Save. From the Save As dialog box that appears, enter a name for your file, choose a location on your computer to store it, then click on Save.

3. Select the first cell in the Price column. To calculate the price (unit price multiplied by quantity), press the = symbol, select the corresponding cell for unit price (F2 in the

ABOVE RIGHT: Customer orders can be processed using Excel.

example), press the asterisk (*) for multiplication, then choose the cell representing the quantity value (G2 in the example). Press Return to complete the calculation. Make sure the calculation is correct, then select the cell to the right of this for VAT. Press = to start the calculation, select the Price calculation you have just created, press the asterisk (*), then enter the number 0.175 (based on VAT at 17.5%). Press Return to complete the calculation and make sure it is correct.

4. There is one more calculation to create. Select the first cell in the Total column. Press the = symbol to start the calculation, select the cell with the corresponding Price calculation, press the + symbol, then select the cell with the VAT amount. Press Return to complete the calculation and make sure the price and VAT displayed in the adjacent cells add up to the same figure shown in this calculation.

5. If the three calculations created in step 3 and 4 are correct, copy these calculations to the other orders in the list. To do this, select all three cells by holding down the left button and moving the mouse across them. Position the mouse pointer over the bottom right corner of these cells (over a small black square) and wait for it to change to a thin black cross. When this happens, hold down the left button and move down the screen to copy these calculations to the other orders. Release the left button to stop copying.

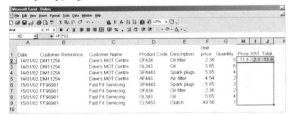

6. Select all of the cells in your orders list. Click on the Data menu, choose Filter and select AutoFilter from the sub-menu. A series of drop-down triangles will appear next to each heading in your list. Click on a drop-down triangle next to a heading and choose an item from the list to filter the chosen data. The triangle will turn blue, but the filter can be switched off by clicking on it again and choosing All.

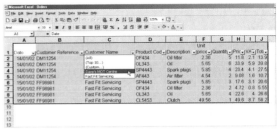

7. You can use AutoFilter to create an invoice. Click on the drop-down triangle to the right of customer name and choose a customer you want to invoice. Click on the drop-down triangle for date and choose the order date you wish to invoice. Only the orders on one day and for one customer will be listed. You will need a grand total. Select the cell at the bottom of the Total list. Click twice on the AutoSum toolbar button (looks like a Greek S symbol). Make sure the grand total figure is correct.

8. To print the filtered list as an invoice, you may want to add a business name to the printout. Click on the File menu and choose Print Preview. From the preview screen that appears, click on the Setup button and use the dialog box to adjust the print settings. Click on the Header/ Footer tab and select Custom Header to add a business name to the top of the invoice. Click on OK to return to the print preview of the invoice, then Print to open a Print dialog box. Click on OK to print the invoice.

9. Returning to the orders list, to switch off the AutoFilter or see a full list of orders, click on the Data menu and choose Filter. From the sub-menu, choose Show All to see all orders, or AutoFilter to show all orders and remove the drop-down triangles.

➡ **SUMming Up**

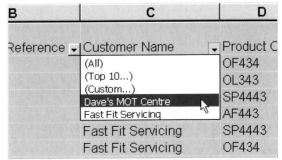

MANAGE YOUR SAVINGS

List your savings accounts in Excel, calculate how much interest will be earned in one year and what each balance will be in the future.

1. Using a new workbook in Excel, select cell A1 and enter the heading, Account. Move across to B1 and enter the heading, Balance. Enter the words, Interest rate, in C1, the title Interest in 1 year, in D1 and finally the words Balance in 1 year in E1. You may need to increase the width of some of the columns. To do this, position the mouse pointer in between the column headings (the letters in grey) and wait for it to change to a cross with two horizontal arrows. Hold down the left mouse button and move to the right to stretch the left column. Release the left button to stop widening the column.

2. Under the heading, Account (in A1), enter the various savings accounts you have and the respective balances in column B. Find out the interest rates for these accounts

TOP RIGHT: Keep an eye on your savings with a spreadsheet.

and enter the figures in column C, making sure you add a % symbol to each figure. If you pay tax on your savings, enter the net interest rates applied to your savings accounts (some savings accounts such as the ISA are tax- free).

3. Select cell D2 (underneath the Interest in 1 year heading). To calculate how much interest will have been generated in one year, press the = symbol to start a calculation, then select cell B2 (the balance on the account), press the asterisk (*) for multiplication, then select cell C2 (the interest rate). Press Return on the keyboard to complete the calculation. Make sure this calculation is correct by entering a balance in B2 of 1000 and an interest rate in C2 of 10%. The amount of interest in one year will be 100.

4. Select cell E2 to calculate the new balance in one year. Press the = symbol to start the calculation. Select cell B2 (current balance), press the + symbol, select cell D2 and press Return to complete the calculation. Check this calculation by selecting B2, then holding down the Ctrl key and selecting D2. With the two cells selected, look at the bottom of the screen for the word Sum=. The total of these two cells will be displayed and should be the same as the figure in E2.

5. To create calculations for interest and balance in one year for the rest of the accounts, first select cells D2 and E2 by holding down the left button and moving across them. Then position the mouse pointer over the bottom left corner of the selected cells (over a small black square) and wait for it to change to a thin black cross. When this happens, hold down the left button and move down the screen to copy the calculations. Move down to the last account listed, then release the left button to stop copying.

6. In column A, enter the word Total at the bottom of the list of accounts. Select the adjacent cell in column B (at the bottom of the list of balances). To calculate a total, click on the AutoSum toolbar button (looks like a Greek S symbol). All of the cells containing balances should be selected. If they are not, hold down the left button and move the mouse across them. Press Return to complete the calculation, then repeat this step for the Interest in 1 year and Balance in 1 year columns.

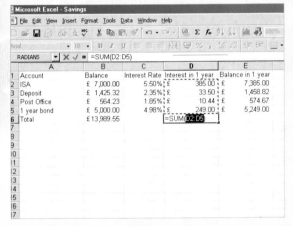

7. Select all the figures under the Balance heading, then hold down the Ctrl key and select all the figures in columns D and E for interest and balance in one year. With these cells selected, click on the Format menu and choose cells. A Format Cells dialog box will appear. Make sure the Number tab is selected, then choose Currency from the list on the left. A £ symbol should be displayed in the middle of the box (click on the drop-down triangle under Symbol if not). Click on OK. All of the selected figures should now have £ symbols against them.

8. Save your Excel file by clicking on the File menu and choosing Save. From the Save As dialog box that appears, enter a name for your file, choose a location on your computer to store it, then click on Save. Returning to your spreadsheet, test the calculations by changing a balance in column B or an interest rate in column C and make sure the interest and balance in one year also change.

9. In the future, you may open another savings account and will need to add it to your spreadsheet. To do this, you will need to insert an extra row. Position the mouse pointer over the row number (left side of the screen, in grey) for the total figures. Make sure the mouse pointer is a large white cross, then right-click and select Insert. An extra row will appear. You can now enter the new account details and copy the calculations for interest and balance in one year.

➡ *Financial Data*

MANAGE YOUR SHARES

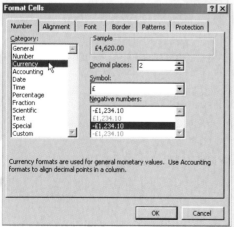

As share prices rise and fall, you can use Excel to calculate the value of your portfolio. The following steps show you how to create a spreadsheet and the necessary calculations to enable you to enter a share price and quantity of shares, then allow Excel to work out how much they are worth. It will also calculate the total value of all your shares.

1. Open Microsoft Excel. Using a new workbook, select cell A1 and enter the title Share Co. In cells B1, C1 and D1, enter the titles Price per share, Number of shares, Total value. Under the Share Co (column A), enter the different shares you own. The width of some columns may need increasing. To do this, position the mouse pointer in between two column letters and wait for it to change to a cross with two horizontal arrows. Hold down the left mouse button and move to the right. The column to the left will be widened. Release the left button to stop widening this column.

2. Select all of the cells under the Price per share heading (hold down the left button and move the mouse down the screen). Click on the Format menu and choose cells. A dialog box will appear. Ensure the Number tab is selected and choose Currency from the list on the left. Make sure that under Symbol the pound sign is displayed (click on the drop-down triangle and change it if not) with two decimal places. Click on OK, then repeat this step for the cells under Total value.

3. Create a calculation to work out the total value of shares for each listing. Select cell D2 (the first cell in the Total value column). Press the = sign on the keyboard to start the calculation. Use the mouse to select cell B2 (the price per share). Press the asterisk symbol (*) on the keyboard, then use the mouse to select cell C2 for the number of shares. Press Return on the keyboard to complete the calculation.

4. Select the cell with the calculation you created in step 3. We are going to copy this calculation to other cells in the Total value column. Position the mouse pointer over the bottom right corner of the selected cell (over a small black square). When the mouse pointer changes to a small, thin black cross, hold down the left mouse button and move down the screen to copy your calculation into the other cells in the Total value column. Release the left button to stop copying.

5. Test your calculations to make sure they are correct. For example, enter a value of £1.00 for a particular price per share and 100 for the number of shares. The total value should be £100. If any of the calculations are incorrect, select the calculation in question and look at the formula bar (above the column headings) to see the contents of the calculation. Make sure it refers to the correct cells. If some or all of your calculations are incorrect, repeat steps 3 and 4.

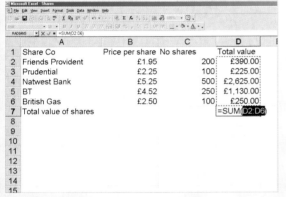

6. Create a calculation to find out the total value of all of your shares. Select the cell at the bottom of the Total value list (cell D7 in this example). Click on the AutoSum toolbar button (looks like a Greek S symbol). The cells in the Total value column will be selected. If they are not, use the mouse to select them. Press Return on the keyboard to complete the calculation.

7. Add some colour to your share table. Position the mouse pointer in cell A1, hold down the left button, then move down and across your table to select all of the cells inside it. Release the left button to finish selecting. All of the cells in your table should be highlighted in black (apart from cell A1). Click on the Format menu and choose AutoFormat. A dialog box will appear with a list of formats that can be applied to your table. Select any of the table formats listed. Click on OK to close this dialog box and add this formatting to your own table. You will need to select a cell outside the table to see the colouring.

8. Save your workbook. Click on the File menu and choose Save. From the Save As dialog box that appears, choose a location to save this file and enter an appropriate name for it. Click on the Save button to close this dialog box and save your file. You can now close this file, then reopen and use it in the future, making changes to share prices or quantities and allowing Excel to automatically recalculate any values.

The share values displayed are not based on the true values of the companies listed. Please refer to an up-to-date listing for current values of your shares.

➡ *Financial Data*

ABOVE: Shareholders may find it easier to manage their shares with Excel.
LEFT: Whatever your shares are in, you can calculate their values in Excel.

MAPS

If you collect and analyse data for a particular country or geographic region, you can create a map from the values in the worksheet. The map will be

the left-hand side of the box and a list of commands associated with a menu name or type.

Select the Insert category from the Categories list box. Search in the Commands list box to find a command

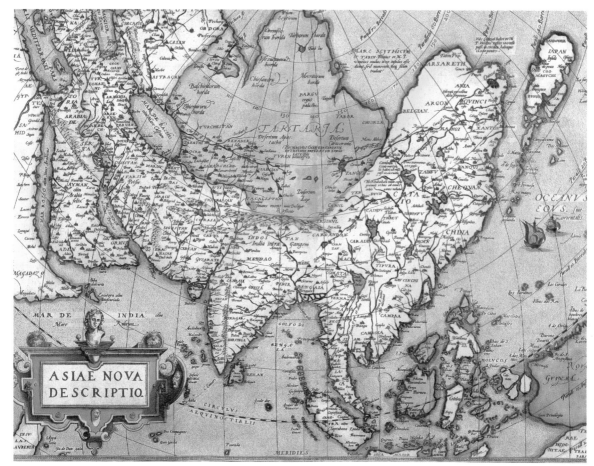

embedded into the worksheet alongside the data and can be formatted to make the worksheet visually appealing.

Microsoft Map is a tool which comes with the Office suite, and as such, you must choose to install it during setup. To be able to use this feature regularly, it would be useful to add the Map toolbar button to a toolbar. To do this, click the Tools menu and choose the Customize option. The Customize dialog box will be displayed. Click the Commands tab. You will see a list of categories down

ABOVE: Maps can be created from the values in the worksheet.

called Map (it has a globe icon next to it). Click and drag the globe icon to one of the toolbars on the screen. Click the Close button to close the dialog box. The Map button should appear on the designated toolbar.

Microsoft Map comes with a set of templates which include the world, Europe, the United States, Canada, Australia, Asia, Mexico and South Africa. You can focus in on specific areas of each map to make for more detailed presentation of data.

A sample workbook containing demographic and geographic information is installed with the Microsoft Office suite. You might find it useful to study the workbook to see what naming conventions and abbreviations have been used to represent country and region names. To see the sample, open C:\Program Files\Common Files\Microsoft Shared\Datamap\Data\Mapstats.xls. The top row of each sheet contains sample data such as the total world male population based on the most recent UN data.

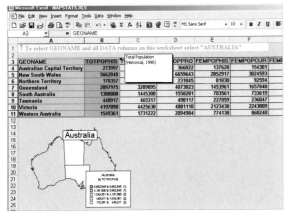

Let's say, for example, that you have taken a geographic region like Europe and entered values which represent revenue, productivity, population statistics or other trends. When you select the data for your map, Excel will look to see if it recognizes the regional names that you have recorded and it will try to apply an appropriate map template to your data.

Before creating a map, spend a little time making sure that data is set up correctly in the worksheet. Enter the names or abbreviations of geographic regions into a column. Arrange all other information, such as figures relating to productivity or sales for these regions, in subsequent columns. If postcodes form part of your data, format the cell as text and then enter the postcode. This will ensure that any zeros at the beginning of the code will be retained.

Select the data which will be used to create the map and include column headings. Click the Map button on the toolbar. Click and drag an area of the worksheet to hold the map. Based on the regional names that it finds in the worksheet, Microsoft Map will attempt to choose a matching template. For example, if a column includes the names of countries in Europe, it will insert a map of Europe. If it does not recognize the data, a Multiple Maps Available dialog box will be displayed. You can now

choose a map from the list provided. The map will be generated, the data plotted and the Microsoft Map Control, Map toolbar and menu will be visible. The values in the selected data will be divided into ranges. In the legend, or key, you will be able to see the number of regions which fall within a range.

The Map toolbar, Map Control and menu provide tools for making amendments. If they are not visible, double-click the map. The Map toolbar includes tools to move a map around a window (grabber), add labels and textboxes, produce a custom pin map, zoom and refresh data. Use the Insert menu to insert additional geographical data and the Map menu to save the edited map as a template, to be used in creating other maps or to add map features.

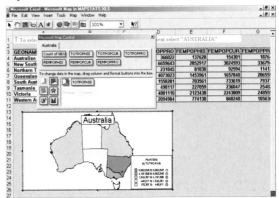

The Microsoft Map Control box can be used to change the format of the map and to add or remove data. At the top of the box you will see icons which represent the columns of data that have been selected. If you select extra data, an icon for the data would appear at the top of the box. To plot this data on the map, drag the icon into the selection area in the middle of the box labelled Column. The selection area illustrates what column of data is currently being used and what format it takes.

On the left of the box, a set of map formats is visible. Dot density displays each geographic area in dots, the density of which corresponds to the value for that area. Other formats include pie charts. Click and drag a format over an existing format in the selection area, or for a newly plotted area, drag over the box labelled Format.

➥ Drawing and Graphics

MATHEMATICAL AND TRIGONOMETRICAL FUNCTIONS

The range of math and trigonometry functions provides the facility to perform simple and complex mathematical calculations. This section will consider some of the simpler and more commonly used functions.

The ABS function returns the absolute value of a number. The argument for the function is either a number or the reference of the cell containing the number to be made absolute. The absolute value of a number disregards sign, so ABS(4) equals 4 and ABS(-4) equals 4.

The INT function returns the integer value of a number. The argument for the function is either a number or the reference of the cell containing the number to be returned as an integer. The integer value of

ABOVE: Excel has features designed to simplify mathematics and trigonometry.
RIGHT: There are functions to perform a wide range of calculations.

a number disregards any decimal places by rounding down the number to an integer, for instance INT(4.6) equals 4 and INT(-4.6) equals -5. To return the decimal part of a positive real number, subtract the integer value from the number. For example, 4.6-INT(4.6) equals .6.

The EVEN function rounds up a numeric value to return an even number. The argument for the function is either a number or the reference of the cell containing the number to be displayed as an even number. The function will round up the number to an even number whether it is positive or negative. For example, EVEN(3.5) equals 4 and EVEN(-3.5) equals – 4.

The MOD function provides the remainder when one number is divided by another. The function has two arguments, number and divisor. Number is the value for which you want to find the remainder and divisor is the number by which you want to divide the number. For example, MOD(5,2) equals 1, MOD(-5,2) equals 1, MOD(5,-2) equals –1 and MOD(-5,-2) equals –1. If the divisor is 0, MOD will return the #DIV/0! error value.

The SQRT function returns the square root of a number. If the number is negative, the SQRT function will return the #NUM! error value. For example, SQRT(25) equals 5, SQRT(-25) equals #NUM and SQRT(ABS(-25)) equals 5.

The POWER function returns the result of a number raised to a power. The function has two arguments, number and power, where number is any real base number and power is the exponent. The "^" operator can be used instead of POWER function. For example, POWER(4,2) equals 16, POWER(3,3) equals 27 and 5^2 equals 25.

➥ *Functions, Paste Function Button*

MICROSOFT'S EXCEL PAGE

Microsoft's page for Excel is at *www.microsoft.com/office/excel*. A lot of it is hype for the latest version of the software, but there are some useful sections.

On the left-hand side of the page is a list of links. The most helpful is probably 'Support' (or go straight there with *www.microsoft.com/office/excel/support*). For a start, it holds the 'Help' files for both Excel 2000 and Excel 2002 online. But if you have a problem, you've probably already tried using these.

There are lists of some common problems with Microsoft, which you can find by clicking on your version of Excel from the list on the main support page. This lets you look at the top issues for your version, as well as a longer list of frequently asked questions. If you find your problem listed, you will find the symptoms, cause and resolution, along with links to more detailed help articles.

The next line of support is the online Microsoft Knowledge Base (again, click on the link from the Support home page). You need to choose your exact version of Excel from the drop-down menu in step one, then your preferred search method: the last option, 'Keyword search using All Words', is a good starting point. In step three, you enter your query. The answers may be helpful, but you may need to experiment with different wordings to find what you need. (Hopefully you'll find the answer somewhere inside this book first.)

ABOVE: Excel's web site can answer your queries and help with problems.

If you can't figure out the problem using the Web, this section also holds useful email addresses and phone numbers (click on the phone number link from the support home page). US and Canadian customers can go through this site for the contact details, UK users should look at *www.microsoft.com/uk/support*. The UK site is, incidentally, the place to visit for help with 'local' issues: support with euro currency, for example, as well as with any software that has been customized for UK requirements.

Free help is usually only available for installing the software, and this only applies if you bought the software directly from Microsoft. Most people 'buy' Excel and other Microsoft software as part of the price of their computer. If that's the case, Microsoft says contact your computer manufacturer, which may or may not be helpful. (The sites mentioned do have links to many manufacturers, known as 'OEMs' in industry jargon.)

This may be expensive, however: the UK-based Dixons Group, which owns Dixons, The Link, PC World and Currys, charges £1 a minute for its Microsoft support phone line.

In general, you'll need to work it out for yourself. Hopefully, with this book and the web sites listed, you'll find a way.

Clicking on the left-hand link marked 'Using Excel' offers different kinds of assistance. There's a fairly short list of 'Tips and tricks', although many of these apply only to the latest version of the software. Next, there's 'How-to Articles', a much more comprehensive set of online tutorials. Bear in mind that these are designed to work with the Office suite of software as a whole, and some have nothing to do with Excel. Still, the list may be worth a glance for new ideas.

There are also sections on training courses, book purchases (designed for US customers) and newsgroups for discussing Excel.

The 'Downloads' section may provide some useful add-ons to your software. It uses a colour-coding, with blue denoting useful extras, red showing downloads that sort out security breaches or improve the basic software, and yellow for converter software. This list is regularly updated, and you shouldn't have any problems with downloads, given they come straight from Microsoft itself.

It's worth downloading the red-coded material for patching security flaws: particularly with newer versions of Microsoft software, the company often unearths many security problems only after release. You can check for these more easily by using the 'Products Update' link. This automatically checks your software and compiles a list of the most important

updates needed to tackle known security problems, such as vulnerabilities to viruses. It is good sense to at least download any required 'Critical Updates' suggested by this process. These are usually fairly small in size.

It is equally worthwhile to do the same thing for Windows overall: this can be done by visiting *http://windowsupdate.microsoft.com*, or by choosing 'Windows Update' from the 'Start' menu.

The 'Previous Versions' link offers the ability to check what's available in any version of Excel, from 95 to 2000. If you want to find out more about the latest version, click on the Evaluation link, which at time of writing includes the chance for US and Canadian customers to order a 30-day only copy of Office XP for a small price (UK customers can find a similar offer at *www.microsoft.com/uk/office*), as well as offering a guide to the latest features.

If you want to upgrade your spreadsheet but don't want to pay Microsoft for an upgrade, it's well worth considering Star Office, a suite that works in a similar way to Microsoft Office, but which can be downloaded for free from www.sun.com/staroffice, or bought on CD from shops for a small price.

➡ **Help with Help**

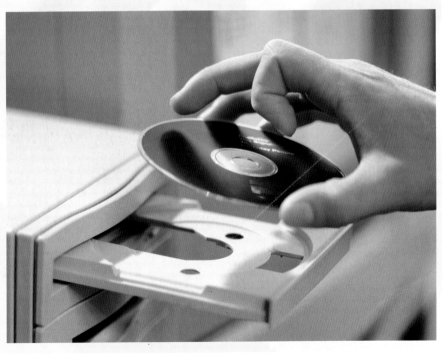

MOUSE AND EXCEL

A mouse is a pointing device predominantly used for selecting menu and toolbar options, data, objects and charts, but it has a great many uses besides. You can use the mouse to drag and drop data between areas of a workbook, different workbooks or even different programs. You can also use it to access task-related functions, which may not be available through any other means.

You can use the mouse to help you build an in-depth knowledge of many toolbar and dialog box options. Most dialog boxes display a question mark button to the left of the Close button. Click and the mouse pointer will change into a question mark. Point and click the question mark into an option to display context-sensitive help. To familiarize yourself with toolbar options quickly, hover the mouse over a toolbar button until a ScreenTip appears.

The mouse can be used to perform drag and drop editing. This is a particularly useful feature, allowing you to pick up data or objects and move or copy them to another location.

To drag and drop the contents of cells in a worksheet, select the cells whose contents you want to move or copy and point into the border of the selected area. The mouse pointer will change to the shape of an arrow. Hold down the left mouse button and start to drag to a new location. As you drag, you will see an outline of the selected cells and the cell references of the current location. Release the mouse when you have reached the desired location.

To copy the cell contents, hold down the Ctrl key while dragging. A Plus symbol will be displayed to the right of the mouse pointer, indicating that drag and copy is active. To switch off drag and drop editing, click the Tools menu and select Options followed by the Edit tab. Uncheck the Allow cell drag and drop box.

ABOVE RIGHT: The mouse is not always easy to control.

Drag and drop editing is a feature of the Microsoft Office suite, making it possible for you to move or copy information between applications. Open the source and destination documents and arrange the application windows so that you can see them both at the same time. If you drag and drop using the left mouse button, the information will be removed from the source document and placed in the destination document. If you drag and drop using the right mouse button, a shortcut menu will appear. Depending upon the type of information selected, you can then choose to move or copy the information, create a link to an Excel object, or create a shortcut or hyperlink.

The left and right mouse buttons perform different operations. In the main, the left button is used to select items. The right button provides a shortcut to options, which are specific to the task in hand. right-click a column heading and you will see the option to change the column width or hide the column. Reduce the size of the workbook window, right-click the Title bar and you will have the option to create a new window or arrange windows. Whenever you are carrying out a task, it is worth viewing the options, which are available via the right mouse shortcut menu.

When you are working with charts and objects, you will find the use of the mouse invaluable. In most charts, you can control the shape and size of the plot area, chart area and legend box and reposition chart titles. To resize an item, select the item and point to a handle. When the pointer changes to a double-headed arrow, drag the handle to the size that you want.

If you have created pie or doughnut charts, use the mouse to drag the slices out of the chart. You can also drag a data point for a particular series to a new position and Excel will reflect the change in the worksheet to which it is linked.

If you have installed a Microsoft IntelliMouse, you can move quickly around your workbook without scrolling or clicking buttons. Roll the wheel backwards or forwards to scroll up or down a few rows at a time. To scroll continuously through the worksheet, hold the wheel down and drag the pointer away from the origin mark.

To begin scrolling automatically, click the wheel and move the mouse in the direction you want to scroll. You can speed up or slow down this process by dragging away from or towards the origin mark. Click any mouse button to stop AutoScrolling.

If you would prefer to use the wheel as a means of zooming in on a worksheet rather than scrolling, click the Tools menu and select Options followed by the General tab. Check the box labelled Zoom or roll with IntelliMouse.

You can customize the mouse buttons or the wheel so that they perform frequently used commands. You can even record and assign a keystroke to a button, such as Ctrl + S to save. The wheel and buttons can be set to perform different tasks in different applications.

➠ *Features for those with Disabilities*

MULTIPLYING AND DIVIDING

Calculations using * and /. The beauty of an electronic spreadsheet is the ability to manipulate the data once it has been entered. Performing simple or complex calculations is easy as long as you remember the rules: multiplication and division have their set place in the order of operations.

To multiply or divide values entered in your spreadsheet, you need to create a formula. All formulae start with the equal sign (=). The equal sign is followed by a number or the address of a cell containing a number. Formulae also contain operators to determine the type of calculation to be carried out. The operator for multiplication is * rather than a lower case x. This is usually obtained by holding down Shift and typing '8'. The operator for division is near the bottom right of the keyboard.

To create a simple formula to multiply the two numbers 6 and 4, select an empty cell and type =6*4. This will appear in the Formula bar at the top of the screen as you type it. Click on the green Tick button on the Formula bar to confirm. The result of 24 will be displayed in the selected cell. Equally, if the cell B3 contains the value 6 and B6 the value 4, the formula can be entered as =B3*B6.

Formulae can contain several operators and can be as complicated as you like. You must remember that Excel has its rules. In any formula Excel performs the series of operations from left to right, giving some operators precedence over others. Excel will carry out multiplication and division operations before any addition or subtraction, irrespective of order. Round brackets () take precedence over all the other operators. For example, by typing a formula as =(B3+B6)/10, Excel will add the contents of the cells B3 and B6 and then divide the result by 10. Without the brackets, Excel will divide the content of B6 by 10 and then add the value in B3, producing a different result.

Instead of the '*' arithmetic operator you can use the PRODUCT() function. To use this function click on the Paste Function button on the Standard toolbar, or select the Function option from the Insert menu. Select Math and Trig from the options and scroll down the box on the right and click on the Product option. You can type either numbers or cell addresses in the Type boxes. A maximum of 30 numbers can be multiplied. The result is displayed at the bottom of the dialog box. Click on the OK button to confirm.

➡ **Brackets, Functions, Paste Function Button**

NUMBER FORMATS (OTHER)

Working with numbers. The main component of a spreadsheet is numbers. Numbers can be displayed in their raw form or formatted to include special symbols, separators and other presentation styles.

The purpose of the commonly used formats is fairly obvious, for example Currency, Percentage and Date and Time. The usefulness of some of the remaining formats may be less clear.

The General format is the default, the number in its raw state. If a cell has had no previous format applied to it, any series of digits typed into the cell will appear in the General format. Sometimes this is exactly what you want. Also, if you have been experimenting with different number formats, you may want to return the contents to how they were. To do this, select the cell or range of cells, access the Format menu and select the Cells option. Select the General option and click on OK to confirm.

The Number format provides three options. You can specify how many decimal places you want to display, select whether or not to display a comma (,) between thousands and choose from a range of ways to display negative numbers. Two of the negative number options allow you to display numbers in red. This can greatly enhance the presentation of a spreadsheet.

The Fraction format provides the option to display the decimal part of a number as a fraction. There are nine different fraction formats to choose from.

The Scientific format displays numbers in exponential notation (with an E). For example, 200,000 will display as 2.00E+05. Sometimes Excel will display a number in this format if the cell is not wide enough to display the whole number.

RIGHT: As part of Microsoft Office, Excel is very easy to open and close.

The Custom format allows you to create your own customized formats. It is easiest to use an existing format as a starting point for creating your new format. In this way you will be sure to use the correct characters (known as placeholders) when defining the format.

To do this, first select the existing format in its own category and then select the Custom format at the bottom of the dialog box. Once you have made the changes and created your format you can preview the result in the Sample box. When you are happy with the result click on the OK button to save the format. The Custom format is saved with the worksheet.

➠ *Paste Function Button*

OPENING AND CLOSING

Excel is part of the Microsoft Office Suite of applications. The applications are integrated in such a way that it is easy to move between them and combine information from different applications into one document. Once Excel is installed, there are many ways in which you can start the program.

Possibly the simplest and most convenient method used to open an Office application is via the Windows Start menu. The Windows Start button is located in the bottom left-hand corner of the screen. Click the button and choose the Programs option. A list of available programs will be displayed. Select Microsoft Excel. If the Microsoft Office shortcut bar is visible you can also click the Excel icon on the bar. In addition, you can double-click an Excel file from within Windows Explorer. Explorer will launch Excel and open the file.

If you use Excel frequently and would prefer to have it automatically open when you switch on your computer, you can do this by making changes to the settings in Windows. Click the Start button followed by the Settings option and then Taskbar. The Taskbar Properties dialog box will be displayed. Click the Start Menu Programs tab and then the Add button. You will be prompted to type in the location of the file which will start the Excel application running. Click the Browse button and search through the folders on your computer until you find Excel. More often than not, Excel will be installed in C:\Program Files\Microsoft Office\Office. Double Click Excel.exe or the name of the file which is identified as the application. The path to its location will appear in the box. Click the Next button. You will be prompted to select a folder. Select the Startup folder and Click the Next button. Type in a name, for example, Excel and click the Finish button.

When you are ready to close Excel, select the Exit option from the Excel File menu. You will be prompted to save any work that has not been saved. If you look at your screen you will also see a cross in the top right-hand corner. This is an application close button. If there are two crosses, the top one will close Excel. If you select the cross underneath, the current workbook will be closed but Excel will continue to run.

➠ *Passwords*

ORDER A LIST

Worksheets often contain lists of information, price lists, lists of customers, and salary details, to name but a few. It is useful to be able to display and print your lists in different orders, by date, by highest to lowest or perhaps in alphabetical order. Excel provides a number of methods for doing this.

information in any one row needs to be kept together. For example, take a table containing the names and addresses of your clients. If you decide to sort the list in order of surname, the last thing you want is for the names to move into alphabetical order but the addresses to stay put. The entire row of data needs to be kept together and not shuffled about. Excel decides the extent of your table by

Rearranging the order of the rows within a list is called sorting. The simplest way to sort is to click on a cell somewhere in the column you want to sort and then click on the Sort Ascending button on the Standard toolbar.

If you cannot see the Standard toolbar, right-click on the currently selected toolbar, deselect it and select the Standard toolbar instead. Excel automatically sorts the list into ascending order: A to Z, lowest to highest, first to last. The Descending button sorts the list into the reverse order: Z to A, highest to lowest, last to first.

If your list forms part of a table, the Ascending and Descending buttons do not just sort the column containing the selected cell. Excel determines how many rows and columns make up your table and sorts all the rows. This is usually what you want because the

looking for empty columns or rows. As soon as it comes across an empty column or row, it assumes that it is the end of the table. So make sure your table does not include a row or column that is completely empty (it can have some empty cells) or only part of your table will be sorted.

You also need to be careful if your table includes formulae. If a formula only refers to cells in the same row, there will not be a problem. However, if a formula refers to cells elsewhere in the table or outside of the table, the formulae will not be correct when the table is sorted.

ABOVE: Lists are important for keeping track of information within Excel.
RIGHT: You may not always wish your name to be on a list, but Excel is useful for ordering data..

In this case you must ensure that your formulae contain absolute cell references. If you do come across any problems, access the Edit menu and select the Undo Sort option. You must do this immediately after sorting the data to reset the table to the previous sort order.

On occasion, you may need to perform a more complex sort. For example, take an employee table that contains department and name details. As there are several people in each department, you need to sort on a second key, possibly name. This will result in the list being ordered by department, and within each department, employees being listed in order of name. You can also take this a stage further if there are two or more employees with the same surname. By performing a third-level sort on first name, John Smith from Accounts will be listed before Mary Smith from Accounts. To sort on more than one column, access the Data menu and select the Sort option. The Sort dialog box is displayed.

If your table contains column headings that are formatted slightly differently from the rest of the table, Excel will assume that the headings are labels and not part of the table to be sorted. In this case, the column headings will be displayed in each of the drop-down Sort by boxes. If you have not included column headings, the drop-down boxes will contain the column name, for example Column E. Select the appropriate columns for the first, second, and if needed, third sort lists. Make sure the Header row or No header row buttons are checked, depending on whether your table has a header row. If you get this wrong you will find that your headings are sorted with the rest of the table! At this point, click the OK button to sort the table. Don't forget you can always select Edit, Undo if the sort does not work as expected.

The Sort dialog box also provides further options. If you click on the Options button within the Sort dialog box the Sort Options box is displayed. There are three options:

- The First key sort order allows you to create a custom sort. There are four default options designed to sort by month or day. For example, if the column contains the entries Monday through to Sunday, you would want all the rows containing Monday before Tuesday, and so on. This is a special order, not alphabetic.
- The Case sensitive option takes note of case and will sort upper-case letters before lower-case letters if sorting in ascending order.
- The Orientation option allows you to sort the table horizontally as well as vertically.

➡ *Keeping Cells Still*

LISTE
DES
GUILLOTINÉS

SUR la place de la Révolution, et au ci-devant Carrouzel

1 LOUIS-DAVID Collenot, dit d'Angremont, ci-devant secrétaire de l'administration de la garde nationale à la maison-commune, commandant en chef la bande assassine, convaincu de conspiration.

2. La Porte, ci-devant intendant de la liste-civile, convaincu de conspiration.

3. Durosoi, homme-de-lettres, et ci-devant rédacteur de la *Gazette de Paris*, et d'une autre feuille intitulée *Le Royalisme*, convaincu de conspiration.

4. Jean Julien, ci-devant charretier à Vaugirard, convaincu de conspiration

5. Jacques-Joseph-Antoine-Léger Backman, natif du canton de Claris, âgé de 59 ans, militaire depuis son jeune âge, demeurant à Paris, rue Verte, fauxbourg St-Honoré, ci-devant major-général des ci-devant gardes-suisses, convaincu de conspiration.

6. Nicolas Roussel, natif de Ville-Rosoi, département de la Moselle, âgé de 49 ans, ci-devant employé dans la régie générale, convaincu de conspiration.

7. Jeanne-Catherine Leclerc, âgée de 50 ans, cuisinière, convaincue de conspiration.

8. Anne-Hyacinthe Beaujour, ci-devant colonel du 3e. régiment d'infanterie commandé par Dumouriex,

A 2

Fac-similé de la liste des guillotinés vendue dans les rues sous la Terreur.

ORDER A LIST CASE STUDY

Excel uses the term list to describe a database stored in a spreadsheet. A list, or database, can be defined as an organized collection of information; the first row containing descriptive labels with the following rows containing values or text. The columns in the list are often referred to as fields and the rows as records. This case study shows that, by viewing a list in a different order, people with different interests can see the records that are relevant to them.

The scenario is that of a training and development company. Details of all the courses that have been run by the company are saved as an Excel list. The list provides details of sales by month, showing the type of sale, the revenue from that sale and also the Account Manager who made the sale. As soon as a course is booked, the Account Manager making the sale enters a record into the list. To make this operation as simple as possible, records can be added using a data form. Each Account Manager has received a brief training session on how to add the information.

The list is designed to include all the relevant information that will be needed by all areas of the business. It has been typed into a worksheet using the fieldnames as column headings. In order to keep the columns as narrow as possible, the column headings have been wrapped around, within the cell. To do this, select the column headings, access the Format menu, select the Cells option and click the Alignment tab. Check the Wrap Text box and click the OK button.

The Account Managers enter all of the information apart from the invoice number. The invoice number is entered by the accounts clerk once an invoice has been issued. The last two columns on the sheet, revenue and month, are calculated automatically using simple formulae.

The revenue information is calculated by multiplying the daily rate by the number of days. The formula $=H2*I2$ has been entered into cell J2. The formula in cell J2 has then been copied to the cells below in readiness for a year's worth of records to be entered.

The month information, in column K, is calculated from the date entered in column B. A lookup table has been entered in cells M2 to N13. The first column contains the numbers 1 to 12 and the second column contains the months of the year. The formula $=LOOKUP((MONTH(B2)),\$M\$2:\$N\$13)$ has been typed into cell K2 and then copied down the column. The formula looks up the month part of the date in cell B2, finds the corresponding month number in the first column of the lookup table and returns the relevant month from the second column of the table.

Once the column headings have been entered and the formulae entered into columns J and K, the worksheet is ready for the Account Managers to start logging the sales.

They have been trained to open the worksheet and click somewhere within the list. They then access the Data menu and select the Form option. The following data form is displayed and they can enter a new record by clicking the New button.

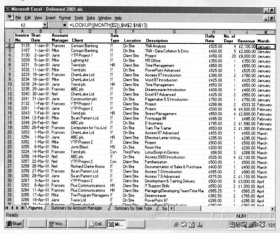

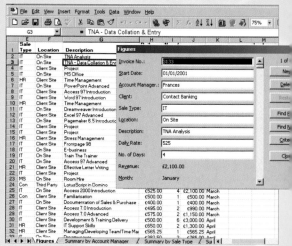

Once the data has been entered, a number of people use the worksheet. The Accounts Clerk enters the invoice number once the work has been completed and the client invoiced. She likes to be able to see the information in order of invoice number. To do this, click within the list, access the Data menu and select the Sort option. The Data Sort dialog box is displayed. To sort the list in order of the invoice number, use the Sort by drop-down list to select the Invoice No field. Make sure Ascending is checked and click the OK button.

	A	B	C	D	E
1	Invoice No.	Start Date	Account Manager	Client	Sale Type
74	3319	15-Nov-01	Neil	ChemLake Ltd	IT
75	3320	16-Nov-01	Neil	Contact Banking	IT
76	3321	5-Dec-01	Mike	ChemLake Ltd	IT
77	3277&32	16-May-01	Frances	Plus Communications	Con
78		25-Apr-01	Frances	Plus Communications	IT
79		9-Jul-01	Neil	ChemLake Ltd	IT
80		11-Jul-01	Neil	ChemLake Ltd	IT
81		16-Jul-01	Frances	ChemLake Ltd	IT
82		16-Jul-01	Frances	ChemLake Ltd	IT
83		6-Nov-01	Frances	Peter Lindon Assoc	Con
84		13-Nov-01	Jane	Kave Handling	IT
85		20-Nov-01	Frances	ChemLake Ltd	IT
86		23-Nov-01	Frances	Contact Banking	IT
87		6-Dec-01	Mike	ChemLake Ltd	IT
88		13-Dec-01	Frances	ChemLake Ltd	IT
89		10-Dec-01	Neil	First Technologies	MS
91					
92					
93					
94					
95					

The Accounts Clerk can instantly see that she has not invoiced for a number of courses earlier in the year. In fact, the course in April was cancelled and the courses for ChemLake in July where paid for in the previous financial year. The November courses however are overdue and need invoicing straightaway.

Frances, one of the four Account Managers, is interested in her sales during the period. She wants to view the records in date order but with her sales grouped together. She would also like to see the most recent first. To do this, she needs to firstly sort on the account manager field in ascending alphabetical order, i.e. A to Z. This will display all Frances's records followed by Jane's, then Mike's and finally Neil's. To make sure that each Account Manager's records are in date order, a secondary sort needs to specify the start date in descending order, i.e. latest to earliest. Frances can easily do this by accessing the Data menu, selecting the Sort option and specifying the appropriate sort keys.

	A	B	C	D	E
1	Invoice No.	Start Date	Account Manager	Client	Sale Type
2		13-Dec-01	Frances	ChemLake Ltd	IT
3		23-Nov-01	Frances	Contact Banking	IT
4		20-Nov-01	Frances	ChemLake Ltd	IT
5		6-Nov-01	Frances	Peter Lindon Assoc	Con
6	3317	1-Nov-01	Frances	First Technologies	MS
7	3302	26-Oct-01	Frances	Kave Handling	Con
8	3317	26-Oct-01	Frances	First Technologies	MS
9	3310	4-Oct-01	Frances	DCT	Con
10	3308	18-Sep-01	Frances	Contact Banking	IT
11	3303	3-Sep-01	Frances	ChemLake Ltd	IT
12	3298	14-Aug-01	Frances	TMD	IT
13	3299	1-Aug-01	Frances	First Technologies	MS
14	3295	27-Jul-01	Frances	ChemLake Ltd	IT
15	3293	24-Jul-01	Frances	ChemLake Ltd	IT
16		16-Jul-01	Frances	ChemLake Ltd	IT
17		16-Jul-01	Frances	ChemLake Ltd	IT
18	3285	11-Jun-01	Frances	First Technologies	MS
19	3281	24-May-01	Frances	Plus Communications	Con
20	3282	24-May-01	Frances	ChemLake Ltd	IT
21	3280	17-May-01	Frances	ChemLake Ltd	IT

Frances can see at a glance her latest sales and the date the training took place. This provides the information she needs to telephone her clients to make sure the courses went well.

OUTLINES

If you frequently work with large worksheets, you will enjoy using the Outline feature. Outlining allows you to identify and display key information whilst temporarily hiding more detailed information from view.

Those of you familiar with Microsoft Word will know that if you view a document in Outline view, Word will collapse the main body of the text until just the key headings are visible. Outlines in Microsoft Excel are based on a similar concept. At the click of a mouse you can hide all data except for the rows or columns that contain key headings or summary information.

Excel can display up to 8 levels of outline. The highest level (level 1) will display top-level information such as a row containing a grand total. The next level down (level 2) will display the row containing the grand total and those rows holding the sub-totals, which contribute to the grand total. If you have no further summary information in the worksheet, outline Level 3 will display the data on which the sub-totals have been based.

There are several ways in which you can create an outline. You can use the Auto Outline feature to have Excel automatically generate an outline from your worksheet information or you can create your own outline, manually. Excel will also create an outline when you use the Subtotals feature.

The data Subtotals feature will produce sub-totals and a grand total from information displayed in a structured list. To use this feature successfully, however, the data must be organized in a particular way. The first row of the list should contain descriptive column headings and subsequent rows must hold related information, as in the following illustration.

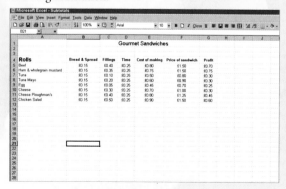

Click the Data menu followed by the Subtotals option. In the Subtotals dialog box, click the down arrow to the right of the At Each Change In box and select the column containing the items that you want to calculate subtotals for. From the Use Function box choose the type of function (for example Sum or Average) on which your subtotals should be calculated. Finally, click the check boxes to indicate which columns should display subtotals.

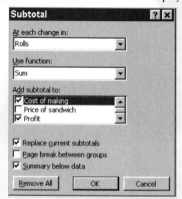

In the following illustration, the cost of making different types of bread roll and the profit from each roll have been calculated, along with a grand total.

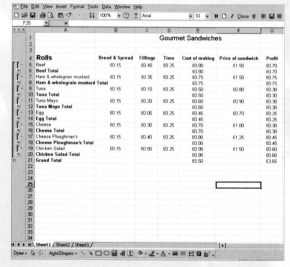

To have Excel automatically outline a worksheet, click the Data menu and select the Group and Outline option followed by Auto Outline. Before using this feature, it is important to have your worksheet set up in a structured and consistent way. Excel will search the worksheet for rows containing related information and rows that make use of summary functions, such as Sum and Average.

Whichever method you use to create an outline, Excel will place outline level markings and brackets to the left or top of the screen, illustrating each group of information and its subgroups, in a hierarchical fashion.

Click an outline number to display the required level of detail. Click Number 1 to view only the grand total. Click Number 2 to see the grand total and the subtotals that contribute to the grand total figure. Where an outline has been collapsed, you can click the plus symbol to the right of the bracket to expand and view corresponding detailed information again and you can click the minus symbol to collapse and hide detail.

The following illustration displays outline level 2 details for all rows, except the first, which has been expanded to show a third level of detail.

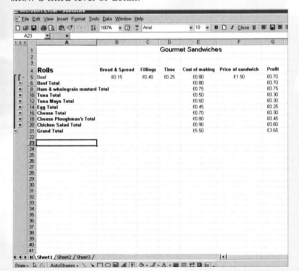

If you want to assign an outline to a small portion of your worksheet or if your worksheet does not contain many formulae, you can create a manual outline. You do this by using the group command to apply a hierarchical structure to your data.

Select rows or columns which contain the detail (do not include rows which contain subtotals). Click the Data menu, select the Group and Outline option followed by Group. If you wish, you can select and group a subset of rows within the original group. Excel will create a corresponding number of outline levels which you can expand or collapse to show or hide detail, using the methods described previously.

To clear an outline, select any cell in the range and click the Data menu followed by Group and Outline and Clear Outline.

If your outlines don't quite work out as you expect, check the options set in the outline Settings dialog box. You can display this by choosing the Settings command from the Group and Outline sub-menu. Excel will use these settings to determine how to group and outline your worksheet data. For instance, if the Summary rows below detail box remains unchecked, Excel will search for summary information above a group of data. If it is checked, Excel will assume that summary information will be located below a set of data. Similarly, you can specify that summary columns are located to the right or left of detail. Click the Create button and check the Automatic Styles box to have Excel use pre-defined styles for each of the outline levels.

OUTLINES CASE STUDY

Simon Parker runs a small mobile catering business, which involves selling ready-made sandwiches and soups to businesses located in out-of-town retail parks. Simon is approaching retirement age and has a potential buyer for his business but the buyer wants to be sure that he can sustain the level of profit achieved by Simon. He has asked Simon to produce a report detailing the number and types of sandwiches sold each day, the cost of each sandwich to make, the price to the customer and the profit. In essence, he wants a breakdown of the income and expenses so that he can decide which lines are most profitable.

Simon prepares the following worksheet.

Gourmet Sandwiches

Expenses	Rolls	Beef	Ham & mustard	Tuna	Tuna Mayo	Egg	Cheese	Pestrami	Chicken Salad
Bread & Spread		£0.15	£0.15	£0.15	£0.15	£0.15	£0.15	£0.15	£0.15
Fillings		£0.40	£0.35	£0.10	£0.20	£0.05	£0.30	£0.40	£0.50
Cost of time		£0.25	£0.25	£0.25	£0.25	£0.25	£0.25	£0.25	£0.25
Total cost of making		£0.80	£0.75	£0.50	£0.60	£0.45	£0.70	£0.80	£0.90
Price to customer		£1.50	£1.50	£0.80	£0.90	£0.70	£1.00	£1.75	£1.50
Profit per roll		£0.70	£0.75	£0.30	£0.30	£0.25	£0.30	£0.95	£0.60
Number sold each day		20	150	250	250	190	45	500	35
Daily profit for rolls		£14.00	£112.50	£75.00	£75.00	£37.50	£13.50	£475.00	£21.00
Total daily profit for rolls	£823.50								

Expenses	Ciabatta	Hot beef & onions	Parma ham & avocado	Tuna & red onions	Corn fed chicken	Egg & bacon	Brie & red grapes	Three cheeses & salad
Bread & Spread		£0.30	£0.30	£0.30	£0.30	£0.30	£0.30	£0.30
Fillings		£1.00	£1.20	£0.50	£2.00	£0.40	£0.60	£0.80
Cost of time		£0.30	£0.30	£0.30	£0.30	£0.30	£0.30	£0.30
Total cost of making		£1.60	£1.80	£1.10	£2.60	£1.00	£1.20	£1.40
Price to customer		£1.50	£1.50	£1.50	£1.50	£1.50	£1.50	£1.50
Profit per ciabatta		-£0.10	-£0.30	£0.40	-£1.10	£0.50	£0.30	£0.10
Number sold each day		350	100	100	50	250	20	20
Daily profit for ciabatta		-£35.00	-£30.00	£40.00	-£55.00	£125.00	£8.00	£2.00
Total daily profit for ciabatta	£53.00							

Expenses	Wraps	Tuna mayo, sweetcorn & salad	Chilli con carne	Cajun chicken & sour cream	Pork & plum sauce	Smoked salmon & cream cheese	Fresh salmon
Bread & Spread		£0.20	£0.20	£0.20	£0.20	£0.20	£0.20
Fillings		£0.40	£0.40	£0.90	£0.60	£1.20	£1.00
Cost of time		£0.40	£0.40	£0.40	£0.40	£0.40	£0.40
Total cost of making		£0.90	£1.00	£1.50	£1.20	£1.90	£1.60
Price to customer		£1.20	£2.00	£2.00	£1.80	£2.00	£2.00
Profit per wrap		£0.30	£1.00	£0.50	£0.80	£0.00	£0.40
Number sold each day		200	200	200	200	200	200

To create this worksheet, click in cell A2 and type 'Expenses', move to cell B2 and type 'Rolls' and so on. When you have completed the column headings, click in cell A3 and type 'Bread and Spread'. Continue down column A until you have typed 'Total Daily Profit for Rolls' in cell A11. Save the worksheet as Gourmet Sandwiches 2.xls

In cell C3, enter 0.15 as the cost of the Bread and Spread. Format cell C3 to display currency. To do this, click the Format menu and select the Cells option. In the Format Cells dialog box, click the Number tab and select Currency from the Category list. Set the number of decimal places to 2 and check that £0.15 appears as the sample.

RIGHT: With the help of Excel Simon Parker runs a small, yet profitable, mobile catering business.

As the cost of the Bread and Spread is the same for all rolls, copy the information in cell C3 through to cell J3. To do this, click in cell C3 and point the mouse into the bottom right-hand corner handle. The mouse pointer will change to a small black cross. Hold the mouse down and drag across the row to cell J3.

Rows 4, 5, 7 and 9 do not contain formulae. Enter the figures for these rows as per the illustration.

To calculate the total cost of making each roll, select cell C6 and click the AutoSum button. Point the mouse into cell C3, hold the mouse down and drag through to cell C5. The formula should read =SUM(C3:C5). Press Enter to complete the formula. Copy this formula across the row to cell J6.

To calculate the profit per roll, click in cell C8 and enter the formula =C7-C6. Copy the formula across the row to cell J8. To calculate the daily profit per roll, click in cell C10 and enter the formula = C9*C8. Copy across the row.

Finally, click in cell C11 and use the AutoSum button to create the formula =SUM(C10:J10).

Although the worksheet contains all the necessary information, the potential buyer wants to be able to see key information at a glance. To achieve this, use the Data Outlines feature in Excel to hide some of the detail.

Before using this feature, check that the first row of each section contains the column headings and that subsequent rows hold related information. The next step is to select the area to outline. To select and outline the entire worksheet, click in the cell to the left of column A and above row 1.

To generate an outline, click the Data menu and select the Group and Outline option followed by Auto Outline. Excel will search the worksheet for rows containing summary functions. Outline level markings and brackets will be displayed to the left or top of the screen, illustrating each group of information and its subgroups, in a hierarchical fashion. The following illustration shows Simon's worksheet after the Auto Outline feature has been applied.

You will see from the illustration that Excel has grouped the information and assigned five outline levels. Each level expands to include the information shown at the previous level. For example, level 1 shows only the total profit per day whereas level 2 shows the total daily profit and the daily profit per roll. The final level, level 5 shows all detail, including rows 3-5, the figures for which are added together to yield the total cost of making the product.

The report looks good when Simon selects the highest outline level (level 1) and reveals the total profit per day. He is sure that the buyer will be keen to proceed. However, when he clicks outline level 2 to see the daily profit for each product, it becomes apparent that he has been making a loss on some of his lines! By clicking on outline level 4 he can see that some products cost more to make than the price charged to customers.

		Gourmet Sandwiches							
		Beef	Ham & mustard	Tuna	Tuna Mayo	Egg	Cheese	Pastrami	Chicken Salad
2 Expenses	Rolls								
3 Bread & Spread		£0.15	£0.15	£0.10	£0.15	£0.15	£0.15	£0.15	£0.15
4 Fillings		£0.40	£0.35	£0.10	£0.20	£0.05	£0.30	£0.40	£0.50
5 Cost of time		£0.25	£0.25	£0.25	£0.25	£0.25	£0.25	£0.25	£0.25
6 Total cost of making		£0.80	£0.75	£0.50	£0.60	£0.45	£0.70	£0.80	£0.90
7 Price to customer		£1.50	£1.50	£0.80	£0.90	£0.70	£1.00	£1.75	£1.50
8 Profit per roll		£0.70	£0.75	£0.30	£0.30	£0.25	£0.30	£0.95	£0.60
9 Number sold each day		20	150	250	250	150	45	500	35
10 Daily profit per roll		£14.00	£112.50	£75.00	£75.00	£37.50	£13.50	£475.00	£21.00
11 Total daily profit for rolls		£823.50							

		Hot beef & onions	Parma ham & avocado	Tuna & red onions	Corn fed chicken	Egg & bacon	Brie & red grapes	Three cheeses & salad
14 Expenses	Ciabatta							
15 Bread & Spread		£0.30	£0.30	£0.30	£0.30	£0.30	£0.30	£0.30
16 Fillings		£1.00	£1.20	£0.50	£2.00	£0.40	£0.60	£0.80
17 Cost of time		£0.30	£0.30	£0.30	£0.30	£0.30	£0.30	£0.30
18 Total cost of making		£1.60	£1.80	£1.10	£2.60	£1.00	£1.20	£1.40
19 Price to customer		£1.50	£1.50	£1.50	£1.50	£1.50	£1.50	£1.50
20 Profit per ciabatta		-£0.10	-£0.30	£0.40	-£1.10	£0.50	£0.30	£0.10
21 Number sold each day		350	100	100	50	250	20	20
22 Daily profit per ciabatta		-£35.00	-£30.00	£40.00	-£55.00	£125.00	£6.00	£2.00
23 Total daily profit for ciabatta		£53.00						

		Tuna mayo, sweetcorn &	Chilli	Cajun chicken	Pork & plum	Smoked salmon &	Fresh

	A	B	C	D	E	F	G
1			Gourmet Sandwiches				
2 Expenses	Rolls	Beef	Ham & mustard	Tuna	Tuna Mayo	Egg	
10 Daily profit per roll		£14.00	£112.50	£75.00	£75.00	£37.50	
11 Total daily profit for rolls		£823.50					
14 Expenses	Ciabatta	Hot beef & onions	Parma ham & avocado	Tuna & red onions	Corn fed chicken	Egg & bacon	
22 Daily profit per ciabatta		-£35.00	-£30.00	£40.00	-£55.00	£125.00	
23 Total daily profit for ciabatta		£53.00					
26 Expenses	Wraps	Tuna mayo, sweetcorn & salad	Chilli con carne	Cajun chicken & sour cream	Pork & plum sauce	Smoked salmon & cream cheese	
34 Daily profit per wrap		£60.00	£200.00	£100.00	£160.00	£0.00	
35 Total daily profit for wraps		£600.00					
38 Expenses	Bagels	Tuna mayo & red onions	Brie & grapes	Cajun chicken & sour cream	Pastrami	Smoked salmon & cream cheese	
46 Daily profit per bagel		£100.00	£40.00	-£25.00	-£15.00	-£48.00	
47 Total daily profit for bagels		£22.00					
50 Expenses	Soups	Brocoli & gruyere	Parsnip & potatoe	Pumpkin	Carrot & coriander	Celery	
57 Daily profit per soup		-50	-100	0	100	-15	
58 Total daily profit for soups		-£50.00					
61 Total Profit Per Day		£1,448.50					

Outlines and Cons... | Outlining and Con... | Microsoft Excel -... | gourme

Click on outline level 2 so that you can see the daily profit for each of the different breads and fillings and the total daily profit for that product. To look at detailed figures, comparing wraps with ciabatta for example, click on each of the plus symbols to the right of the brackets showing the groupings for wraps and ciabatta. By doing this, you can see which types of bread and filling are the most and least profitable.

PAGES AND WORKBOOKS

Working with more than one sheet. Excel files are known as workbooks. A workbook can contain an unlimited number of pages, with each page being known as a sheet. Sheets that hold rows and columns of data are known as worksheets, whereas those that hold charts are known as chart sheets.

Excel allows you to move freely around and between the worksheets of a workbook and also between different workbooks.

There are many ways to move around the current worksheet. To move to a cell that is in view, simply click the left mouse button on the cell. To move to a cell out of view, use the scroll bars at the bottom and right-hand side of the screen or you can use the Page Up and Page Down buttons (or the Alt key to leap right and left respectively). If you know the address of the cell you want to move, press F5 on the top row of your keyboard. The Go To dialog box is displayed. Type the address of the cell you want to move to and click on the OK button.

ABOVE: You can look at different sheets within a workbook using sheet tabs.

You can switch between worksheets by clicking on the sheet tabs on the lower border of the workbook window or through using Page Up and Page Down buttons with the Control key. When you create a new workbook, there are three worksheets set up for you named Sheet one, Sheet two and Sheet three. To give your sheets more meaningful names, access the Format menu and select the Sheet, Rename options. Change the name on the sheet tab to something more relevant.

If you want more than three worksheets, access the Insert menu and select the Worksheet option. The new worksheet will be inserted before the current worksheet. To change the order of the worksheets, use the mouse to drag the worksheet tab to the left or right.

If you have more than one workbook open at the same time, you can toggle between the workbooks using the key combination Ctrl+F6. Alternatively, you can access the Window menu and click on the name of the workbook from the list.

On occasion, it may be useful to be able to see more than one workbook at the same time. This can most easily be accomplished by choosing Arrange from the Window menu, then selecting 'Tiled' and OK – you can then see books side-by-side.

➡ **Working with Different Views**

PANES AND WINDOWS

Viewing multiple areas of a worksheet. When a table expands beyond the screen size, problems can arise. It becomes difficult to find out where you are if column or row headings have disappeared from view. Equally, it is difficult to understand formulae if cells being referenced are not within the current view. As this is a situation that arises frequently, Excel provides a number of ways that enable you to view different areas of your worksheet at the same time.

1. By opening one or more windows, you can view different areas of a worksheet at the same time. This will allow you to display new views of the active workbook at the same time as the current view.

To open a new window, access the Window menu and select the New Window option. A new window will be created, although this may not be immediately obvious. If

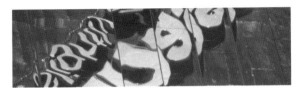

LEFT: You can view multiple areas of a worksheet with Panes and Windows.
BELOW: The zoom tool can be used to enlarge and reduce text size.

your initial window is maximized (taking up the whole screen), the new window will now be on top of it. If you look at the Excel title bar you will see that the window in view has the number two appended to the filename. To see both windows, access the Window menu and select the Arrange option. The Arrange Windows dialog box is displayed. There are a number of different ways to display the worksheets, choose an option and click the OK button. You can now view completely different areas of your worksheet in each open window. The windows are considered as being separate and you can close one or more windows in the usual way without closing them all.

2. Splitting the worksheet into panes provides another way of viewing different areas of a worksheet at the same time. You can split a window into two or four separate panes. There are two ways to do this. One is to drag the split box to the position where you want to divide the window. You will find a split box above the up scroll arrow on the scroll bar at the right of the screen (the vertical scroll bar) and to the right of the right scroll arrow on the scroll bar at the bottom of the screen (the horizontal scroll bar). Drag the split box down the vertical scroll bar to split the screen horizontally or drag the split box to the left along the horizontal scroll bar to split the screen vertically.

To split the window by accessing an Excel menu, position your cell pointer. To split the window horizontally, click in the first cell of the row where you want to split the window. To split the window vertically, click in the first cell of the column where you want to split the window. If you want to split the window into four, click on the cell where the row and column should be split. When your cell pointer is positioned, access the Window menu and select the Split option.

You can now move around each pane independently, providing different views of your data. To remove the split, either double-click on the split separator bar or access the Window menu and select the Remove Split option.

3. If you are working with a large table of information, it can be extremely annoying when row or column headings disappear off the screen. By 'freezing' the rows and columns containing the title information they will remain still while you scroll through the data in your table.

The important part is to position your cell pointer in the right place before you freeze your titles. The cell pointer needs to be pointing to the cell below the row that you want to remain visible as you scroll down, and to the right of the column you want to remain visible when you scroll across. Once positioned, access the Window menu and select the Freeze Panes option. Excel will insert a dark line to show you the frozen rows and columns. As you now scroll through your data, the titles will remain in view.

If you want to unfreeze the titles to return the window to its original state, access the Window menu and select the Unfreeze Panes option.

4. The final method for seeing more data at the same time is generally less useful. It does, however, come into its own if the data you want to see is just outside of the current screen area. By zooming in and out, you can view more data on the screen at the same time. Excel achieves this by increasing or decreasing the 'zoom percentage'. By default, everything you see on screen is set to 100%. In order to see more of your worksheet at the same time, you will need to decrease the size of the cells and data within the cells. To do this, zoom out by using the Zoom tool on the standard toolbar. You can change the 'zoom percentage' from 10% (very small text) to 400% (very large text). Choose the appropriate percentage from the drop-down box or type a percentage to provide maximum screen usage.

➡ *Working with Different Views*

PASSWORDS

If a workbook contains sensitive information, there are several levels of security which can be applied. At the highest level, you can save a workbook with a password and so prevent unauthorized people from opening it. At a lower level you can have a workbook open as read-only and prevent others from saving changes to the content.

Before setting a password, proceed with caution. If you forget the password you will not be able to open the workbook again. To password-protect a workbook, click the File menu and select the Save As option. A Save As dialog box will appear. To the right of the box you will see the Tools drop-down menu. Select General Options from this menu. The Save Options dialog box will be displayed. In the Password to open box enter a password of up to 15 characters and click OK. You will be prompted to confirm the password by typing it a second time into the Re-enter password to proceed box. Make sure that you keep a record of all passwords and the case in which they were written. Click OK. You will return to the Save As dialog box and you will now need to select the Save option. If this file has been saved before but without a password, you will be prompted to overwrite the existing file. Click Yes.

ABOVE: There are security measures for worksheets containing sensitive information.

To remove password protection from the current workbook, select the Save As option from the File menu. From the Tools drop-down menu choose General Options. As before, the Save Options dialog box will be displayed. Delete the asterisks from the Password to open box and Click OK. Save and overwrite the existing file. To prevent changes being made to a workbook, access the Save Options dialog box and type a password in the Password to modify box. Save and overwrite the existing file. In future, a password will be required before changes can be made to the workbook. If the password is not known, the only way to open the file is to click the Read Only button. Changes can be saved by saving a copy of the file with a new name.

If the Read only recommended box has been checked in the Save Options dialog box, Excel will remind you that this file should be opened only as read-only. You can, however, choose to ignore this recommendation.

➡ *Locked and Hidden Cells, Opening and Closing*

PASTE FUNCTION BUTTON

List of available functions. Excel provides far too many functions to remember them all without help. The Paste Function button is designed to make life easier. The button activates the Paste Function dialog box. This lists the available functions with details on what they do. Once a function is selected from the list, the Formula Palette is displayed requesting the information required by Excel to carry out the calculation.

The Paste Function button is located on the Standard toolbar. [include button]. If the Standard toolbar is not displayed, right click on the current toolbar, deselect it and select the Standard toolbar instead. Select the cell to contain the result and click the Paste Function button. The Paste Function dialog box appears.

The column to the left of the box displays the various categories of functions. Click on the category you want. The column to the right will change to display a list of available functions. To help you choose the right function, Excel displays a description at the bottom of the box. If you need to know more, click on the Help button at the bottom-left of the box.

When you have selected your function click OK. The Formula Palette is displayed. The Formula Palette provides text boxes so that you can enter values for the function arguments. The function arguments are simply the information that Excel needs to be able to provide a result. You can either type the information or you can use the Collapse Dialog button situated on the right-hand side of each text box to minimize (shrink) the dialog box so that you can see the worksheet. This enables you to select the cell or range of cells to be referenced in the function. To restore the Formula Palette back to full size, click the Restore Dialog button or press the Enter key. When you have entered all the arguments for the function click OK. The result of the function will be displayed in the current cell.

If you need to make changes to the function, select the cell containing the function and click the Paste Function button. The Formula Palette is displayed – make your changes and then click on OK to confirm.

➠ *Financial Functions, Functions, Statistical Functions, SUMming Up*

PERCENTAGES

Displaying the per cent symbol. It is much easier for someone else to understand your spreadsheet if the data is presented in a clear format. This can include symbols such as £ and % to distinguish number type. Excel provides the tools to format individual cells, ranges of cells or entire columns or rows.

The percentage format automatically converts a decimal number to a percentage by multiplying the number by 100 and adding the percentage symbol (%). For example, if you enter the value .175 in a cell and format the cell as a percentage, the result will display as 17.5%. Conversely, if you enter a number and manually type a percentage sign, Excel will store that number as a decimal. For instance, if you enter 17.5% in a cell, Excel will store the value as .175.

BELOW: The Paste button can be found on the toolbar.

To apply the Percent Style, select a single cell or range of cells and then click the Percent Style button on the Formatting toolbar (%). If the Formatting toolbar is not displayed, right-click on the current toolbar, deselect it and select the Formatting toolbar instead. The value will display with no decimal places. To change the number of decimal places, ensure the cell(s) are selected and click on the Increase Decimal or Decrease Decimal buttons also available on the Formatting toolbar (two buttons to the right of the %).

You can also apply the percentage format by accessing the Format menu and selecting the Cells option. Alternatively, click the right mouse button and select Format Cells. Click on the Number tab and select the Percentage option from the list.

In accounting conventions, when presenting a percentage, the number is usually separated from the percentage symbol by a single space. Excel does not conform to this convention and displays the symbol adjacent to the number. If you are a stickler for convention you can always create your own percentage format. To do this, select Format, Cells and click on the Number tab. Select the last option, Custom. To enter a customized format simply overtype an entry with your own format. In this case, type 0.00 % to produce a percentage format with two decimal places. Remember to leave a space between the last 0 and the percentage sign. To check the result, view your format in the Sample box at the top of the Type box. Click on the OK button to complete the customization.

➠ *Currency Formats, Number Formats (other)*

PIVOT TABLES

Viewing data in different ways. Pivot tables enable you to look at your data in many different ways. Rather than just having a static view of a table of data, you can create a more dynamic approach to data analysis. The term pivot table has evolved due to the ability to pivot from one axis of your table to another, displaying different relationships between the data.

The best approach to understanding the capability and versatility of the pivot table is by example. Consider the following simple database – what does it show? Does it show sales figures for three sales representatives, sales during May to July 2002, or sales for five current clients?

	A	B	C	D	E	F	G
1	Date	Order No	Customer		Order Total	Sales Month	Sales person
2	19/05/2002	102	ABC Ltd	£	225.00	May-02	Marie
3	21/05/2002	103	Blacks plc	£	1,342.00	May-02	John
4	22/05/2002	104	Howard Bros	£	1,222.00	May-02	John
5	31/05/2002	105	ABC Ltd	£	567.00	May-02	Marie
6	05/06/2002	106	ABC ltd	£	7,895.00	June-02	Marie
7	12/06/2002	107	Jones Ltd	£	2,134.00	June-02	Frank
8	14/06/2002	108	Blacks plc	£	1,453.00	June-02	John
9	29/06/2002	109	Ledger plc	£	7,843.00	June-02	Frank
10	01/07/2002	110	Jones Ltd	£	6,592.00	July-02	John
11	02/07/2002	111	Ledger plc	£	987.00	July-02	Frank
12	04/07/2002	112	ABC Ltd	£	215.00	July-02	Marie
13	21/07/2002	113	Blacks plc	£	5,312.00	July-02	John
14							

In fact, it shows all these things and more. The trouble is, it is difficult to extract the answers to specific questions. For example, just by looking at the table, it is difficult to establish sales for Marie for June or total revenue from Jones Ltd for the period, without doing some mental arithmetic, manipulating the table by sorting or filtering the data. Assuming a 'real' table with hundreds of records, mental arithmetic is probably not an option! Filtering or sorting is a possibility but it will only show you the answer to one of the questions at any one time. With pivot tables, it takes only a few seconds to display the answer to a frequently asked question without the use of a single formula.

The following pivot table provides the answers to several questions at the same time. You can see at a glance the total sold during the period by each salesperson and

ABOVE: You can view data in different ways using a pivot table.

the total revenue produced by each customer. The table also provides totals for each customer and salesperson.

	A	B	C	D	E	F	G
1	Sum of Order Total	Customer					
2	Sales person	ABC Ltd	Blacks plc	Howard Bros	Jones Ltd	Ledger plc	Grand Total
3	Frank				£ 2,134.00	£ 8,830.00	£ 10,964.00
4	John		£ 8,107.00	£ 1,222.00	£ 6,592.00		£ 15,921.00
5	Marie	£ 8,902.00					£ 8,902.00
6	Grand Total	£ 8,902.00	£ 8,107.00	£ 1,222.00	£ 8,726.00	£ 8,830.00	£ 35,787.00
7							
8							

A pivot table is simple to create. Access the Data menu and select the PivotTable and PivotChart Report option. The PivotTable and PivotChart Wizard will be displayed, asking you where your data is held. With a simple example, your data will probably be held in an Excel list. Select this option and PivotTable as the type of report to be created. Click on the Next button and the wizard will prompt you to confirm the range of cells containing your database. If your cell pointer was within the table when you accessed the Data menu, Excel will automatically highlight the table. If not, select the range either by typing the cell addresses or by clicking on the button to the right of the Range box to shrink the dialog box. Highlight the required range and click on the button to the right of the minimized dialog box to restore it to normal size. If your database is held in another workbook,

you can use the Browse button to locate the workbook and then select the required range of data. When you have finished, click the Next button.

You will now be asked where you want to put the pivot table – on a new worksheet or on the current worksheet. Click the appropriate button. If you select the New worksheet option, Excel will automatically insert a new worksheet for the pivot table. If you select the Current worksheet option, you will be prompted to select the cell to contain the top leftmost cell of the pivot table.

The next step is to tell Excel how to construct the pivot table. Click on the Layout button.

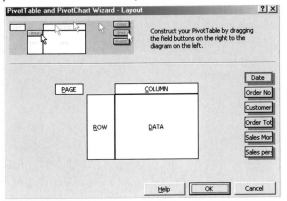

You will see a list of the column headings from your table at the right-hand side of the dialog box. These are known as fieldnames. To create a pivot table, drag the appropriate field button to an area on the plan. The best way to get to grips with using pivot tables is to have a play. Try out different field combinations and see what you get. With the sales example, the Sales Person button is dragged to the Column box, the Customer button to the Row box and the Order Total button to the Data box. If you drag the wrong button or change your mind, simply drag the button off again, back to the list on the right-hand side of the dialog box. When you have made your selection, click on the OK button.

Before you click the Finish button, it is worth considering the range of options available to determine how your pivot table will look. Click on the Options button. Make any changes and click the OK button.

Click on the Finish button to complete the wizard. Your pivot table will be displayed in the selected location.

If the result is not what you expected, you can continue to modify the pivot table until it is exactly what you want. It is useful to display the PivotTable toolbar when working with pivot tables. It is not displayed automatically. You need to access the View menu, select Toolbars and check the PivotTable option.

If you make changes to the source database, Excel does not automatically update any associated pivot tables. To make sure your pivot table is up to date, click the right mouse button anywhere in the pivot table and select Refresh Data from the shortcut menu.

➡ **Database Functions.**

PIVOT TABLES CASE STUDY

Pivot tables provide a dynamic approach to data analysis, pivoting from one axis of the table to another, displaying different relationships between the data. This case study demonstrates how simple it is to use pivot tables to provide valuable management information.

The case study involves a training and development company who use Excel to hold sales details as a list. The types of questions being asked by management are becoming more complex. The sorting and filtering features currently used to interrogate the data are becoming inadequate. It has been suggested that pivot tables may help.

The list contains details of all the courses run in the past 12 months. Management intend to use this information to determine trends and plan for the future of the business.

The types of questions being asked require subtotals, cross-tabulation and frequency distributions. It sounds like a job for a statistician but, in fact, a pivot table can do all this without you having to supply a single calculation. Let us consider each of the questions in turn.

1. How are our Account Managers performing in comparison with each other? Do they all have good and not so good months at the same time or does it vary?

To answer this question you need to provide a figure for total sales for each Account Manager on a monthly basis. To generate a pivot table to do this, position the cell pointer within the list, access the Data menu and select

the PivotTable and PivotChart Report option. The PivotTable and PivotChart Wizard will be displayed asking you where your data is held. Select the Excel list option and select PivotTable as the type of report to be created. Click on the Next button and the wizard will prompt you to confirm the range of cells containing your list. When complete, click the Next button. Select the New worksheet option so that the pivot table will be displayed on a separate worksheet.

The next step is to tell Excel how to construct the pivot table. You will see a list of the column headings from your table at the right-hand side of the dialog box. Drag the Account Manager field to the Row box, the Month field to the Column box and the Revenue field to the Data box.

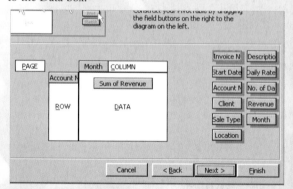

The resulting pivot table provides exactly what is needed to answer the posed question. Before presenting it to the management, it needs some formatting to improve the appearance and clarity. Before making any changes to the format, it is important to ensure that these changes are preserved when the pivot table is recalculated. Position your cell pointer within the pivot table and click the right mouse button. Select the Options option. The PivotTable Option dialog box is displayed. Make sure the Preserve Formatting box is checked and click the OK button. You can now decrease the font size, add currency notation and alter column widths as you feel appropriate.

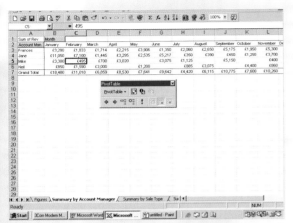

2. The Sales Manager is keen to know the breakdown of sales by client on a monthly basis.

Return to the worksheet containing the list. Create another pivot table, again choosing the option to insert it in a new worksheet. You will be asked whether you want to create this pivot table from the existing pivot table. This question is a bit misleading. What it means is that the second, or subsequent table, will be created from the same data as the first pivot table. It is more efficient in terms of memory to do this, so choose to base the new pivot table on an existing one and click the Next button.

To generate a table that will answer the question, you need to drag the Client field to the Row box, the Month field to the Column box and the Revenue field to the Data box. Format the pivot table to improve the appearance.

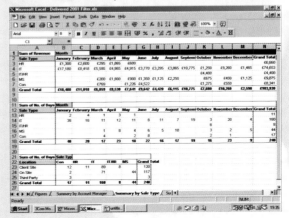

3. The third question relates to the type of sale. The records all contain a sale type code: IT for Information

Technology courses, HR for Soft Skill courses, MS for a Managed Service and Con for Consultancy. The management would like to know the breakdown on a monthly basis for both revenue and the number of training events. They are also interested to know the number of training days based on location and their sale type.

To generate the pivot table to show revenue by month for each sale type, drag the Sale Type field to the Row box, the Month field to the Column box and the Revenue field to the Data box.

To generate the pivot table to show the number of days by month for each sale type, drag the Sale Type field to the Row box, the Month field to the Column box and the No of Days field to the Data box.

To generate the pivot table to show the number of days by location for each sale type, drag the Location field to the Row box, the Sale Type field to the Column box and the No of Days field to the Data box.

PLAN A PROJECT

Excel can help with project planning, especially for calculating costs, time required and start and end dates of tasks. The following two pages show how to plan the construction of a new garage, which requires drawings, planning permission, new foundations and a base. Instructions are provided on calculating total costs, total time required and the total time between the project starting and finishing. Cells can also be linked, so if the project starts later than planned, Excel can still calculate a finish date.

1. Using a new workbook in Excel, select cell A1 and enter the title Task Description. Continue along this row and enter the titles, Time required (days), Estimated cost, Start date and Completion date. The final heading should appear in cell E1. You may want to increase the width of some of the columns in your spreadsheet. Position the mouse pointer in between the column headings (the letters in grey) and wait for it to change to a cross with two horizontal arrows. Hold down the left mouse button and move to the right to stretch the left column. Release the left button to stop widening the column.

2. Decide upon the order of tasks for your project and enter them in the order they will occur in column A along with the time required and estimated cost. Do not enter the start or completion dates. These will be entered in the next step. Save your Excel file regularly by clicking on the File menu and choosing Save. When you do this for the first time, a Save As dialog box will appear. Enter a name for your Excel file and choose a location on your computer to save it. Click on the Save button to return to the spreadsheet. In the future, when you click on the File menu and choose Save, the file will automatically be saved and the dialog box will not appear.

3. Select cell D2 – the start date for the first task on your list. This will be the first task to be started, so enter a date. Then select cell E2 for the completion date of this task. If, for example, you would like the completion date to be based upon the start date + the time required (in cell B2), a calculation can be created to work this out. Press the = symbol to start the calculation, then use the mouse to select cell D2 (the start date). Press the + symbol, then select cell B2 (number of days) and press Return. Try changing the start date and the time required figure in cells B2 and D2. Notice the completion date automatically changes.

ABOVE: Help with project planning includes calculating the costs and time involved.

	B	C	D	E
				=D2+C2
1	Time required (days)	Estimated cost	Start date	Completion
2	4	♦800	15/08/02	=B2+D2
3	1	150		
4	3	250		
5	2	750		
6	3	850		
7	10	2500		
8	4	850		
9	1	450		
10				
11				
12				
13				
14				
15				
16				
17				
18				

the left mouse button and move down all the cells you want to include. Press Return to complete the calculation. Repeat this procedure for calculating total estimated cost.

7. Select the cell below the last completion date for the last task (in column E). We are going to calculate the number of days between the project starting and finishing. Press the = sign to start the calculation, select the cell for the completion date of the last task in your list, press the minus symbol (-), then select cell D2 (the start date of the first task). Press Return to complete the calculation. A date will appear in this cell. Select the cell again, then click on the Format menu and choose Cells. From the dialog box that appears, select the Number tab, choose Number from the Category list on the left, then click on OK to return to your spreadsheet and find out the number of days between your project starting and finishing.

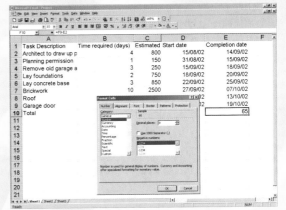

4. Select cell D3 – the start date for the next task in your project. If this task is linked to the first task (e.g. the first task must be completed before the next task can start), a calculation can be created to ensure this happens. Press the = sign to start the calculation, then select cell E2 (the completion date of the first task). If required, add or subtract days to this calculation. Press Return to complete it. Change the time required and start date for the first task and make sure the start date of the second task changes.

5. Continue entering calculations for start and completion dates. You do not have to enter calculations, especially if a task does not rely upon anything starting or finishing. However, make sure any such calculations work properly and automatically update when changing the first start date of the first task and any of the time required figures. Save your Excel file regularly (see step 2).

6. In column A, enter the word Total at the bottom of the list of tasks. Select the cell to the right of this title (in column B) and click on the AutoSum toolbar button (looks like a Greek S symbol). The words =SUM() will appear on the screen and some cells in column B may be selected. Make sure all the cells in column B with time required figures are selected. If they are not, hold down

➡ *Date and Time Formats*

PRICE COMPARISON

If you need to find the best price for an item, there are several facilities available online. They could be useful for planning how to save, or for working out your overall spending. They should also help you save money.

There are several general purpose price comparison engines. In the UK, these include *http://uk.shopsmart.com*, *www.easyvalue.com* and *http://uk.kelkoo.com*. (Kelkoo, a French site, has several versions for other European countries – these can be accessed through *www.kelkoo.com*.) They all cover popular online items such as music, electronics and books. Each has further areas of coverage: Shopsmart and Kelkoo both cover household appliances, and Easyvalue covers insurance.

which also owns the airline EasyJet, and that Shopsmart is owned by Barclays Bank (although both say they are unbiased nevertheless).

Basically, if it's an important purchase, it's well worth using a couple of these sites, and seeing if they come up with the same answer. If it's really valuable, it can't hurt to look at the prices on a few major retailers' web sites too.

Here's how you would use one of the sites, *www.easyvalue.com*, to find the value of a book, let's say, the first Harry Potter novel. On the home page, in the section marked 'Entertainment', click on the link 'Books'. The page that appears lists the top ten books, but if by the time you read this Harry Potter is slightly less popular than at time of writing, you would need to type 'Harry Potter and the Philosopher's Stone' into the box at the top left marked 'Title', 'JK Rowling' into the 'Author' box, and choose 'Paperback' from the drop-down list of formats. You would then hit the orange search button on the right of these boxes.

The system will come back with a range of choices that fit your query. If you had just entered 'Harry Potter'

These sites work by finding out what you want, then going to several suppliers and retrieving their prices for that item. A few health warnings are necessary. Firstly, although these sites don't take commission for helping you, some only list suppliers that pay them a finder's fee. Secondly, don't assume accuracy. These sites often get extras wrong, such as postage and packing charges, which can affect their conclusion as to who you should shop with. Furthermore, many sites charge less for P&P if you buy several items at once.

Thirdly (perhaps obviously), this kind of comparison only works well with standardized products. And fourthly, be aware that Easyvalue.com is owned by EasyGroup,

ABOVE RIGHT: Instead of visiting various car dealers, shop online to compare costs.

FAR RIGHT: Price comparison web sites cover a wide range of products.

as the title, this list would be a lot longer. Let's say you want the 'Adult Edition' (the one with a photo of a steam engine, designed to prevent embarrassment when read on the train to work). You click on the orange 'Compare' button to the right of that entry, and wait for the system to go to the online retailers in question and come back with prices.

In this case, nine shops returned prices from £6.99 to £8.54 (although these prices change regularly). You can then click on the orange 'Buy' button to the right hand of the price you want to pay, and be taken directly into that shop.

If you decide to buy, you should buy from a shop you feel safe with – it should, for example, use security when taking your personal details, especially your credit card number. Security systems are denoted by a padlock appearing in the frame of your web browser, and by web addresses that start with https:// rather than http://. Any reputable site will explain its security on its web site, normally a system called SSL (Secure Sockets Layer). A site that uses SSL is reasonably safe.

You should also look for a UK phone number and address. If the retailer does not have an office in this country, you are unlikely to have any comeback if goods do not arrive or are faulty.

There are some specialist comparison sites. For utilities including gas, electricity, telephones and digital television, *www.uswitch.com* offers comparisons. Although not strictly speaking a comparison service, *www.callforless.co.uk* is an excellent independent web site that specializes in finding the best value phone tariffs.

When it comes to finding flights, it is worth trying online travel agencies such as *www.ebookers.com* or *www.expedia.co.uk*, which compare flights from many airlines, and sometimes have better deals than the airlines will offer direct. However, budget airlines such as *www.ryanair.com*, *www.easyjet.com* and Go, at *www.go-fly.com*, do not use travel agents (which take a commission), so you need to look at their sites separately.

If you are looking at travel sites to budget for a trip, remember that flight seats usually increase in price the nearer you are to the flight date – unless the flight is lightly booked, in which case the airline might try to sell seats cheaply through a site such as *www.lastminute.com*.

➡ *Compare Costs*

PRINTING FROM EXCEL

When you have formatted a worksheet to your satisfaction, you can use the Print button on the Standard toolbar to produce a hard copy of the worksheet contents. If you need to print the entire workbook or limit the print to specific sections of a worksheet, it is better to choose the Print option from the File menu. In the Print what area of the Print dialog box you can choose whether to print only a Selection, the Active sheets or the Entire workbook. You can also specify the range of pages to print and the number of copies. At the bottom of the dialog box you will see a Preview button. Preview is a useful tool because it gives you a feel for how your worksheet will look when it is printed.

If you do not select a specific area to print, the entire worksheet will be sent to print. However, if you want to preview or print targeted areas of a worksheet, you will need to set a print area. Select the areas of the worksheet

BELOW: Printing is not the arduous task that it used to be; new technology means that we can print at the click of a button.

to print. Click the File menu and select the Print Area option followed by Set Print Area. You can also set the print area through the Page Setup dialog box. A dotted line will appear around the print area.

To print multiple areas, simply click and drag the first selection area with the mouse and then hold down the Ctrl key while you click and drag additional areas. Each area will print on a separate page. If you want them to print on the same page, select the cells, columns or rows between each of the selected ranges and hide them. To clear a print area, click the File menu followed by Print Area and then Clear Print Area.

More detailed printing options can be set using the Page Setup dialog box, which can be accessed from the

File menu. The Sheet tab allows you to set the print area, specify titles to print on each page and control the order in which a large worksheet will print. To set the print area through the Sheet tab, click the Collapse Dialog button located at the end of the box. Select the areas of the worksheet to print and click the button again to return to the Page Setup dialog box. You will see that print ranges have been entered.

If printed information spans more than one page, consider setting Print titles. This will allow key information contained in the home area of a worksheet, such as titles or company logos, to be repeated on all pages. Click in the Rows to repeat at top box or Columns to repeat at left. You can either type in the range or click the Collapse Dialog button and select the range in the worksheet. The range will be entered into the box as an absolute reference, which is Excel's way of making sure that it is fixed. Other printing options controlled through this dialog box include printing worksheet gridlines, row numbers, column letters and comments. Where information spills over more than one page, use the Page order area to control the order in which the worksheet should be printed. Specify Down, then Over to have Excel print down the rows first, and then across the worksheet. Use Over, then Down to print across the columns and then down the rows.

Use the Page tab in the Page Setup dialog box to print in portrait (suitable for printing more rows than columns) or landscape (suitable for printing more columns than rows). You can also specify the number of pages into which Excel should condense worksheet contents and choose to have the worksheet centred on a page.

The Margins tab sets the distance from the edge of the page that data, headers and footers will print. You can either select a measurement in this box, or for an easier method, click the Margins tab in the Print Preview dialog box. This second option will provide you with a pictorial representation of the margins and you can click and drag each margin to a new position.

The Header/Footer tab sets text which will print at the top and bottom of every page. Headers and footers are commonly used to illustrate the name of the person producing the report, company names, dates and number of pages. Excel provides a set of built-in headers and footers which can be chosen from the drop-down lists, or you can click the Custom button and type in your own. In addition to entering your own text, the custom option has a range of buttons which can be used to insert standard information such as page numbers. Place text or pictures in the left, centre or right section of the footer area.

Changes to page setup will only take effect in the active worksheet. Press Ctrl and click multiple worksheets or right click the Sheet tabs and choose Select All Sheets to set these options for more than one worksheet.

➡ **Working with Different Views**

PRINTING FROM EXCEL CASE STUDY

This case study is based on the worksheet created in the Outlines Case Study, see page 142. To recap, Simon Parker runs a small mobile catering business, which he is looking to sell. A potential buyer has asked for a report showing a breakdown of daily income and expenses. Simon has prepared the following workbook ready for printing. The workbook contains three sheets, one for each of the retail parks that Simon visits each day. Before printing, follow the stages outlined in the Formatting Case Study to improve the presentation style of the report.

To print the active file or selected worksheet items, click the Print button on the Standard toolbar. To limit the print to specific sections of a worksheet, it is better to choose the Print option from the File menu.

The buyer is particularly interested in the sales figures for the Thornes and Panerton retail parks. To print just these sheets, click on the sheet for Thornes, hold down the Ctrl key and click on the sheet for Panerton. Click the File menu followed by the Print option. In the Print what area of the Print dialog box, select the Active sheets option. Each sheet will print on a new page.

To get a feel for how your worksheet will look when it is printed, click the Preview button at the bottom of the Print dialog box.

Expenses	Rolls	Beef
Bread & Spread		£0.15
Fillings		£0.40
Cost of time		£0.25
Total cost of making		£0.90
Price to customer		£1.50
Profit per roll		£0.70
Number sold each day		20
Daily profit per roll		£14.00
Total daily profit for rolls		£823.50

Expenses	Ciabatta	Hot beef & onions
Bread & Spread		£0.30
Fillings		£1.00
Cost of time		£0.00
Total cost of making		£1.50
Price to customer		£1.50
Profit per ciabatta		£0.10
Number sold each day		5
Daily profit per ciabatta		£35.00
Total daily profit for ciabatta		£53.00

The first thing you will notice is that only the first few columns of each section are displayed on the page. In order to print a whole section on the same page, we can change the position of the page break. Click on the Page Break Preview button and drag the page break to the right hand side of the page. Excel will reduce the font size so that more information fits on the page. Your workbook should resemble the following illustration.

Next we need to set the page margins to give maximum space to printing. Margins set the distance between the data in the worksheet and the edge of the paper. To do this, click the Margins tab in the Print Preview dialog box. You will see a pictorial representation of the margins. Click and drag the left margin further to the left. As you drag, you will see the position of the left margin appear in the bottom left hand corner of the screen. Drag the left margin to approximately 1 cm. Drag the right margin until it is 1 cm away from the right-hand edge of the paper. The top and bottom margins affect the position of headers and footers in the document.

Click the Setup tab. The Page Setup dialog box will be displayed. Click the Page tab. As we have a large worksheet to print, it may be better to change the orientation to Landscape. Notice that because we adjusted the page break in order to fit an entire section on one page, the worksheet has been scaled to around 38% of its normal size! Click the Fit to button and select 1 as the number in the page(s) wide box and 1 in the tall box. This will reduce the worksheet to fit onto the specified number of pages. It is important to remember that changes to page setup will only take effect in the active worksheet. Press Ctrl and click multiple worksheets or right-click the Sheet tabs and choose Select All Sheets to set these options for more than one worksheet.

The report needs to have headers and footers, which appear at the top and bottom of every printed page. Excel provides a set of built-in headers and footers, which can be chosen from the drop-down lists, or you can click the Custom button and type in your own. Click the Header/Footer tab.

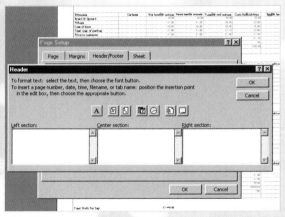

Click in the Right section and type 'Gourmet Sandwiches Confidential Report'. Select the text and click on the letter A. From the Font dialog box, select 9 points in size. Click OK and then choose Custom Footer. Place the cursor in the Left section and click on the Date button. Select the Center section and type "Report prepared by Simon Parker. Click in the Right section and type 'Page'. Click the Page button. Type "of" and click the Number of pages button. Select each piece of text and decrease the

font size to 9 points. If the sample text appears as you expect, click OK.

Click the Sheet tab. Select to print gridlines. In the Page Order area specify Over, then Down to have Excel print across the columns and then down the rows. Click the Print button.

Finally, the buyer would like to be able to compare the figures for rolls and wraps on the same sheet. To do this, select the rows between the rolls section and the wraps section. Click the Format menu followed by the Row option and then Hide to hide the rows. Select both sections and set the print area by selecting the File menu followed by the Print Area option and Set Print Area. A dotted line will appear around the print area. Print the file.

ABOVE: Excel helps to keep Simon Parker's catering business organized.

PROPERTIES

Excel builds a unique picture of each file and stores the information as a set of file properties. File properties include details of the date and time that the file was created, the size and location of the file, and the date that the file was last modified. While some of these details provide a useful source of information, other details, or properties, can be modified. For example, you can record keywords, which can then be used as search criteria. Properties will be saved with a file.

To see a file's properties, click the File menu and select the Properties option. You can also see file properties by accessing the Open dialog box, clicking the Tools menu

FAR RIGHT: Custom properties can be created to make relevant files easier to find.

and choosing the Properties option. There are five tabs. The General tab provides information on the file type, location, size and other attributes. With the exception of file attributes, this information cannot be changed. File attributes can be changed in Windows Explorer: open Windows Explorer, locate the file and right-click the filename. From the shortcut menu, select the Properties option and change the attribute. Properties cannot be changed if a workbook is protected.

Use the Summary sheet to record further details about the file. This might include entering a title, subject, author, keywords and comments. If you make the effort to do this for all files, you will be able to quickly search for and retrieve a group of files, which share the same information. For example, you can retrieve all files by the same author, or all files that contain a keyword. If you check the Save preview picture option which is located at the bottom of the Summary sheet, you will be able to preview the file before opening it in the Open dialog box.

The Statistics sheet provides information relating to the date and time that the file was created, the date it was last saved, the date it was last opened, the name of the author and the number of times that it has been saved.

The Contents sheet provides a detailed list of all worksheets and chart sheets in the file.

In addition to the file information provided by Excel, you can draw attention to a file by adding your own custom property. A custom property can be created from a specific type of data or from a link to the contents of a cell on a worksheet.

To create a custom property, click the Custom tab. Type a name in the Name box or select a category from the drop-down list. Depending on the type of property entered in the first step, choose a data type from the Type box. For example, if you choose Data completed as the property, choose Date as the property type. Choices include Text, Date, Number, or Yes or No.

In the Value box, type a value for the property. The value must relate to data type. For example, if you have selected Number in the Type box, you must type a number in the Value box. Values that do not match the property type are stored as text.

If you want to set a property that is linked to a cell in a worksheet, you must start by defining a name for the worksheet cell. In the Custom sheet, check the Link to content box. In the Source drop-down list you will see a list of all names defined in the worksheet. Select the cell to which the property should be linked. Click the Add button to see the property defined. Where a property is linked to the contents of a cell, a chain symbol will precede the property name.

A property linked to the contents of a cell will display the value of the cell in the Custom sheet. The link between the property and the cell contents is dynamic and will be updated if the contents of the cell are changed in the worksheet. However, as with most links, if you

remove the cell name from the workbook, the link will be removed. In this case, the file property will display the last value for that cell.

This type of property can be a useful way of quickly finding only those files whose contents satisfy a particular target. For example, if you keep a set of files to record departmental revenue and you set a property to link to a worksheet cell which displays departmental revenue, you will be able to see at a glance which departments have exceeded the revenue target. You can view properties via the Open dialog box. This will allow you to see quickly whether or not a file matches a set of criteria, before opening the file.

If you are not used to setting file properties, it would be a good idea to have Excel prompt you to set them the first time that you save a workbook. To do this, click the Tools menu, select Options and then the General tab. Check the Prompt for workbook properties box.

➡ *Opening and Closing*

PUBLICATION DATA

If you use a spreadsheet to keep records of publications – books, CDs, films – you may want to get extra data to fill in any gaps, such as the year of publication/release, details of participants and catalogue numbers. There are several web sites that will tell you all you need to know.

For information on books, it makes sense to refer to the catalogue of a major library. You could try an organization with one of the world's shortest web addresses, the British Library (*www.bl.uk*). The national library has an online catalogue, which can be searched at *blpc.bl.uk* with as little as the author's name (although this should be entered using the surname first, e.g.: 'Orwell George').

The British Library will provide the full title, authors (including dates of birth and death for some), editors, the name of the series, the subject, the publisher, the year and place of publication, the number of pages and even the height of the book (useful for librarians deciding what size of shelf to use). It also tells you the British Library's catalogue number for the book.

The British Library system can get busy, so you might try one of the other copyright libraries – the six institutions that automatically receive copies of every book published in the UK. The Cambridge University Library catalogue is at *www.lib.cam.ac.uk/Catalogues*. It's very fast and holds links to other major libraries around the world.

Online bookseller Amazon (*http://www.amazon.co.uk*) is also reasonably good for searching for books, although it holds a fraction of the titles of a major library. Perhaps

FAR RIGHT: You can use a spreadsheet to keep a record of CDs.

surprisingly, it comes into its own when searching for music, offering sound clips for many recordings, as well as user comments, professional reviews and some of the catalogue data provided by libraries. You can also buy the title, although Amazon's prices are rarely the cheapest. Try using a comparison engine to find a better price.

If you want detail rather than sound clips, it's back to the British Library, and specifically its National Sound Archive (*http://cadensa.bl.uk*). This holds an amazing amount of cross-referenced detail. For example, it can tell you that the title track of The Beatles' *Sergeant Pepper* album started recording on 1 February 1967 in studio two at Abbey Road Studios; that it was produced by George Martin and engineered by Geoff Emerick; and that the performers (apart from the Fab Four) were James Buck, Neil Sanders, Tony Randall and Jo Burden, all of whom played French horn on the track. You can click on the name of any of the 10 participants to see what other works they are involved with. It's only a shame that Excel lacks the charting ability to produce rock family trees.

How about films? Although not owned by a library, the Internet Movie Database (*http://uk.imdb.com*) is as comprehensive a guide as you could hope to find. It predates the World Wide Web, having been created on a Usenet bulletin board by a group of enthusiasts. Its data was first placed on a web site courtesy of Cardiff University and its popularity grew and grew until it became a UK limited company. In 1998, Amazon bought Internet Movie Database as part of a move into selling videos, but let the company continue pretty much as before.

The search facility is great fun. It even includes a quotation facility, so typing in 'No Mr Bond, I expect you to die' returns Auric Goldfinger, in the film *Goldfinger*, 1964. A further click takes you to a wider selection of appalling Bond puns.

But it is the main database that provides the data for spreadsheet completists. Entering 'Goldfinger' as a title returns the director, the writers, the tagline ('James Bond is back in action! Everything he touches turns to excitement!'), plot outline, average user ratings, the cast list and the certificates in various countries (apparently it was a '16' in West Germany).

There are also links to the trailer, a full list of cast and crew, trivia, reviews and linked films – in this case, 19 other Bond films (including a provisional listing for Bond 20, due out in 2002 – Internet Movie Database holds provisional data on films in production), 28 films that reference *Goldfinger* and 15 that spoof it (such as *Austin Powers in Goldmember*, again due out in 2002).

If the video collection you're trying to catalogue includes television as well as film, it can be harder to find information. TV Cream (*http://tv.cream.org*) holds entries on hundreds of programmes shown in the UK, with data such as years of broadcast, production company and a few cast members. It is primarily a review site rather than a database and doesn't have a search engine. It is, however, a lot of fun.

Often, for data on individual programmes, the best thing to do is enter the show's title into a search engine such as Google (*www.google.com*): 'Red Dwarf' came up with 64,000 entries. Helpfully, the official site (*www.reddwarf.co.uk*, which includes a complete list of episodes) comes up first. If the show was shown on a BBC channel, it's also worth searching the corporation's web site at *www.bbc.co.uk*.

➠ *Keep a Library*

SELECTING MULTIPLE CELLS

You will come to recognize the current or active cell in a worksheet because it is clearly visible by its thicker border. The active cell is the one into which Excel will enter any information that you type at the keyboard or to which it will apply the results of your current action. If a cell is active and you click the Bold and Align Right buttons on the Formatting toolbar, these attributes will be applied to the contents of that cell. However, there will be many occasions when you find it useful to perform actions on multiple cells simultaneously. For example, you might want to enter the same information into different cells or apply the same text or numeric format to a range of cells. There are many techniques available for selecting cells. The simplest way to select adjacent cells is to click in the first cell in a range and drag the mouse to include the last required cell. If you are trying to drag the mouse over a large area of cells, however, it can be difficult to control the mouse and make a precise selection. You can achieve a more controlled result by clicking the mouse in the first cell, holding down the Shift key and clicking in the last cell in the range.

To select non-contiguous cells, click in the first cell and hold down the Ctrl key while you click additional cells. You can also use a combination of the Ctrl and Shift keys to select adjacent and non-contiguous cells.

To select an entire row or column, click in the row number at the left of the worksheet or the column letter at the top of a worksheet. To select an entire worksheet, click the cell above row 1 and to the left of column A. Use any combination of the techniques described here to select rows or columns that are adjacent or non-contiguous. Try selecting multiple non-contiguous cells, type text into the active cell and press Ctrl + Enter to see it entered into all selected cells.

Use the Go To option on the Edit menu to save time in selecting special cells. For instance, you can click on the Special button and choose to select only those cells which contain comments or formulae or are visible and not hidden.

➠ *SUMming up*

SHORTCUT KEYS

Although you may prefer to make the most of Excel's functionality through using a combination of mouse and menu options, numerous keyboard shortcuts are available to give you greater flexibility and control. There are too many keyboard shortcuts to mention here, so a few of the more useful ones have been selected and categorized according to their function or type. It is worth investing a little time to learn some of the most commonly used keys.

Shortcut keys are particularly useful for moving around a worksheet. Each worksheet contains 256 columns and 65,536 rows, so using a mouse to select areas other than the home page can be cumbersome and time-consuming.

To move around a worksheet quickly, use the following keys:

CTRL + HOME
Moves to the first worksheet cell, usually cell A1

CTRL + END
Moves to the cell, which is at the intersection of the last working column and row

HOME
Start of a row

ARROW KEYS
One cell in any direction

CTRL + ARROW KEYS
Moves in the direction of the arrow key to the last cell in the current range

PAGE DOWN
Down one screen

PAGE UP
Up one screen

ALT + PAGE DOWN
One screen to the right

ALT + PAGE UP
One screen to the left

CTRL + PAGE UP
Next sheet in a workbook or first record in a data form

CTRL + PAGE DOWN
Previous sheet in a workbook or new record in a data form

Function keys provide access to commonly used features and dialog boxes. They are quick to use and easy to remember. The most useful ones are outlined in the next section:

F2
Places the insertion point at the end of the active cell

F4
Toggles between absolute and mixed cell references

SHIFT F4
Finds next occurrence of the contents entered into the Find what box in the Find dialog box

F5
Go To dialog box

SHIFT F5
Find dialog box

F6
Moves to the next worksheet pane

SHIFT F6
Moves to the previous worksheet pane

F7
Spelling dialog box

F11
Creates a chart from selected cells

SHIFT + F11
Inserts a new sheet in a workbook

ALT + F8
Macro dialog box

F10
Makes the menu bar active, closes a visible menu and sub-menu

SHIFT + F10
Displays a shortcut menu

As printing is something that most people do frequently, the print shortcut key can be a very useful one:

CTRL + P
Print dialog box

Entering data into a worksheet is what Excel is all about, so it stands to reason that shortcut keys for inserting data will be among the most useful to memorize:

ENTER
The Enter key will enter data into the active cell and move to the cell below. If a range or multiple range is selected, the Enter key will move the active cell, from top to bottom, down the columns of the active ranges. To change the direction in which the Enter key moves, click the Tools menu followed by the Options command and then the Edit tab. In data forms, Enter will take you to the first field in the next record.

SHIFT + ENTER
Enters data and moves up to the next cell in the column. If the direction of the Enter key has been changed in the Edit tab, Shift + Enter will move in the opposite direction from the Enter key. In data forms, Shift + Enter will take you to the first field in the previous record.

ALT + ENTER
Use to enter multiple lines of text within a cell

CTRL + ENTER
Copies the current cell entry to all other cells in selected ranges

CTRL + SHIFT + ENTER
Enters a formula as an array formula

TAB
Enters data and moves a cell to the right in the selected range. Moves to the next field to edit in a data form

SHIFT + TAB
Moves right to left, one cell at a time

CTRL + PERIOD (.)
Where a range has been selected this key combination will move from one corner to the next

Editing shortcut keys are extremely useful, especially when you need to manipulate information in a formula bar or dialog box:

ESC
Cancels

DELETE
Deletes the character in front of the insertion point

BACKSPACE
Deletes to the left of the insertion point

CTRL + DELETE
Deletes text from the insertion point to the end of the line

HOME OR END
Start or end of the line being edited

CTRL + RIGHT OR LEFT ARROW
Forward or backwards one word at a time

Some of the formatting shortcut keys will come in very handy too:

CTRL + 1
Format Cells dialog box

CTRL + B
Bold

CTRL + I
Italics

CTRL +U
Underline

CTRL + SHIFT + $
Currency format with two decimal places

CTRL + SHIFT + %
Percentage format with no decimal places

There are several shortcut keys which are common to the Office suite. They are as follows:

CTRL + C
Copy

CTRL + X
Cut

CTRL + V
Paste

CTRL + Z
Undo

➡ *Help with Help*

SPELLCHECK

A dictionary is installed as part of Microsoft Office and is made available to all programs in the suite. Excel will spell-check the contents of the current worksheet, using the dictionary as a reference. Headers and footers, cell comments, cell values, text boxes and embedded charts will all be included in the spellcheck process. Formulae and words in a protected worksheet will not be checked.

To check one cell entry, click in the formula bar and select the word or entry. To check a range of cells, select the range. To spellcheck an entire worksheet, click in any cell. After each of these actions click the spellcheck icon or click the Tools menu and choose the Spelling option.

The Spelling dialog box will be displayed. Excel will search the worksheet and display the first word it encounters that does not match a word in its dictionary. The word will be displayed in the Not in dictionary box and, when available, will be accompanied by a list of suggested spellings. You can select a word from this list or enter the correct spelling in the Change to box. Click the Change button to replace the text in the worksheet with the text in the Change to box. Click the Change all button if you want to change all occurrences of the text in the worksheet.

You can also opt to leave the spelling as it is currently found in the worksheet. You would do this by either clicking the Ignore button which would leave the word

ABOVE: The Microsoft Office dictionary checks spellings in all of the suite's programs.

currently selected as is, or by clicking the Ignore all button which would leave all occurrences of this word unchanged. Alternatively, you may prefer to delete the word from the worksheet by deleting the word from the Change to box and clicking the Delete button.

If you find that you frequently mistype a particular word, you can make sure that it gets automatically corrected for you as you type. Either select an alternative spelling from the list of suggested spellings or make changes to the word in the Change to box and then click the AutoCorrect button. From now on, if you type the misspelled word, Excel will automatically replace it with your chosen alternative. You can delete an AutoCorrect entry by selecting the AutoCorrect option from the Tools menu, selecting the entire entry and clicking the Delete button.

➡ *Words in Excel*

STAROFFICE

Most of us never buy a Microsoft product – we find them foisted upon us when buying a computer. However, at some point you may find yourself considering whether to pay to buy or upgrade Microsoft Office, the suite that includes Excel. Don't – until you've checked whether StarOffice could do the job instead.

StarOffice, from US software giant Sun, is a parallel product to Microsoft Office, with one rather big difference: it's free if downloaded over the Web. (If you buy it in shops, it will still cost you far less than Microsoft Office.) The web site at *www.sun.com/staroffice* provides information, and the downloads. You will be able to use your existing Excel files, as StarOffice supports these file types.

The latest version, 6.0, will block up a normal 56k modem for about six hours, rather less if you have a broadband connection.

Fortunately, it can be downloaded in ten blocks. There's a detailed guide to downloading at *www.guardian.co.uk/Archive/Article/0,4273,4284561,00.html*. It's available for Microsoft Windows, as well as operating systems including Solaris and Linux, although not currently for the Apple Mac.

Once you have the software in place and initialized, you should find a little butterfly icon at the bottom-right of the screen. Right-click on the logo (or find StarOffice on the Programs section of the Start menu). Then choose the 'Spreadsheet' option. This opens a new workbook.

What you'll see is very similar to Excel. The grid of cells is the same. The line with '=' before it is there at the top of the screen, for entering and editing formulae. And if you open an Excel file, you will find it looks pretty much as it did in Excel.

The differences are mostly to do with presentation. A line at the top of the screen shows information on the font type and size. There's also a quick way to choose the most popular formats for a cell: currency, percentage and normal, which you can choose by clicking on the pile of coins, the percentage symbol and the arrow under a dollar and percentage sign respectively. The two symbols immediately to the right of these three allow you to, respectively, add and subtract a decimal place from the cell or cells highlighted.

In the grid itself, one small difference is that StarOffice shows when a cell has more in it than can be shown in the column width by putting a little red arrow at the end of the cell. Otherwise, the grid works in much the same way: if you want to widen a column, for example, you do so by clicking on its edge in the bar at the top of the grid.

When first opened, you will see two floating toolbars on the screen. One is called 'Cell Formats', and if you click on the square just to the left of the cross in the top right corner, it will expand to give a choice of preset cell formats. The Navigator bar lets you jump to any cell or sheet on the workbook or to another file. These tasks can be done through menus, as in Excel – these bars are just another method. If they get annoying, click on the cross in the top right corner and they vanish. If you want to move them around, just click on them, hold the button down and move the mouse. The bar will move with it.

The left-hand side of the screen contains shortcuts to facilities which, although available in Excel, are in some cases hidden away. To find out what does what, rest the cursor over an icon and leave it still for a second or two (without pressing any buttons on the mouse). A little box will appear explaining it. Some of the more useful shortcuts here include the second from the top, which creates a floating toolbar for adding columns and rows, and the 'ABC' symbol with a tick under it, which activates a spellchecker.

When saving, which is by choosing 'Save' from the 'File' menu as in Excel, you have a wide range of options. Sun knows that Excel is the most popular spreadsheet, so it allows you to open Excel files and also save files in Excel's own formats – from any version of Excel from 5.0 to the latest, XP. You can also save in the StarOffice format, which has the advantage of easy password protection straight from the 'Save' dialog box. But if you do this, you won't be able to open the file in Excel. The StarCalc formats listed simply refer to earlier versions of StarOffice's spreadsheet – it's not a different program.

If you've downloaded StarOffice, you don't just own a free spreadsheet. By right-clicking on the appropriate words in the butterfly menu, you can create and work on text documents, presentations and drawings. As the spreadsheet is designed to work with Excel files, so the text editor works with Microsoft Word files and the presentation producer with Microsoft PowerPoint – and both can save their output in the formats of their Microsoft equivalents. There's also a database available as a separate download.

➡ *Do I Need to Upgrade Excel?*

STATISTICAL FUNCTIONS

Excel provides numerous statistical functions from the most commonly used SUM and AVERAGE functions (see specific entries on these) through to

obscure functions such as the cumulative beta probability density function. Some of the functions are designed for specialist use but many prove useful in every day worksheets. A few are described below:

Unless otherwise stated the following functions can have up to 30 arguments. These arguments can be values or array/cell references – see the table for worked examples.

The COUNT function counts the number of cells within a range containing numbers. If the arguments contain no numbers, COUNT returns zero.

ABOVE: Functions allow complex formulae, composed of smaller parts, to be easily applied by the user.

RIGHT: The various functions work with the data to provide detailed information.

The COUNTA function counts the number of cells that are not empty. It will return the number of cells containing any type of data, even an error message, excluding those that are empty.

The MAX and MIN functions return the largest or smallest value in a set of values. Only numbers are included within the functions' calculations and if the arguments contain no numbers, MAX and MIN return zero.

The MEDIAN function returns the median of a set of values. The median is the number in the middle of a set of numbers. Half the numbers will have values that are greater than the median, and the other half values that are less than the median. Only numbers are included within the functions' calculations and if the arguments contain no numbers, MEDIAN returns zero. Cells containing the value zero are included within the calculation. When there is an even number of numbers in the set, MEDIAN calculates the average of the two numbers in the middle and returns this value as the median.

The MODE function will return the value that appears most frequently in an array or range of data. The function can have up to 30 arguments and can also use a single array or a reference to an array instead of arguments separated by commas. If there are no duplicate values, MODE returns the #N/A error value.

The QUARTILE function is often used in survey data to divide populations into groups. For example, you can use QUARTILE to find the top 25 per cent of incomes in a population. The function has two arguments,

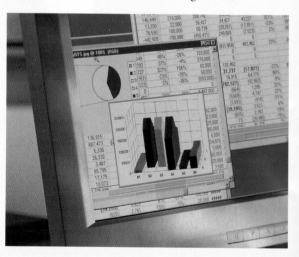

QUARTILE(array,quart). Array is the array or the range of cells containing the numeric values to be included in the calculation. Quart is a number in the range 0 to 4 specifying which value to return.

0	Minimum value
1	First quartile (25th percentile)
2	Median value (50th percentile)
3	Third quartile (75th percentile)
4	Maximum value

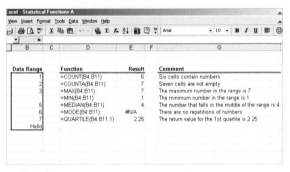

➠ *Functions*

SUMMING UP

Adding together values in cells. One of the most common tasks when using Excel is summing up values you have entered into cells. There are several tools and methods available to help you with this task, the most useful being the AutoSum tool. AutoSum will automatically sum the values in selected cells.

The quickest way to add a row or column of figures is to use the AutoSum button, located on the Standard toolbar. If the Standard toolbar is not displayed, right-click on the current toolbar, deselect it and select the Standard toolbar instead. First select an empty cell immediately to the right of the row of numbers or directly below the column of numbers that you want to sum.

Double-click the AutoSum button. Excel will automatically sum the contents of the cells above or to the left of the selected cell up to the first empty cell.

If you just want to have a look at the total figure without saving it in a cell, simply highlight the cells you want to total and view the result on the Status bar at the bottom of the screen. This is known as the AutoCalculate feature.

BELOW: The Autosum tool, as its name suggests, sums up values automatically.

If there are empty cells within the range of cells you want to sum, you can still use AutoSum. Select the cell to hold the result as before, but instead of double-clicking the AutoSum button, single-click. AutoSum will assume you want to sum the cells to the left or above up to the first empty cell. The range will be highlighted by a dashed box around the cells, known as a marquee (often referred to as marching ants!). To change the selection use the mouse to drag over the cells you want to include. To complete the calculation, press the Enter key.

AutoSum can also be used to sum values in non-adjacent cells or cell ranges. First, select the cell to hold the result and single-click the AutoSum button. While holding down the Ctrl key, select all the cells to be included in the sum. To complete the calculation, click the AutoSum button a second time. In all cases, the AutoSum tool uses the SUM function to calculate the result. You can, of course, use the SUM function from the Number tab of the Formula Palette or type the formula manually. In most cases this is more time-consuming and open to error.

➠ *Adding and Subtracting, Functions, Selecting Multiple Cells*

TEMPLATES

Making a model workbook. Creating a template file is one of the most useful features of Excel, yet few users make the most of it. Creating a worksheet that acts as a starting point for future worksheets can save you a lot of time. You can also farm out work to other people in the confidence that what you get back will at least be in the expected format even if you cannot guarantee its accuracy!

A template is essentially a model on which you can base your new workbook. It can contain any or all of the components of a workbook, including data and formatting. Templates come into their own when you need to produce a number of similar worksheets on a regular basis. This could be a monthly report, weekly sales statistics, or you may just want all your workbooks to have a similar look and feel: same header and footer, font, text formatting etc. Templates are also useful if a number of people are generating worksheets that will then be consolidated. By setting up a template, you can ensure that numbers and totals are entered into the same cells on each sheet, enabling you to 'add the sheets together'.

New workbooks are always created on the basis of a template. A template is just a sample workbook and Excel makes a copy of it each time you select the New option from the File menu. Excel comes with a General workbook template and a number of its own solution templates. Before you create a template of your own, it is worth checking if any of the Excel templates fit the bill. If they come close, you can make adjustments rather than starting from scratch.

To create your own template workbook, first decide on a starting point. To start from scratch access the File menu, select the New option and click on the workbook called Workbook under the General tab. To use one of the Excel solution templates, click on the Spreadsheet Solutions tab or select a template from the Templates subdirectory. Singleclick to preview a template and doubleclick to open the file. The third alternative is to use a workbook you have already created as a basis for your template.

Whichever option you choose, you need to consider carefully what to include in the template and what to leave out. In general, you should follow these rules:

- Include formulae, constant values and text that will be needed in the workbook.

- Include standard formatting for page and print settings, fonts, colours etc.

- Format cells that are currently empty but will contain values, as well as those containing constant values.

- Do not enter any data into the workbook that will have to be deleted from subsequent workbooks.

In a nutshell, only include elements that will be common to all workbooks. When you have included all the common elements (and removed any workbook-specific elements), save the template by accessing the File menu and selecting the Save As option. The Save As dialog box is displayed.

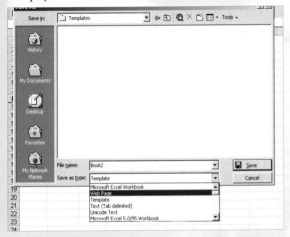

Enter a name for your template in the File name text box. Directly below, you will see the Save as type drop-down list; select the Template option. Your template will be saved in a subdirectory called Templates. If you do not select a different folder or create a new folder, your template will be saved in the root of this subdirectory alongside the General Workbook and will be instantly available each time you select New from the File menu. Decide where you want your template saved and click on the Save button to confirm.

If you want to make changes to the template at any time, simply open the file by selecting the Open option from the File menu, make the changes and save the file again as a template.

You can also make changes to Excel's default workbook. To do this, you need to create two special templates, book.xlt and sheet.xlt. These two templates determine the default settings for new workbooks and new worksheets. To create book.xlt, open a new worksheet and make any changes you want. You can change many of the defaults by selecting Options from the Tools menu.

Default formatting options can be changed by modifying the settings for Normal.sty. To do this, access the Format menu and select the Style option.

When the workbook is changed to your satisfaction, select File, Save As and enter book.xlt for the filename. Save the file in the \XLStart folder. The exact location of this folder will depend on the version of Excel you are using. If you then close the file and restart Excel, you can create a workbook based on your template. Your template will automatically be used if you open a new workbook by clicking on the New button on the Standard toolbar or if you use the key combination Ctrl+N

Use the same process to create sheet.xlt but create a workbook with just one sheet. Again, make sure you save the template in the \XLStart folder. Each time you insert a new sheet into a workbook, the sheet will have the settings defined by sheet.xlt.

➡ *Opening and Closing*

TEMPLATES CASE STUDY

The previous entry discussed the use of templates within Excel. This case study provides a practical example which shows you the benefits and advantages of using templates when consolidating data.

ABOVE: Cliff Redford is responsible for producing the monthly accounts for a charity.

The scenario is that of Cliff Redford who is responsible for producing the monthly accounts for a Charity. This involves gathering information from 20 fundraising offices and consolidating it into reports that can be forwarded to the Head Office. Cliff is familiar with Excel and confident in its use. Unfortunately, the majority of the fundraisers are not! All the fundraisers have access to Excel but the format and quality of data received is variable. Cliff is determined to make his life easier and has decided to create template worksheets that are foolproof. All the fundraisers will need to do is type their figures into the appropriate cells and email a copy to Cliff. By using a standard template, he can ensure that all comparative entries appear in the same cell. For example, the total revenue from the Charity Shops will appear in

the same cell for each of the 20 reports. In this way, he can simply add all the figures from each sheet to produce a report with the totals for the region. To make life as easy as possible, Cliff has highlighted the cells where data needs to be entered and included comments to provide guidance. He has also protected the cells that do not need data entry.

The worksheet he has designed for summary information looks like this:

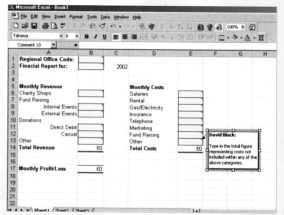

To create a template, access the File menu and select the New option. Make sure the General tab is selected and click on the template called Workbook. This is the default template workbook that comes with Excel and provides a blank canvas for customizing your own template. To save this file as a new template, access the File menu and select the Save As option. Enter the name of the file as Monthly Summary Report and select Template from the Save File As Type drop-down list. Click on the Save button to save this template so that it is instantly available each time you create a new worksheet. Remember to save regularly during the development of the template.

Type the label 'Regional Office Code' in cell A1 and 'Financial Report For' in cell A2. Move down to cell A5 and type 'Monthly Revenue'. Enter the labels for the types of revenue in the cells below but do not worry about the positioning of the text within the cell. Type Total Revenue in cell A14 and 'Monthly Profit/Loss' in cell A17. Move across to column D and type the labels for the cost information. To make a label bold type, press Ctrl+B.

Increase the widths of columns A and D to accommodate the longest label. To do this, point the mouse to the right-hand side of the column heading and drag the column to the required width. To move some of the revenue labels to the right of the cell, select the cell containing the label, and click on the Right Align button on the Formatting toolbar.

To shade a cell with colour, select the cell, access the Format menu and select the Cells option. Click on the Patterns tab, select the required colour from the palette and click on the OK button. To put a border around the cell, select Format, Cells and click on the Border tab. Select the Outline option and click the OK button. Once you have coloured one data entry cell you can copy the formatting to all the other cells using the Format Painter on the Standard toolbar (the paintbrush symbol). Click on the cell you have already formatted, click on the Format Painter and than click on the cell to be formatted. This handy tool can save loads of time.

To add a comment to a cell, click on the cell, access the Insert menu and select the Comment option. A box is displayed for you to type in an appropriate comment. To save the comment, click away from the box. The

BELOW: Excel can help you plan ahead with your business.

comment will display whenever the mouse moves over the cell. You can identify that a cell has an associated comment by the red triangle in the top right-hand corner of the cell.

Format the cells that will contain figures for currency notation. Select the appropriate cells and click on the Currency button on the Formatting toolbar. The currency symbol will not appear until the data is entered.

Enter the year in cell C2 by using the formula =YEAR(NOW()) which will provide the year part of the current date.

To total the revenues and costs, select the cell directly below a column of figures (B14 or E14) and click on the AutoSum button on the Standard toolbar. Ensure the cells to be summed are selected and press the Enter key. To determine whether a profit or loss has been made, enter the formula =B14-E14 into cell B17.

Last but certainly not least, protect the worksheet so that only the blue cells can have data typed in. To do this, follow the instructions in the entry titled Locked and Hidden Cells.

TEXT FUNCTIONS

Text functions enable you to manipulate text strings in a variety of ways. The following example demonstrates extracting the first name and surname from the full name by using a number of text functions.

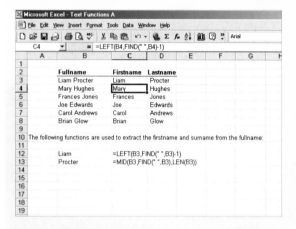

The calculations include:

LEFT(text,num_chars), where text is the text string that contains the characters you want to extract. And num_chars specifies how many characters you want to extract from the left.

FIND(find_text,within_text,start_num), where find_text is the text you want to find, within_text is the text containing the text you want to find and start_num specifies the character at which to start the search. If start_num is omitted, the search will start at the first character.

MID(text,start_num,num_chars) where text is the text string containing the characters you want to extract, start_num is the position of the first character you want to extract in text (the first character in text has a start_num of 1) and num_chars specifies how many characters to return from text. This function is used to extract characters from the middle of a string.

ABOVE RIGHT: Text can be manipulated using a variety of functions.
RIGHT: Text functions can be used to extract words form cells.

LEN(text) where text is the text whose length you want to find (spaces count as characters).

Let us consider how these functions work in the example to extract the surname and first name. The function to extract Liam is entered as =LEFT(B3,FIND(" ",B3)-1). The text string that you want to extract from is held in cell B3 (Liam Procter) and you are going to extract from the left of this string. Determining how many characters you need to extract to separate the first name involves finding the space between the first name and surname. The FIND function locates the first space

in the text held in B3 and returns its position. In this case it is a five as the space is the fifth character. The number of characters you want to extract from the left is therefore five minus one. If you do not subtract one, the space character will be included as well as the first name.

To extract the surname, you will need to determine the length of the string. The function =MID (B3, FIND (" ",B3) +1, LEN (B3)), takes the text held in B3 and finds the first space character in the string which denotes the character before the start point for the extraction – the '+1' moves the start to the first letter after the space. The third argument dictates up to what point to extract (how many characters from the start point). In this case you want to extract up to the end of the string so the LEN function is used to return the length of the string which also denotes the last character. Although the length of the whole string is longer than the surname alone, Excel is tolerant of this.

➡ *Words in Excel*

TEXT POSITIONING

Excel treats any combination of characters, numbers and spaces as text. By default text will appear aligned to the left of a cell, numbers will appear to the right and logical or error values will be centred. Excel provides a range of alignment options to help you maximize the appearance of key material.

The simplest way to alter the position of text or data is to use the buttons visible on the Formatting toolbar. For example, to position text in the centre or to the right of a cell click the Center or Align Right buttons. Changing alignment will not affect the type of data that the cell contains. A number will still be recognized as a number even if it is positioned to the left of a cell.

To create the appearance of a little more space before the text in a cell, use the Increase Indent button on the Formatting toolbar. Each time you click this button it will move text forward by one character width of the standard font. The Merge and Center buttons will allow you to select two or more adjacent cells and merge them into one single cell. The text in the upper left cell will be placed into the centre of the newly created cell. Data entered into cells other than the top left will be lost.

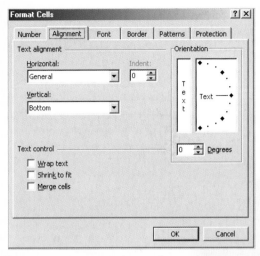

You can exert a greater degree of control over how text is positioned using the Format Cells dialog box. To access the dialog box, select the cells containing the text, right-click the mouse and choose Format Cells. Alternatively, click the Format menu and select the Cells option. Select the Alignment tab. From here you can change horizontal and vertical alignment as well as text orientation. For example, the Center across selection option in the Horizontal box will align text in the centre

of a range of selected cells. The Vertical box will adjust text alignment in relation to the row. The default is for text to appear aligned to the bottom of a row but you can choose to have it aligned to the top, centre or be justified. Changes in vertical alignment are most noticeable where the height of a row has been increased or the font size is small.

Text can be rotated vertically or at an angle. Select the appropriate position from the Orientation box. Text angle can be increased or decreased one degree at a time.

➡ *Words in Excel*

TOOLBARS

If you were to paint a picture, you would assemble a set of tools that would help you do a good job: maybe an easel, a set of paints, a set of brushes and a knife for creating textures. You would also use a slightly different set of tools depending on the effect that you want to create. A toolbar in Excel is based on the same concept. Excel provides you with a range of tools to suit the job in hand.

The first time that you use Excel, two toolbars are visible. The Standard toolbar contains all the tools that you require to carry out basic functions such as saving files, creating new files and printing. The Formatting toolbar provides tools to control the way text and numbers appear. They share a row underneath the menu. Because they share the same row, there is not enough space to see all toolbar buttons in one go.

In addition to the two most frequently used toolbars, Excel will make other toolbars available depending upon the nature of the work that you are doing. For example, if you select a chart, the Charting toolbar will appear. If you use WordArt, the WordArt toolbar will be displayed. To see a list of toolbars, click the View menu and select the Toolbars option or right-click on any toolbar. Some toolbars may not be listed. To see a full complement of toolbars, right-click any toolbar and choose Customize from the pop-up list. Select the Toolbars tab in the Customize dialog box.

Office 2000 embraces new toolbar technology in the form of personalized toolbars. Excel will build up a picture of the personal choices that you make over time and will place the most frequently used tools on display in the toolbar. Where more tools are available, you will see double-headed arrows. Tools that are rarely, if ever, used will be highlighted grey. If you choose one of the additional buttons, Excel will make it available from the toolbar. It will remain on the toolbar until you stop using it or until a more frequently used tool replaces it.

You can control the way toolbar buttons and menus appear. You can add and remove toolbar buttons and you can create your own toolbar. Click the Tools menu followed by the Customize option to access the Customize dialog box.

There are three tabs to choose from: Options, Commands and Toolbars. The Options page allows you to control the way that personalized menus and toolbars operate. To place the Standard and Formatting toolbars on separate rows of the screen, uncheck the Standard and Formatting Toolbars Share One Row box.

BELOW: Toolbars can be customized to include the tools necessary for the task in hand.

FAR LEFT: Excel provides you with a range of tools to suit any job.

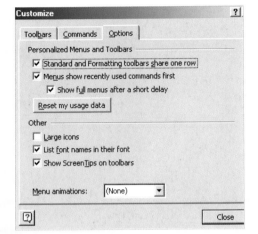

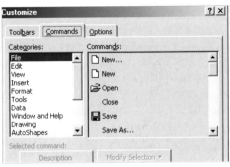

If you notice that a toolbar has been extensively personalized, you can use the Reset my usage data button on the Options page. This will reset the toolbar to show the default set of visible buttons. It will not, however, restore any buttons that you have removed nor will it remove any buttons that you have added through the Customize dialog box. If you would prefer not to have toolbars or menu items personalized at all, uncheck the 'Menus show recently used commands first box'.

You can choose to view additional toolbar buttons by clicking the More Buttons button on the toolbar and selecting the Add or Remove Buttons option. Choose from the list of buttons associated with this toolbar. Buttons that are preceded by a tick are currently available on the toolbar. Click to add or remove a button.

If you want to add a button which does not appear in the toolbar list, you will need to customize the toolbar. Display the toolbar and select the Commands tab in the Customize dialog box. To the left of the box you will see a list of categories such as File, Edit, View, Insert, and to the right of the categories you will see a set of commands which correspond to each category. Select a command and drag the button to a location on the toolbar. To customize the button further, with the Customize dialog box still open, right-click the button and choose from the menu.

To remove a button from a toolbar, open the Customize dialog box and drag a button off a toolbar. If you make a mess of adding and removing buttons and you want the toolbar to take on its default characteristics, click the Toolbars tab in the Customize dialog box and then the Reset button.

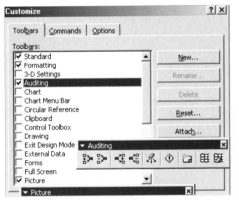

To create your own toolbar, select the Toolbars tab and click the New button. A very small empty toolbar will appear in the worksheet. Use the Commands tab in the Customize dialog box to add buttons to it. You can delete a custom-built toolbar but not a built-in toolbar.

Hyperlinks can be assigned to a button. Click the Commands tab and select the Macros category. Drag a custom button to the toolbar. Right-click the button and choose Assign Hyperlink and Open. You can link to an existing file or web page, to a document or an e-mail address. Enter the name of the file to link to.

➠ *The Euro, Fonts, Undo*

TRACKING CHANGES

Do you work as part of a team? Do you make a contribution to other people's workbooks? Are workbooks produced as a joint effort? If the answer to any of these questions is yes, Excel has a useful set of tools which can help you track changes to a workbook which have been made by other people. To share a workbook via a network, select the Tools menu followed by the Share Workbook option. Click the Editing tab and check the Allow changes by more than one user at the same time box. You will be prompted to save the workbook with these changes.

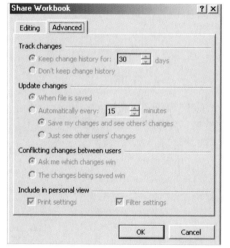

Tracking options can now be set in the Share Workbook dialog box. Click the Advanced tab. It is recommended that the Keep change history for option is selected and that you record the length of time for which it should be kept. This will allow you to see a record of changes that have been made, who made them and when. You will also be able to view the original content. If you choose not to keep a change history, you will not be able to review changes or merge workbooks.

Although you may have put quite a lot of effort into making changes to a document, the changes will not be visible to another user until the file is saved or a specified amount of time has elapsed. Indicate your preference by either selecting the When the document is saved or

ABOVE RIGHT: If you can work as part of a team, Excel has a useful set of tools, which can help you track changes to a workbook.

Automatically after a specified number of minutes option and then select the number of minutes.

If two or more people make changes to a document at the same time there are bound to be conflicts over which changes should take precedence. You can set options in the Conflicting changes between users box to dictate what should happen in the event of conflict.

Choose the Ask me which changes win option if you want to be informed of conflicts and given the opportunity to determine how they should be resolved. The Resolve Conflicts dialog box will appear. You can choose to work through each amendment and accept those made by you or those made by the other user. You can also accept all of your amendments or all amendments made by another user. If The changes being saved win option is selected, the most recently saved version of amendments will take precedence. Print and filter settings can also be saved with your copy of the workbook.

If you have not yet shared your workbook, you can still track changes. Click the Tools menu and select the Track Changes option followed by the Highlight Changes option. Check the box to Track changes while editing. Note that this option will also make a workbook available to share.

Click the When box and select an option from the drop-down menu. You can choose to see all changes, only those changes made since you last saved, only those changes which you haven't reviewed or changes made since a specified date. Select an option from the Who box to specify whose changes you want to track, i.e. changes made by specified users, changes made by all users or changes made by all users except you. Finally, select the Where box so that you can track changes that have been made to a particular area of the workbook.

During the tracking process, changes can be highlighted on the screen or placed in a new sheet. If you choose the

Highlight changes on screen option, Excel will highlight those cells which have been changed, inserted or deleted. Different colours will be used to represent the changes made by individual users. Cells which have been changed can be easily identified by a small triangle in the top left-hand corner and a coloured border. To see who, when and what changes have been made, hover the mouse over the triangle area. A comment will display change details.

Placing changes in a new sheet provides additional benefits over just highlighting changes on screen. It provides a full change history and has AutoFilter already switched on. This makes it easy to filter important tracking information quickly, such as just those changes that have been made to a particular cell or changes made on a particular date. This sheet will not be saved with the workbook but can be copied to a new workbook, saved and printed.

If you want to methodically review changes at any time you can do this by clicking the Tools menu, selecting the Track Changes option and then Accept or Reject Changes. The Select changes to the Accept or Reject dialog box will be displayed.

You can specify which changes to review by selecting options in the When, Who and Where pull-down menus. Excel will filter and display changes which meet the criteria specified. Details of each change will be displayed in the Accept or Reject dialog box.

➠ *Adding Comments, Collaboration*

TRAVEL INFORMATION

You can use a spreadsheet to calculate aspects of travel: distances may be required to calculate and budget for fuel use, or for tax or expenses claims. The Web can provide you with accurate information on mileages for these purposes. The RAC's web site, at *www.rac.co.uk*, has a facility for producing such data within Europe.

From the home page, there are links on the left and right of the page marked 'Plan Route'. There might be a slight delay connecting to the service.

When you get to the page marked 'Plan Your Journey', you need to enter a departure and destination and can choose to enter points en route. Say you want to go from London to Edinburgh, via Manchester. You would enter

BELOW: Wherever you are going on your holiday, Excel can help you plan it.

these in the white boxes below 'Departure', 'Destination' and 'I want to go via', and then click on the orange 'Calculate' symbol at the bottom-right of the page.

The page then appears with drop-down menus against each place name – the RAC's software holds multiple locations within each city. Perhaps you are going from Heathrow to central Edinburgh, picking up someone from Manchester University's Woolton Hall residence. To pick the first, you can scroll down the list offered for London to find 'London; Heathrow; (LHR) Airport (GB)'.

Alternatively, you can enter airports directly through their three-letter codes (found on luggage tickets). Heathrow is LHR, Gatwick is LGW and Manchester is MAN.

For the second, you will have to know the postcode of your friend. You could use the Post Office's postcode finder (qv), but in this case it's M14 6WS. The system doesn't need the last two letters of the postcode. For the third, using the 'EH1.1' postcode is a good bet – 1.1 is usually in the centre of any city. This doesn't quite work for London, which uses eight postcode areas, but Londoners normally know their postcode. Other tips for entering locations are given at the bottom of this web page.

Having picked your precise way-points, you need to decide whether you want to take the fastest route, or the shortest route (through clicking on the button to the left of these options), then click on 'Calculate' once more. The software calculates the length of your route and the expected journey time: in this case (for 'fastest' route) your mileage will be 415.6 miles, taking an estimated eight hours and seven minutes.

➠ *Keep Track of your Mileage*

UNDO

Excel provides a very useful set of tools that allow you to restore data that you have deleted, or reverse some recently performed actions. Although this section will concentrate on the Undo feature, it is worth noting that this is not the only tool available for making good your work. Other useful options include Reset (which can be used to reset default toolbars, pictures and borders) and None (to undo AutoFormat and chart data labels).

If an action can be reversed, you will be able to undo it using the Undo button on the Standard toolbar. If you click the Undo button once, only the last action will be undone. If you click the Down arrow next to the Undo button, you will see a list of the 16 most recently performed actions, with the most recent action at the top.

You can undo several actions in one go by pointing the mouse down the list. Click on an action lower in the list to undo all actions from that point up to the current point.

It is easy to become over-zealous with the Undo button and undo actions that you really want to apply. To redo an action you have undone, click the Redo button on the Standard toolbar. The Down arrow next to the button will list up to 16 actions that you can re-perform.

Your last action will also be displayed at the top of the Edit menu. If you undo the last action, the action prior to that will be available to undo. Once you have undone an action, you can choose the Redo option from the Edit menu.

The Redo option can also be used to repeat an action for other cells. For example if you have underlined text in

one cell, select another cell or group of cells and choose the Repeat Format Cells option from the Edit menu.

Useful shortcut keys include, F4 to repeat the last action, Ctrl + Z to undo and Ctrl + Y to redo.

There are some important operations, which cannot be undone. The most obvious of these are the commands, which appear on the File menu. For instance, once you complete a file save, the save is permanent. Similarly, you cannot undo changes made in the Tools menu and Options tab.

➡ **Backing up Files**

USING CELLS ON OTHER PAGES

A worksheet can be likened to a piece of paper divided into columns and rows. At the intersection of each column and row there is a rectangle, known as a cell. Each cell has a unique address (or reference) taken from the column letter and row number. The first cell in a worksheet is cell A1.

A cell can contain references to other cells on the same worksheet, other sheets in the same workbook and other workbooks. To refer to another cell simply type equal (=) into the current cell and enter the cell address or click the cell to be referenced. Formulae are the basis of mathematical operations and often include references to other cells. For example, the formula =C6+C7 would add the contents of cell C6 to the contents of cell C7.

To reference cells on another sheet of the same workbook, type = and then click on the sheet name at the bottom of the page – you will then see that sheet. Click the cell that you want to reference and press the Enter key. The contents of this cell will be visible in the original

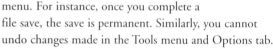

RIGHT: Cells have their own addresses and can be referred to from other pages.

sheet or its contents used in a formula. Look at the Formula bar. You will notice that the cell reference begins with the sheet name followed by an exclamation mark, e.g. Sheet 1!H12.

To produce a summary report you can amalgamate data stored in other workbooks. To do this, you will need to create external references or links. The simplest way of achieving this is to open the workbook or worksheet that you are linking to, select the cells that you want to refer to and press the Enter key. Excel will precede the cell reference with the workbook name in square brackets followed by the sheet name, e.g. [Wheat Production]Australia!$B$20. When a formula refers to cells in a workbook that is closed, you will need to enter the workbook location before the name, e.g. C:\My Documents\[Wheat Production]Australia!$B$20].

As a rule of thumb, when making changes to linked workbooks, open them before you begin. To see a list of files which are linked to the current file, click the Edit menu and select the Links option. In the Edit Links dialog box you can select to open source files and update the current workbook to include changes made in other linked workbooks.

➡ *Brackets, Keeping Cells Still*

VERSIONS OF EXCEL

During the past decade, major enhancements have been made to Microsoft Excel and launched as part of a new release of the software. If you have been using Excel for some time, you may be familiar with some of the earlier versions of Excel, such as 4.0 and 5.0. In recent years these have been superseded by Excel 97, Excel 2000 and Excel 2002, all of which combine superior software functionality with a high degree of integration with the World Wide Web.

With each successive release Microsoft aims to provide increasingly 'intelligent' applications, which are easy to install, set up, use and personalize. Excel 97 and later releases make extensive use of IntelliSense™ technology, which is designed to automate repetitive tasks. For example, the AutoCorrect function, will correct 15 typical formulae-related mistakes. Most enhancements introduced in Excel 97 have been incorporated, in one form or another, into subsequent releases. They include:

Range Finder Double-click a cell containing a formula and Excel will colour-code those cells, which are referenced in the formula. Click a data series on a bar chart and the source range will be highlighted in the worksheet.

Merging Cells Multiple cells can be merged into one.

Charts The Chart Wizard now includes all available chart tools.

Additional chart types and formatting options are available. They include bubble charts and transparent fills. Chart tips indicate the current area of the chart and the value of a particular data series.

Viewing page breaks You can view what will be printed on each page and drag page breaks to a new location. Excel will adjust the layout to provide the best fit.

Conditional Formatting Click the Format menu followed by the Conditional Formatting command to apply automatic formatting rules to your worksheet. You can set colours, patterns or textures to different types of results.

Integration with the Web You can publish worksheets in HTML format, which can be viewed via a web browser. Users do not have to have Excel installed to view the worksheets.

Searching for files The Open dialog box can now be used to search for documents.

Send a workbook electronically Click the File menu and select Send To.

Custom view Create having to have the View Manager add-in program installed.

ABOVE: The newer versions of Excel include a lot of interaction with the Web

Hyperlinks Allow you to jump quickly to another document or web address.

Automatic formatting Can be applied to a cell which meets set criteria.

Track changes Multiple users can contribute to a workbook and changes merged into a summary workbook.

Excel 2000 provides functionality over and above that found in Excel 97. The main focus has been on streamlining the process by which users collaborate or share information across a network, Intranet or Internet.

Excel 2000 web features make light work of publishing worksheets as interactive web pages and allow data to be viewed and analyzed by anyone with a web browser.

Powerful collaboration capabilities provided through MS Office Server Extensions allow users to take part in group discussions, receive e-mail notification of changes to web pages and 'meet' with other users on the Internet.

Excel 2000 also contains sophisticated analysis and reporting tools, which make it an ideal front-end system for analysing corporate intranet data and producing reports. It is easier than ever to use and has many new functions, which increase user productivity. A few of these are listed below.

List AutoFill When you add information to a list, Excel will work out which formulae and formatting can be extended, based on the information in preceding cells.

Euro currency Excel 2000 has a currency format for the Euro which allows you to format Euro-denominated data correctly.

See Through View Selected cells are lightly shaded so that you can 'see through them'.

Personalized menus and toolbars Frequently used commands are made visible on toolbars.

Excel 2002 was launched as part of Microsoft Office XP. Although it is similar in functionality to Excel 2000, it has a different 'look and feel' due to the fact that 'intelligent' assistance is provided for many tasks. Key drivers for Microsoft developers

included increasing user product knowledge and confidence, file security and extending the power of team collaboration.

Excel 2002 makes use of new technologies such as SharePoint Team Services, which encourages team members to communicate via their own web site. Using only a web browser, team members can canvas the opinions of other members, create task lists and set up a document library.

Some of the exciting new features are described below:

Smart Tags Task-focused buttons, which provide options for completing an action. For example, when you copy data, Smart Tags paste options allow you to copy the data with the original formatting or change the formatting to fit the destination document.

Task Panes Important related tasks are grouped on the screen. For example, if you copy two pieces of information, the Office Clipboard will open as a task pane.

Web Queries Web site information can be analysed in Excel. Paste it into Excel and a Smart Tag will provide the option to create a refreshable query.

➡ *Do I need to Upgrade Excel?*

VIRUSES

A virus is a computer program that has been written with the intent of corrupting the data on your PC or rendering your PC unworkable. An analogy is made between a biological virus, which invades the human body, and a computer virus, which affects the way your computer works.

Although viruses are not the only type of program that can cause serious damage to a computer, they are distinct from other programs in that they have the ability to replicate and copy themselves to other programs. Other destructive programmes include Worms (which change or delete data generated in data-processing programs), Trojan Horses (so called because they hide themselves in other programs) and Logic Bombs, which are timed to cause maximum disruption.

Although a virus may consist of just a few lines of programming code, it can be very easily disguised within other programs and difficult to detect. Some viruses are relatively harmless, like the famous Stoned virus, which

ABOVE: Computer viruses are destructive and can cause serious damage.
RIGHT: A virus could be activated at any time, depending on its programming code.

leaves a message on the infected computer saying: "This computer is stoned." Others can infiltrate the operating system and cause serious damage.

Viruses can be activated as soon as they infect the host program or be set to trigger at a particular date, time, or when a user presses a particular set of keystrokes. They can be introduced to your machine from many different sources. Nowadays, people are much more familiar with using a computer and are increasingly able to access information from a wider range of sources. We all know people who regularly access files from the Internet and download them to their PC.

There are in excess of 50,000 known viruses, so as a preventative measure, you would be wise to install dedicated anti-virus software onto your PC or network. The software will scan your hard disk, network drives or floppy disk looking for viruses and, where possible, remove or repair. Visit the web site of your anti-virus software provider to get detailed information on viruses, including what effect they have on your system and how to get rid of them.

Viruses are sometimes stored as a macro within a Microsoft Office document or add-in program. When you open the workbook, the virus is triggered. Once triggered, it will be copied to Personal.xls, a hidden workbook, or another hidden location on your machine. The virus will probably be activated in every new workbook that you create. The creators of the virus rely on users sharing 'virus-infected' documents so that the virus can infiltrate as many systems as possible.

Excel does not have a built-in scanning facility but it does recognize when a document contains programming code. If you open a document which contains a macro, the Macro Alert dialog box will be displayed. This doesn't mean that the document contains a macro virus; simply that it contains a macro. If you are sure of both the author and the content of the document you are about to open, you can choose to open the document with the macros available. If you are not sure, then choose to open the document with the macros disabled. A macro virus can be harmful only if it is allowed to run, so disabling the macros allows you to open the workbook safely.

There are three levels of security that you can set for macros. To change the security level, click the Tools menu and select the Macro option followed by Security. The Security dialog box will appear. Click the Security Level tab.

Setting a Low level of security is not recommended. If you choose the Low option, you are basically leaving yourself unprotected from potential macro viruses. You should only use this option if you either have anti-virus software installed or you feel confident that all documents you open will be from trusted sources. Irrespective of the selected level of security, a workbook will be scanned for known viruses if Office 2000-compatible anti-virus software has been installed.

If you set a Medium level of security, you will have the option of choosing whether or not to run a macro. With the macros disabled, you can still look at the code on

BELOW: If you are a victim of a virus, you may need to completely rebuild your computer.

which the macro is based. If the code looks legitimate, you can then choose to run the macro. It is better to be safe than sorry!

If you set a High level of security, you will only be able to run a macro that is accompanied by a digital signature from a trusted source. You can build a list of trusted sources. When you open a workbook which has been received from a source on the list, the macros will be available to use.

Program developers can assign a digital signature to a macro. The signature is a way of recording the author and the integrity of the source. When you open a workbook, you will receive a certificate containing this information. Of course, a digital signature is not, in itself, proof that a macro is free from viruses. If you have any doubts, pay careful attention to the certificate or choose to disable macros.

➠ *Backing up Files*

WEB PAGES FROM EXCEL

Excel 2000 contains many new web features which make light work of publishing your workbooks on the Internet. This hasn't always been the case. Until

recently, it was difficult to publish Excel files on the Internet without losing the rich complexity of non-text based information and associated formatting.

Hypertext Markup Language (HTML) is the commonly used medium for marking web page content so that it can be viewed through a browser. HTML codes, or tags, provide the browser with information relating to both the web page content and instructions on how to display it.

FAR RIGHT: Excel workbooks can be saved as pages to post onto the Internet.

All browsers have the facility to read HTML tags. Unfortunately, HTML works well with text-based documents but is less able to support Excel workbooks because they are written in binary format and contain numeric data and formulae. They also have their own brand of formatting. So, with Office 2000, Microsoft provided Excel with the use of two additional standards: Cascading Style Sheets (CSS), which increases your ability to format styles in an HTML document, and Extensible Markup Language (XML), which provides a means of storing information which cannot be presented through HTML.

Many of these new web features require you to have Office Server Extensions (OSE) installed on a web server. OSE is a web feature that comes with Office 2000 and provides Office applications with the facility to navigate around web-based documents, open documents produced in HTML format, and create and save application-specific documents in HTML format.

You don't have to know or understand HTML code to publish a document on the Internet. Excel will automatically convert the formats saved with your worksheet into HTML tags.

Start off by creating a web folder. Click the File menu and select Open. Click the Web Folders button and then the Create New Folder button. In the Add Web Folder dialog box type the URL (address) of the web site to which the document will be published. Proceed through the remaining steps.

Before saving an Excel workbook as a web page, click the File menu and select the Web Page Preview option to see how it will look through a browser. If you are happy to proceed, select Save as Web Page. Click the Web Folders button and choose a web site to publish to. If you select the Entire Workbook option, each sheet will be saved as individual web pages and will be available when you open the file on the Web. To publish a restricted range, select the range before starting the Save As procedure and choose the Selection Sheet option. If you haven't made a selection, only the current sheet will be saved as an HTML file.

➥ *Collaboration, Hyperlinks*

WHAT-IF ANALYSIS

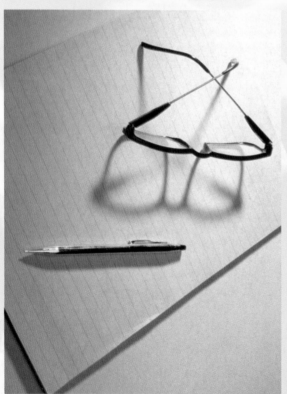

Making changes. Once a worksheet has been created you can easily make changes to the values in one or more cells and observe the effect on the worksheet as a whole. This is known as what-if analysis. At a simple level this can be achieved by manually altering values. If a more complex scenario is required, the Excel Data Table feature can be used to display the result of the change without affecting the original data.

One of the fundamental rules when designing a worksheet is to provide maximum flexibility. In general, values should not be included in formulae. It is good practice to store a value in a separate cell and then refer to that cell when creating a formula. This is certainly the case with worksheets containing fluctuating values such as VAT, interest rates and exchange rates. If you include the value within the formula you could be faced with the difficult task of working through the sheet, cell by cell, ensuring that all references to that value have been altered.

Storing values externally to formulas also provides scope for carrying out manual what-if analysis. For example, if you have a worksheet that calculates values based on the current interest rate, that rate should be stored in a separate cell. You can then simply change the interest rate and all the formulae within the worksheet referencing the cell containing the interest rate will change automatically. By changing the value in one cell, the whole worksheet will reflect the change. If you want to preserve this change you can always save the worksheet with a new name. To restore the worksheet to how it was, simply replace the interest rate with the original value.

This is adequate for simple what-if analysis but it can become messy if you need to change more than one value. There is also the danger that you will forget to change the cell content back to the original value. The Excel Data Table feature allows you to change the value in one or two cells and display the resulting change to another cell in a separate table. Data tables are best explained by example.

	A	B	C	D	E	F
1	**Repayment Model**			B12	=B7	
2						
3	Loan Amount	£25,000				
4	Interest Rate	5.25%				
5	Term	10				
6						
7	**Monthly repayment:**	£268.23		<--- =ABS(PMT(B4/12,B5*12,B3))		
8						
9	Total Payments	£32,187.51		<--- =B7*12*B5		
10	Interest paid	£7,187.51		<--- =B9-B3		
11						
12	£268.23	5	7	10	12	
13	**4.00%**	£460.41	£341.72	£253.11	£218.88	£184
14	**4.25%**	£463.24	£344.60	£256.09	£221.93	£188
15	**4.50%**	£466.08	£347.50	£259.10	£225.00	£191

The repayment model used in the Financial Functions entry serves as a good example.

The PMT function calculates the monthly repayment based on a loan taken out at a specified interest rate, over a specified term. By generating a data table you will be able to see how that repayment will alter if any of the three variables change.

A one-input data table displays the resulting changes to a cell or cells if the content of just one cell is changed. For example, how will the monthly repayment alter if the interest rate goes up from 6% to 6.25%, 6.5% or even higher? You could systematically change the value in cell

B4 and see how it effects the result in cell B7. This is exactly what the data table feature will do for you. Firstly, enter the range of values you want to enter into cell B4 (the interest rate). For this example the values 6% through to 8% have been entered in increments of .25%. These figures have been entered as a column. You now need to enter the address of the cell that you are interested in, the cell containing the result. In this example the result cell is B7, the cell containing the formula to calculate repayment. This needs to be entered one column to the right and one row above the series of interest rates.

The Table dialog box is displayed, prompting for the address of the input cell. As you have entered the input values in a column the input cell should be entered in the Column input cell box. If you had created your table with the input values across a row, then you would enter the input cell address in the Row input cell box. In this example the input cell is B4, the cell containing the interest rate. The data table feature will take each value in the first column of the table in turn and systematically calculate the formula referenced at the top of the second column of the table. The results will be entered in the second column.

	A	B	C	D
3	Loan Amount	£10,000		
4	Interest Rate	6%		
5	Term	10		
6				
7	Monthly repayment:	-£111.02		<--- =PMT(B4/12,B5*12,B
8				
9				
10		-£111.02		
11	6.00%			
12	6.25%			
13	6.50%			
14	6.75%			
15	7.00%			
16	7.25%			
17	7.50%			
18	7.75%			
19	8.00%			
20				

	A	B	C	D	E	F	G	H
3	Loan Amount	£10,000						
4	Interest Rate	6%						
5	Term	10						
6								
7	Monthly repayment:	-£111.02		<--- =PMT(B4/12,B5*12,B3)				
8								
9								
10	Interest Rate	-£111.02		Term	-£111.02		Loan Amount	-£111.02
11	6.00%	-£111.02		5	-£193.33		£5,000	-£55.51
12	6.25%	-£112.28		10	-£111.02		£7,500	-£83.27
13	6.50%	-£113.55		15	-£84.39		£10,000	-£111.02
14	6.75%	-£114.82		20	-£71.64		£12,500	-£138.78
15	7.00%	-£116.11					£15,000	-£166.53
16	7.25%	-£117.40					£17,500	-£194.29
17	7.50%	-£118.70						
18	7.75%	-£120.01						
19	8.00%	-£121.33						
20								
21								
22								
23								
24								
25								
26								

Sheet1 / Sheet2 / Sheet3 /

Ready

The formula =B7 has been entered in cell B10. It displays as the current value for the monthly repayment. This is meaningless and the cell content can be hidden if you find it distracting. To calculate the values, highlight the table area, in this case cells A10 to B19, access the Data menu and select the Table option.

Figuratively speaking, 6% is put into cell B4 (the input cell), the formula in cell B7 is calculated and the result displayed in cell B11. The second value in the column, 6.25% is then put into cell B4, the formula in B7 calculated and the result displayed in B12, and so on.

The other two data tables are created in the same way using B5 and B3 as the input cells, respectively. The following case study provides an example of a two-input data table.

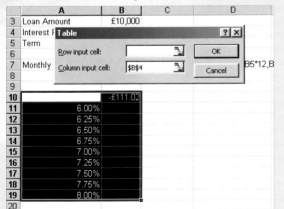

	A	B	C	D
3	Loan Amount	£10,000		
4	Interest	Table		
5	Term			
6		Row input cell:		
7	Monthly	Column input cell:	$B$4	B5*12,B
8				
9				
10		-£111.02		
11	6.00%			
12	6.25%			
13	6.50%			
14	6.75%			
15	7.00%			
16	7.25%			
17	7.50%			
18	7.75%			
19	8.00%			
20				

WHAT-IF ANALYSIS CASE STUDY

By using Excel data tables you can determine what-if scenarios without actually changing your data. A one-input data table allows you to vary the contents of a single cell and observe changes in a number of other cells. The two-input table allows you to vary the content of two cells and observe the changes to one other cell. This case study uses both types of data tables to help make a vital business decision.

The scenario concerns a training and development company. Management has been considering training room occupation and has decided that it may be time to set up one or two more training rooms at the centre. In order to do this, they will need to borrow capital to buy computers, desks chairs and teaching aids. They have calculated that it will cost in the region of £12,500 to fully kit out one room. They have been offered a fixed interest rate of 5.25% or a variable interest rate of 4.75%. They are interested to know how much more they might pay for the loan if they go for the variable rate and the rate subsequently goes up. They would also like to be able to compare the rates and total payments for a number of different payment terms. All of these queries can be addressed by using data tables.

The first step is to create the initial model. Enter the loan amount in cell B3 as £25,000, the interest rate in cell B4 as 5.25% and the term in cell B5 as 10. The monthly repayment is calculated in cell B7 using the PMT function. Total payment and interest payment over the period are calculated as shown.

Using this fixed interest rate scenario, borrowing £25,000 over 10 years at an interest rate of 5.25% will cost £268.23 per month. Over the ten-year period they will pay £32,187.51 of which £7,187.51 will be interest.

Management wants to compare this with interest rates fluctuating from 4% to 6.5% over the same ten-year term. Rather than systematically entering the different interest rates in cell B4, and observing the changes to the values in B7, B9 and B10, it is decided to display the information as a one-input data table. The input cell will be the interest rates with the output cells being repayment, total payment and interest paid.

Enter the range of interest rates in a column. The easiest way is to use the Fill option. Type the value, 4%, in the first cell of the column. Highlight this cell and at least ten cells below. Access the Edit menu and select the Fill, Series options.

Set the Step value to .25% and the Stop value to 6.5%. Click OK to confirm. The values 4% through to 6.5%, in increments of .25%, will display in the column.

You now need to enter the addresses of the cells that you are interested in, the output cells. In this example the output cells are B7, the cell containing the formula to calculate repayment, B9, the cell containing the total payments and B10, the cell containing the interest paid. These need to be entered in the columns to the right of the series of interest rates, one row above the first interest rate. To generate the data table, highlight the column of interest rates and the three columns to the right including the cells referencing the output values. In this example the data table includes cell A13 through to cell D24. Access the Data menu and select the Table option. The Table dialog box is displayed. The Column input cell is B4, the cell containing the interest rate. Click the OK button. The values will be displayed for the different interest rates. Format the table to display currency notation if required.

	Repayment	Total Payment	Interest		
	£268.23	£32,187.51	£7,187.51	B13	=B7
4.00%	£253.11	£30,373.54	£5,373.54	C13	=B9
4.25%	£256.09	£30,731.26	£5,731.26	D13	=B10
4.50%	£259.10	£31,091.52	£6,091.52		
4.75%	£262.12	£31,454.32	£6,454.32		
5.00%	£265.16	£31,819.65	£6,819.65		
5.25%	£268.23	£32,187.51	£7,187.51		
5.50%	£271.32	£32,557.88	£7,557.88		
5.75%	£274.42	£32,930.77	£7,930.77		
6.00%	£277.55	£33,306.15	£8,306.15		
6.25%	£280.70	£33,684.03	£8,684.03		
6.50%	£283.87	£34,064.39	£9,064.39		

You can hide the values in cells B13, C13 and D13 if you find them distracting.

Management now has a clear idea of how fluctuations in the interest rate may effect their payments. The next task is to consider how payments might alter with fluctuation of interest rates over differing terms. This requires a two-input data table. The two input values are the term and the interest rate and the output value is the monthly repayment.

To create this table, enter the range of interest rates in a column in the same way as the one-input table. Enter the range of terms, from 5 to 15, as a row, above the interest rates, starting one column to the right. The address of the cell containing the output value, =B7, is

entered in the right-hand corner of the table. Highlight the entire table, A12 to F23, access the Data menu and select the Table option.

The Table dialog box is displayed. There are two input cells when generating a two-input data table. The Row input cell is B5, the cell containing the term. The Column input cell is B4, the cell containing the interest rate. Click on the OK button.

The data table shows the various permutations between interest rate and the term of the loan.

WORDS IN EXCEL

Working with text. You would be right to think a spreadsheet is all about numbers, but words also play an important part. Without some explanation, a spreadsheet can be extremely difficult to decipher. Excel can only distinguish between text and numbers. If the cell contains spaces or characters, it will be considered as containing text.

When you start a new worksheet, Excel uses the default font and font size, Arial font in point 10 size. Changing the way your words look is quick and easy using the Formatting toolbar. If the Formatting toolbar is not displayed, click the right mouse button on the current toolbar, deselect it and select Formatting instead.

The first options on the Formatting toolbar allow you to change the font style and size. There is a full range of styles available, so experiment to see which you prefer. The next three buttons provide an easy way to change the text style. The options are Bold, Italic or Underline.

These are the most commonly used font formats. For more options access the Format Cells dialog box. To do this, access the Format menu and select the Cells option. Alternatively, click the right mouse button and select Format Cells from the Shortcut menu. Click on the Font tab. Here you will find extra formats for underlining your text and other special effects such as Strikethrough, Subscipt and Superscript. There is a Preview box in the bottom left of the dialog box to show you how your text will look. Click the OK button to confirm your changes.

If you want to remove all the font formatting and return to the default setting, access the Format Cells dialog box by clicking the right mouse button and selecting Format Cells from the Shortcut menu. Click on the Font tab and check the Normal Font box. Click on OK to complete.

The third group of buttons on the toolbar allows you to change the alignment of text within a cell. Spreadsheets have a set way of displaying values in cells. Numbers are

ABOVE: By using the toolbar you can format your text to make it easier to interpret.

always right-aligned in a cell with text being left-aligned. The toolbar provides four options for changing the alignment of text within the cell: Align Left, Centre, Align Right, and Merge and Centre. The Merge and Centre option allows you to merge adjacent cells either horizontally or vertically. This is an extremely useful option when you want headings to span more than one column or row.

Further horizontal and vertical alignment options are available from the Format Cells dialog box. Right-click, select Format Cells and click the Alignment tab.

The Alignment tab also provides two other options for Text control. If you have text that is too wide to fit the column and you don't want it to spill over adjacent cells you can use the Wrap or Shrink options. The Wrap Text option will display the text on multiple lines in the cell while the Shrink to Fit option reduces the size of the text to fit the cell width. You can manually wrap text in a cell by pressing the Alt and Enter keys at the same time. Pressing Enter on its own will move you down a cell.

The fourth group of buttons provide shortcuts for formatting numbers. The next two buttons will decrease or increase the indent of the text. Each click will move the text one character either to the left or right.

The last group of buttons provides formatting options to enhance the presentation of your sheet and can be used for both numeric and text entries. You can put borders around cells, fill cells with colour or change the colour of text.

On occasion you may need to enter text into a cell that is made up entirely of numeric values. For example, you may need to enter telephone numbers or numeric codes. As long as you do not intend to perform any type of numeric calculation on these numbers you can format the values as text.

If you want to change the cell format to text for the occasional cell, the simplest method is to type an apostrophe (') before the number. Excel will register the ' and automatically format the cell for text. To format a range of cells as text, select the cells and click the right mouse button. Select the Format Cells option and click the Number tab. There are two available text options, Text and Special. Text will simply save the contents of the selected cells as text rather than numeric values. The Special option provides a number of predefined formats for zip codes, phone numbers and social security numbers. If your text number starts with one or more zeros, you must either use the ' or format the cells before you type in the entry, otherwise Excel will remove the leading zeros.

➡ *Automatic Text, Fonts, Keeping Cells Still, Text Positioning*

WORKING WITH DIFFERENT VIEWS

As a workbook grows, it can become increasingly difficult to find and print key information. You can change display and print settings to make viewing your workbook easy and then save each different view of the workbook as a custom view. Excel also comes with a set of built-in views.

Most of the built-in views can be found on the View menu. The first option on the View menu is Normal. This is the default view required to complete most tasks within Excel. If you have selected a different view for a time, you would switch back to this view to enter text and numbers, create formulae and create charts or complete many of your usual activities.

ABOVE: The different ways of viewing your work can help with layout issues.

The Page Break Preview option offers you a preview of how a worksheet will print with the page breaks clearly visible. This will give you some idea of what information will print on what page, and gives you the opportunity to alter the position of the page breaks before sending a worksheet to print. You can move the page break boundaries to the left or right, up or down, by clicking and dragging them with the mouse. Excel will change the scale of the worksheet so that the columns and rows fit the new page size.

Where you have a lot of information concentrated in a particular area of a worksheet, you might find it useful to use the Full Screen option. This will hide most screen elements so that you can view more of your data. You can switch back by either selecting the Full Screen option again or pressing the Esc key. Alternatively, select the Close Full Screen button from the Full Screen toolbar. If you want to magnify or reduce the size of a worksheet on the screen, select the Zoom option. This will not affect the printing size of the document. It will simply make it easier to focus on a particular area or navigate around a larger area.

Print Preview is a very useful tool because it gives you a feel for how your worksheet will look when it is printed. You can preview each worksheet as you work by clicking the Print Preview button on the Standard toolbar. You can also select Print Preview from the File menu. Use Print Preview to check for problem areas or enhance the general design. For instance, make sure that column widths are wide enough to display the entire contents of a column, change the position of page breaks and margins, and add headers and footers. If you

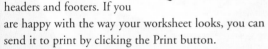

are happy with the way your worksheet looks, you can send it to print by clicking the Print button.

Experiment with the way your worksheet looks and prints and save a unique combination of settings in a custom view.

Set different display options, many of which can be found by clicking the Tools menu, selecting Options and then the View tab. For example, by selecting options in the Show box, you can choose to display the Formula bar and Status bar. In the Comments area, you can control the way comments are displayed. In the Objects area, you can choose to display all objects (which may slow up the process of scrolling through a document) or only object placeholders (which would indicate where objects would be placed if they were visible). In the Windows options, you can choose to display page breaks, formulae, gridlines, gridline colour, row and column headers, sheet tabs and scroll bars. Other display options that you might like to set include changing the size and position of the worksheet window, splitting the worksheet screen, freezing panes and setting data filter options.

You can also set and store print settings like margins, headers and footers, and print areas, in a custom view. A custom view will be saved for the whole workbook. When you use a custom view you will see any cells or sheets that were active at the time of saving the view. Hidden sheets will not be visible and multiple sheets from the same workbook will be displayed.

To create a custom view, select the View menu and then the Custom Views option. Click the Add button in the Custom Views dialog box and type a name for the view. You may find it useful to include the name of the sheet in the name of the view because a workbook can have many different views associated with it and the view name will remind you of the sheet that was active at the time of creating the view. Choose whether to save the view to include Print settings, hidden rows, columns and filter settings. To delete a view, select the name of the view and click the Delete button and reset settings. To switch between different views and view or print the worksheet with those particular display settings, select the view name from the Custom Views dialog box and select the Show option.

➡ *Printing from Excel*

WORK OUT YOUR TAXES

If you run a sideline business such as a holiday home or selling home-made items, you need to declare this information to the Inland Revenue.

Calculating how much tax you have to pay on the earnings from such a business is reasonably straightforward with Excel. The following two pages show you how to calculate the total income generated from a couple of sideline businesses, work out the expenses incurred and calculate how much tax is to be paid. The step-by-step instructions assume you have a full-time job and this is some additional income, but there are appropriate sections to enter tax allowances. You will need to contact your local tax office to find the current tax rates or see the section in this book under web sites for working out your taxes.

ABOVE: Excel can make declaring your taxes more straightforward.

1. Open Excel. With a new workbook on the screen, select cell A1 and enter the word Income. List the different sources of income you receive from your business(es) and enter the corresponding amounts in column B. At the bottom of this list (in column A), enter the words Total Income, then select the cell next to this in column B. Click on the AutoSum toolbar button (looks like a Greek S symbol). The cells above the currently selected one will be highlighted. If these are all the cells you want to total, press Return. If some are excluded, reselect all the cells to be included by holding the left button down and moving the mouse pointer down them. Press Return to complete the calculation.

2. Move down a few cells in column A and enter the title Expenses. List the different expenses you have incurred through your business(es) and enter the corresponding figures in column B. Add the words Total Expenses to the bottom of the list (in column A) and add up your expenses using the AutoSum toolbar button (as described in step 1).

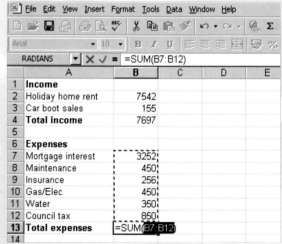

3. Check your total calculations. Select all the cells in column B for income by holding the left button down and moving the mouse pointer over them. All the cells will be highlighted. Look at the bottom of the screen for the word Sum= and a total figure. Make sure the figure displayed is the same as the Total Income calculation created in step 1. If, however, a different type of calculation is displayed here, right-click on it and choose

Sum from the list that appears. Repeat this step for checking your total expenses.

4. You may need to increase the width of column A. To do this, position the mouse pointer in between the column headings A and B, and wait for it to change to a cross with two horizontal arrows. Hold down the left mouse button and move to the right to stretch column A. Release the left button to stop widening this column. Save your Excel file by clicking on the File menu and choosing Save. From the Save As dialog box that appears, enter a name for your file, choose a location on your computer to store it, then click on Save.

5. Move down a few cells in column A (below the total for expenses) and enter the words Income-Expenses. Select the cell next to this title (in column B) and press = to start a calculation. Select the total figure for income, press the minus symbol (-), then select the figure for total expenses. Press Return to complete the calculation and check the result to make sure it is correct.

6. If you have a tax allowance, type the word Allowance below the Income-Expenses title from step 5. Select the cell next to this title in column B and enter the amount for the allowance. Enter the title Net Profit underneath the title for Allowance. Select the cell next to this in column B. Press the = symbol to start a calculation, select the figure calculated in step 4 (for income less expenses), press the minus symbol (-), select the cell displaying the amount of allowance and press Return to confirm the calculation.

7. When you have found out which tax rate(s) apply to your net profit, enter the words Tax Rate in column A, below the Net Profit, then select the cell next to this in column B and enter the rate. Use the % symbol on the keyboard to make sure the tax rate is displayed as a per cent figure. If this is additional income, you may find this income moves you into a higher tax bracket for a proportion of the net profit. If this is the case, you will need to divide your net profit figure into two amounts (one for a lower tax rate and the other for the higher rate).

8. To calculate how much tax you have to pay, move down a few cells in column A (below the Tax Rate title), enter the words Amount of tax to pay, then select the cell next to this in column B. Press the = symbol to start a calculation, select the figure for your net profit, press the asterisk (*) for multiplication, select the cell containing the tax rate per cent and press Return on the keyboard to complete the calculation. If you have a lower and higher tax band to calculate, you will need to complete two calculations, then SUM the amounts (see step 1 for using AutoSum).

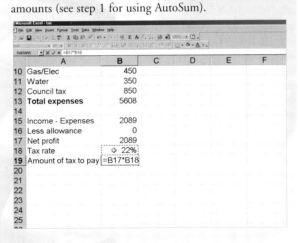

FREQUENTLY ASKED QUESTIONS

GENERAL

How do I start Excel?

Click the Windows Start button located in the bottom left-hand corner of the screen and choose the Programs option. A list of available programs will be displayed. Select Microsoft Excel. If the Microsoft Office shortcut bar is visible you can also click the Excel icon on the bar.

How do I close all Excel files at the same time?

Hold down the Shift key, click the File menu and select the Close All option. You will be prompted to save any unsaved files.

How do I Print?

Click the Print button on the Standard toolbar. Alternatively, click the File menu and select the Print option.

How do I save my work?

Click on the Save button (disk) on the Standard toolbar or click the File menu and choose the Save option.

How do I apply a border to a cell?

Click the down arrow to the right of the Borders button on the Formatting toolbar and choose a border.

How do I apply colour to worksheet cells?

Select the cells and click the down arrow to the right of the Fill Color button on the Formatting toolbar. Choose a colour from the palette.

What is the shortcut key for spell-check?

It is F7.

How do I send a copy of my worksheet via e-mail?

Click the File menu and select the Send To option. Choose the Mail Recipient (as Attachment) option to send the entire workbook as an e-mail attachment. Choose the Mail Recipient option to send the contents of the current workbook as the main body of the e-mail.

How do I insert a hyperlink into a worksheet?

Right click in a cell and choose Hyperlink from the shortcut menu. Click one of the images displayed down the left-hand side of the Insert Hyperlink dialog box to select the type of object you want to link to.

How do I create a chart?

Organize your data into columns and rows of related information, select the area to be represented on the chart and press F11. This will create a chart based on the default chart type. Instead of pressing F11, you can also click the Chart Wizard button on the Standard toolbar and work through the options presented.

How can I make changes to a chart?

If the chart has been created in a separate sheet from the worksheet, click on the Chart sheet tab to make it active. If the chart has been created as part of a worksheet, make sure that the chart is selected. Select from the range of available chart menu options. Generally, you can also double click on an area of a chart to make changes to that area.

How do I begin a formula?

Click in the cell in which you want to create a formula and type an equal sign (=).

Can I use an Excel chart in a Word document?

Yes. Select the chart in Excel. Click the Edit menu and choose the Copy option. Switch to Microsoft Word. Position the cursor at the point in the document that you want to insert a copy of the chart. Click the Edit menu and select the Paste option.

ERROR MESSAGES

What does the error message, ##### mean?

If the cell is filled with hash characters (#), Excel is letting you know that the numeric value entered into the cell is too wide to display within that cell. This could be a number, date or the result of a formula. The solution is to resize the column by dragging the boundary between the column headings.

What does the error message #VALUE! mean?

Excel will display the #VALUE! error when the wrong type of argument or operand is used within a formula. For example, when text is entered into a formula but the formula requires a number or a logical value.

What does the error message #DIV/0! mean?

The #DIV/0! error message will be displayed whenever a formula attempts to divide by zero. This error mainly occurs when you refer to a blank cell or a cell containing zero as a divisor within a formula.

What does the error message #NAME? mean?

The #NAME? error message will be displayed if Excel fails to recognize text in a formula. This can happen if you have deleted a name that is used in the formula, misspelt the name or if you have used a name that does not exist. If this error occurs, check that the name exists by accessing the Insert menu and selecting the Name, Define options. If the name is not listed, add the name by using the Define command.

What does the error #N/A mean?

The #N/A error message is displayed when a value is 'not available' to a function or a formula. If there are cells within your worksheet that contain data that is not currently available, enter #N/A in those cells. Formulas that refer to those cells will then return #N/A instead of attempting to calculate a value.

What does the error #REF! mean?

The #REF! error message occurs when a cell reference is not valid. This can happen when you delete cells that are referred to by other formulae.

TROUBLE-SHOOTING

Printing

If I have set a print area of less than one page, can I expand the print scale so that the contents will fill an entire page?

In the Page Setup dialog box click the Adjust To option and select a scale that is larger than 100 per cent. Depending upon the scale chosen, the contents may spill on to an additional page. If this happens, manually adjust rows and columns until the contents fit on one page.

Publishing to a web page

Why does my Pivot Table look different when I publish it to a web page?

Most cell formatting is lost when you publish a Pivot Table to a web page, including cell borders and patterns, alignment, fonts and number formatting. If you want to make sure that you keep the correct number formatting, apply the format through the PivotTable Field dialog box.

Each time I publish a worksheet as a web page, the file size increases. Why?

Excel places a blank line above the <HEAD> tag in the HTML file and this increases the HTML file size by approximately two bytes each time. To prevent this happening, delete the blank lines from the HTML file.

AutoCorrect

I don't seem to be able to use AutoCorrect lists. Why?

One possible cause is that you are using a third-party Windows keyboard driver. This problem can be rectified by restoring the default Windows keyboard driver but it is important to be aware that doing so may affect the way your computer functions. If you decide to restore the default driver, click the Start button on the Windows taskbar and select the Run option. Type System.ini in the Open box. This file will open in Notepad. Search for a line that reads keyboard.drv=kb123.drv (or similar). This sets the Windows keyboard driver. Type a semicolon (;) at the beginning of the line and insert a new line just after the existing keyboard driver line. Type keyboard. drv=keyboard. drv to reset the default driver setting. Save the file and restart the computer.

Why do I get a message telling me that my file is read-only when I try to save it to a network drive?

It is likely that you have not been assigned network permissions to save your file to that drive. Speak to your Administrator or try saving the file to your hard disk and then copying it to the network drive.

FUNCTIONS

Excel provides literally hundreds of built-in functions. Some you may use on a daily basis, others only occasionally. The majority you will probably never use but there may be the odd occasion when it is just what you need. The following pages provide a complete list of all the functions available within Excel. The most commonly used functions are readily available from the Paste Function dialog box. Some of the lesser-used functions may not be currently available. If this is the case, run the Setup program to install the Analysis ToolPak. After you have installed the Analysis ToolPak, enable it by selecting the Add-Ins option on the Tools menu.

DATABASE FUNCTIONS

The database functions, known collectively as the Dfunctions, are used to analyze data that forms part of a list or database. To use these functions, data needs to be entered so that Excel recognizes it as a list or database.

DAVERAGE(database,field,criteria)
Calculates the average of the values in a column based on the conditions specified.

DCOUNT(database,field,criteria)
Counts the number of cells containing numbers in a column based on the conditions specified.

DCOUNTA(database,field,criteria)
Counts all the cells in a column that are not blank based on the conditions specified.

DGET(database,field,criteria)
Extracts a single value from a column based on the conditions specified.

DMAX(database,field,criteria)
Returns the largest (maximum) number in a column based on the conditions specified.

DMIN(database,field,criteria)
Returns the smallest (minimum) number in a column based on the conditions specified.

DPRODUCT(database,field,criteria)
Multiplies the values in a column based on the conditions specified.

DSTDEV(database,field,criteria)
Estimates the standard deviation of a population based on a sample, using the numbers in a column based on the conditions specified.

DSTDEVP(database,field,criteria)
Calculates the standard deviation of a population based on the entire population, using the numbers in a column based on the conditions specified.

DSUM(database,field,criteria)
Adds (sums) the numbers in a column based on the conditions specified.

DVAR(database,field,criteria)
Estimates the variance of a population based on a sample, using the numbers in a list based on the conditions specified.

DVARP(database,field,criteria
Calculates the variance of a population based on the entire population, using the numbers in a list based on the conditions specified.

GETPIVOTDATA(pivot_table,name)
Returns data stored in a PivotTable.

DATE AND TIME FUNCTIONS

Date and time functions enable you to work with date and time values in your worksheet displaying full or part information. They also provide tools for analyzing and calculating date and time values.

DATE(year,month,day)
Displays the serial number of a given date.

DATEVALUE(date_text)
Converts a date represented by text to a serial number.

DAY(serial_number)
Displays the day of the month as an integer ranging from 1 to 31.

DAYS360(start_date,end_date,method)
Designed for Accountants working on a 360-day year (twelve 30-day months), this function provides the number of days between two given dates.

EDATE(start_date,months)
Returns the serial number for the date that is a specified number of months before or after a given date (start date).

EOMONTH(start_date,months)
Returns the serial number for the last day of the month that is a specified number of months before or after the start date.

HOUR(serial_number)
Displays the hour as an integer (ranging from 0 (12 a.m.) to 23 (11 p.m)), based on the given serial number.

MINUTE(serial_number)
Displays the minute as an integer (ranging from 0 to 59) based on the given serial number.

MONTH(serial_number)
Returns the month as an integer (ranging from 1 (January) to 12 (December)), based on the given serial number.

NETWORKDAYS(start_date,end_date,holidays)
Displays the number of whole working days between the given start and end date (excludes weekends and any dates identified as holidays).

NOW( )
Displays the serial number of the current date and time (based on the computer's clock).

SECOND(serial_number)
Returns the second as an integer (ranging from 0 to 59), based on a given serial number.

TIME(hour,minute,second)
Returns the serial number of a particular time as a decimal fraction ranging from 0 to 0.99999999.

TIMEVALUE(time_text)
Converts a time represented as text into a serial number.

TODAY( )
Returns the serial number of the current date.

WEEKDAY(serial_number,return_type)
Returns the day of the week as an integer (ranging from 1 (Sunday) to 7 (Saturday)).

WORKDAY(start_date,days,holidays)
Returns the serial number of a date that is a given number of working days before or after the start date (excludes weekends and any dates identified as holidays).

YEAR(serial_number)
Displays the year as an integer (ranging from 1900 to 9999), based on a given serial number.

YEARFRAC(start_date,end_date,basis)
Calculates the fraction of the year based on the number of whole days between two given dates.

ENGINEERING FUNCTIONS

The engineering functions are designed for those performing engineering analysis. In general, the functions are used for one of the following three operations:

- Working with complex numbers
- Converting values between decimal, hexadecimal, octal, and binary systems
- Converting values between different measurement systems

BESSELI(x,n)

Returns the modified Bessel function (equivalent to the Bessel function evaluated for purely imaginary arguments).

BESSELJ(x,n)

Returns the Bessel function.

BESSELK(x,n)

Returns the modified Bessel function (equivalent to the Bessel functions evaluated for purely imaginary arguments).

BESSELY(x,n)

Returns the Bessel function (also known as the Weber function or the Neumann function).

BIN2DEC(number)

Converts a binary number to a decimal number.

BIN2HEX(number,places)

Converts a binary number to hexadecimal number.

COMPLEX(real_num,i_num,suffix)

Converts real and imaginary coefficients into a complex number of the form x + yi or x + yj.

CONVERT(number,from_unit,to_unit)

Converts a number from one system of measurement to another; for example, ounces to grams or meters to yards.

DEC2BIN(number,places)

Converts a decimal number to a binary number.

DEC2HEX(number,places)

Converts a decimal number to a hexadecimal number.

DEC2OCT(number,places)

Converts a decimal number to an octal number.

DELTA(number1,number2)

Tests to see whether two values are equal. Returns 1 if the values are equal and 0 if not.

ERF(lower_limit,upper_limit)

Returns the error function integrated between the specified lower and upper limits.

ERFC(x)

Returns the complementary ERF function integrated between x and infinity.

GESTEP(number,step)

Returns 1 if number $\geq$ step; returns 0 (zero) otherwise.

HEX2BIN(number,places)

Converts a hexadecimal number to a binary number.

HEX2DEC(number)

Converts a hexadecimal number to a decimal number.

HEX2OCT(number,places)

Converts a hexadecimal number to an octal number.

IMABS(inumber)

Returns the absolute value (modulus) of a complex number in x + yi or x + yj text format.

IMAGINARY(inumber)

Returns the imaginary coefficient of a complex number in x + yi or x + yj text format.

IMARGUMENT(inumber)

Returns the argument, theta, an angle expressed in radians.

IMCONJUGATE(inumber)

Returns the complex conjugate of a complex number in x + yi or x + yj text format.

IMCOS(inumber)

Returns the cosine of a complex number in x + yi or x + yj text format.

IMDIV(inumber1,inumber2)

Returns the quotient of two complex numbers in x + yi or x + yj text format.

IMEXP(inumber)

Returns the exponential of a complex number in x + yi or x + yj text format.

IMLN(inumber)

Returns the natural logarithm of a complex number in x + yi or x + yj text format.

IMLOG10(inumber)

Returns the common logarithm (base 10) of a complex number in x + yi or x + yj text format.

IMLOG2(inumber)

Returns the base-2 logarithm of a complex number in x + yi or x + yj text format.

IMPOWER(inumber,number)

Returns a complex number in x + yi or x + yj text format raised to a power.

IMPRODUCT(inumber1,inumber2,...)

Returns the product of 2 to 29 complex numbers in x + yi or x + yj text format.

IMREAL(inumber)

Returns the real coefficient of a complex number in x + yi or x + yj text format.

IMSIN(inumber)

Returns the sine of a complex number in x + yi or x + yj text format.

IMSQRT(inumber)

Returns the square root of a complex number in x + yi or x + yj text format.

IMSUB(inumber1,inumber2)

Returns the difference of two complex numbers in x + yi or x + yj text format.

IMSUM(inumber1,inumber2,...)

Returns the sum of two or more complex numbers in x + yi or x + yj text format.

OCT2BIN(number,places)

Converts an octal number to a binary number.

OCT2DEC(number)

Converts an octal number to a decimal number.

OCT2HEX(number,places)

Converts an octal number to a hexadecimal number.

FINANCIAL FUNCTIONS

Financial functions perform common business calculations, often those related to borrowing or saving money.

ACCRINT(issue,first_interest,settlement,rate,par,frequency,basis)
Returns the accrued interest based on a security paying periodic interest.

ACCRINTM(issue,maturity,rate,par,basis)
Returns the accrued interest for a security paying interest at maturity.

AMORDEGRC(cost,date_purchased,first_period,salvage,period,rate,basis)
Returns the depreciation for each accounting period (provided for the French accounting system).

AMORLINC(cost,date_purchased,first_period,salvage,period,rate,basis)
Returns the depreciation for each accounting period. (provided for the French accounting system).

COUPDAYBS(settlement,maturity,frequency,basis)
Returns the number of days from the beginning of the coupon period to the settlement date.

COUPDAYS(settlement,maturity,frequency,basis)
Returns the number of days in the coupon period that contains the settlement date.

COUPDAYSNC(settlement,maturity,frequency,basis)
Returns the number of days from the settlement date to the next coupon date.

COUPNCD(settlement,maturity,frequency,basis)
Returns a number that represents the next coupon date after the settlement date.

COUPNUM(settlement,maturity,frequency,basis)
Returns the number of coupons payable between the settlement date and maturity date, rounded up to the nearest whole coupon.

COUPPCD(settlement,maturity,frequency,basis)
Returns a number that represents the previous coupon date before the settlement date.

CUMIPMT(rate,nper,pv,start_period,end_period,type)
Calculates the cumulative interest paid on a loan between a given start and end period.

CUMPRINC(rate,nper,pv,start_period,end_period,type)
Returns the cumulative principal paid on a loan between a given start and end period.

DB(cost,salvage,life,period,month)
Returns the depreciation of an asset for a specified period (usies the fixed-declining balance method).

DDB(cost,salvage,life,period,factor)
Returns the depreciation of an asset for a specified period using the double-declining balance method or some other method you specify.

DISC(settlement,maturity,pr,redemption,basis)
Returns the discount rate for a security.

DOLLARDE(fractional_dollar,fraction)

Converts fractional dollar numbers to decimal numbers.

DOLLARFR(decimal_dollar,fraction)

Converts decimal numbers to fractional dollar numbers.

DURATION(settlement,maturity,couponyld, frequency,basis)

Returns the Macauley duration for an assumed par value of $100.

EFFECT(nominal_rate,npery)

Returns the effective annual interest rate, given the nominal annual interest rate and the number of compounding periods per year.

FV(rate,nper,pmt,pv,type)

Returns the future value of an investment based on periodic, constant payments and a constant interest rate.

FVSCHEDULE(principal,schedule)

Calculates the future value of an investment with a variable or adjustable rate.

INTRATE(settlement,maturity,investment, redemption,basis)

Returns the interest rate for a fully invested security.

IPMT(rate,per,nper,pv,fv,type)

Returns the interest payment for a given period for an investment based on periodic, constant payments and a constant interest rate.

IRR(values,guess)

Returns the internal rate of return for a series of cash flows represented by the numbers in values.

MDURATION(settlement,maturity,coupon,yld, frequency,basis)

Returns the modified duration for a security with an assumed par value of $100.

MIRR(values,finance_rate,reinvest_rate)

Returns the modified internal rate of return for a series of periodic cash flows.

NOMINAL(effect_rate,npery)

Returns the nominal annual interest rate, given the effective rate and the number of compounding periods per year.

NPER(rate, pmt, pv, fv, type)

Returns the number of periods for an investment based on periodic, constant payments and a constant interest rate.

NPV(rate,value1,value2,...)

Calculates the net present value of an investment by using a discount rate and a series of future payments (negative values) and income (positive values).

ODDFPRICE(settlement,maturity,issue,first_coupon,rate,yld,redemption,frequency,basis)

Returns the price per $100 face value of a security having an odd (short or long) first period.

ODDFYIELD(settlement,maturity,issue,first_coupon,rate,pr,redemption,frequency,basis)

Returns the yield of a security that has an odd (short or long) first period.

ODDLPRICE(settlement,maturity,last_interest,rate,yld,redemption,frequency,basis)

Returns the price per $100 face value of a security having an odd (short or long) last coupon period.

ODDLYIELD(settlement,maturity,last_interest,rate,pr,redemption,frequency,basis)

Returns the yield of a security that has an odd (short or long) last period.

PMT(rate,nper,pv,fv,type)

Calculates the payment for a loan based on constant payments and a constant interest rate.

PPMT(rate,per,nper,pv,fv,type)

Returns the payment on the principal for a given period for an investment based on periodic, constant payments and a constant interest rate.

PRICE(settlement,maturity,rate,yld,redemption,freque ncy,basis)

Returns the price per $100 face value of a security that pays periodic interest.

PRICEDISC(settlement,maturity,discount, redemption,basis)

Returns the price per $100 face value of a discounted security.

PRICEMAT(settlement,maturity,issue,rate,yld,basis)

Returns the price per $100 face value of a security that pays interest at maturity.

PV(rate,nper,pmt,fv,type)

Returns the present value of an investment.

RATE(nper,pmt,pv,fv,type,guess)

Returns the interest rate per period of an annuity.

RECEIVED(settlement,maturity,investment, discount,basis)

Returns the amount received at maturity for a fully invested security.

SLN(cost,salvage,life)

Returns the straight-line depreciation of an asset for one period.

SYD(cost,salvage,life,per)

Returns the sum-of-years' digits depreciation of an asset for a specified period.

TBILLEQ(settlement,maturity,discount)

Returns the bond-equivalent yield for a treasury bill.

TBILLPRICE(settlement,maturity,discount)

Returns the price per $100 face value for a treasury bill.

VDB(cost,salvage,life,start_period,end_period,factor, no_switch)

The variable declining balance function calculates the depreciation of an asset for any given period.

XIRR(values,dates,guess)

Calculates the internal rate of return for a schedule of cash flows that is not necessarily periodic.

XNPV(rate,values,dates)

Calculates the net present value for a schedule of cash flows that is not necessarily periodic.

YIELD(settlement,maturity,rate,pr,redemption,frequen cy,basis)

Returns the yield on a security that pays periodic interest (use to calculate bond yield).

YIELDDISC(settlement,maturity,pr,redemption,basis)

Calculates the annual yield for a discounted security.

YIELDMAT(settlement,maturity,issue,rate,pr,basis)

Calculates the annual yield of a security that pays interest at maturity.

INFORMATION FUNCTIONS

The Information functions provide status information regarding the selected value. The majority of the information functions are referred to collectively as the IS functions. They can be used to check the type of value and return TRUE or FALSE depending on the outcome.

CELL(info_type,reference)

Provides details of formatting, location, or contents of the upper-left cell in a given reference.

COUNTBLANK(range)

Counts empty cells in a given range of cells.

ERROR.TYPE(error_val)

Returns a number representing an Excel error value.

INFO(type_text)

provides information on the current operating environment.

ISBLANK(value), ISERR(value), ISERROR(value), ISLOGICAL(value), ISNA(value), ISNONTEXT(value),

ISNUMBER(value), ISREF(value), ISTEXT(value)

Each of these nine worksheet functions, referred to collectively as the IS functions, checks the type of value and returns TRUE or FALSE depending on the outcome.

ISEVEN(number)

Returns TRUE for an even number and FALSE for an odd number.

ISODD(number)

Returns TRUE for an odd number and FALSE for an even number.

N(value)

Converts a value to a number.

NA( )

Returns the error #N/A, (no value is available).

TYPE(value)

Indicates type of value (i.e. number, text).

LOGICAL FUNCTIONS

The logic or conditional functions are used to test whether a specified condition is true or false. The IF function is widely used to return two different values depending on whether a condition is true or false whereas the other functions within this category simply return a true or false value.

AND(logical1,logical2, ...)

Returns TRUE if all its arguments are TRUE; returns FALSE if one or more arguments is FALSE.

FALSE( )

Returns the logical value FALSE.

IF(logical_test,value_if_true,value_if_false)

Returns one value if a condition you specify evaluates to TRUE and another value if it evaluates to FALSE. Use IF to conduct conditional tests on values and formulas.

NOT(logical)

Reverses the value of its argument. Use NOT when you want to make sure a value is not equal to one particular value.

OR(logical1,logical2,...)

Returns TRUE if any argument is TRUE; returns FALSE if all arguments are FALSE.

TRUE( )

Returns the logical value TRUE.

LOOKUP AND REFERENCE FUNCTIONS

The lookup and reference functions provide the facility to locate a specific value from a list or find a reference for a specific cell. Probably the most commonly used functions from this category are the lookup functions.

ADDRESS(row_num,column_num,abs_num,a1, sheet_text)

Generates a cell address as text, using the given row and column numbers.

AREAS(reference)

Returns the number of areas (a range of contiguous cells or a single cell) in a reference.

CHOOSE(index_num,value1,value2,…)
Selects one of up to 29 values based on the given index number.

COLUMN(reference)
Returns the column number of the given reference.

COLUMNS(array)
Returns the number of columns in an array or reference.

HLOOKUP(lookup_value,table_array,row_index_num, range_lookup)
Searches for a value in the top row of a table and returns a value in the same column from a row you specify in the table or array.

HYPERLINK(link_location,friendly_name)
Creates a shortcut or jump that opens a document stored on a network server, an intranet, or the Internet.

INDEX(array,row_num,column_num)
Returns the value of a specified cell or array of cells within array.

INDEX(reference,row_num,column_num, area_num)
Returns a reference to a specified cell or cells within reference.

INDIRECT(ref_text,a1)
Displays the reference specified by a text string. Used to change the reference to a cell within a formula without changing the actual formula.

LOOKUP(vector) and LOOKUP(array)
The vector form of LOOKUP looks in a one-row or one-column range for a value and returns a value from the same position in a second one-row or one-column range. The array form of LOOKUP looks in the first row or column of an array for the specified value and returns a value from the same position in the last row or column of the array.

MATCH(lookup_value,lookup_array,match_type)
Locates the relative position of an item in an array that matches a specified value in a specified order.

OFFSET(reference,rows, cols,height,width)
Returns a reference to a range that is a specified number of rows and columns from a given cell or range of cells.

ROW(reference)
Displays the row number for a given reference.

ROWS(array)
Calculates the number of rows in a given reference or array.

TRANSPOSE(LINEST(Yvalues,Xvalues)) and TRANSPOSE(array)
Transposes a vertical range of cells to a horizontal range, or vice versa.

VLOOKUP(lookup_value,table_array,col_index_num, range_lookup)
Searches for a value in the leftmost column of a table, and returns a value in the same row from a column you specify in the table.

MATH AND TRIGONOMETRY FUNCTIONS

The range of math and trigonometry functions provide the facility to perform simple and complex mathematical calculations.

ABS(number)
Displays the absolute value of a number (the number without its sign, ABS(-9)=9).

ACOS(number)
Returns the arccosine of a number in radians (range 0 (zero) to p (pi)).

ACOSH(number)
Returns the inverse hyperbolic cosine of a number.

ASIN(number)

Returns the arcsine of a number in radians (range -p/2 to p/2).

ASINH(number)

Returns the inverse hyperbolic sine of a number.

ATAN(number)

Returns the arctangent of a number in radians (range -p/2 to p/2).

ATAN2(x_num,y_num)

Returns the arctangent of the given x- and y- coordinates.

ATANH(number)

Returns the inverse hyperbolic tangent of a number.

CEILING(number,significance)

Rounds up a number (away from zero), to the nearest multiple of significance.

COMBIN(number,number_chosen)

Calculates the total possible number of groups for a given number of items.

COS(number)

Returns the cosine of the given angle.

COSH(number)

Returns the hyperbolic cosine of a number.

COUNTIF(range,criteria)

Counts the number of cells in a given range based on a specified criteria.

DEGREES(angle)

Converts radians into degrees.

EVEN(number)

Rounds up a number to the nearest even integer.

EXP(number)

Returns e raised to the power of number. The constant e equals 2.71828182845904, the base of the natural logarithm.

FACT(number)

Returns the factorial of a number. The factorial of a number is equal to 1*2*3*...* number.

FACTDOUBLE(number)

Returns the double factorial of a number.

FLOOR(number,significance)

Rounds a number down, toward zero, to the nearest multiple of significance.

GCD(number1,number2, ...)
Calculates the largest common divisor of two or more integers (the largest integer that will divide all the given numbers without leaving a remainder).

INT(number)
Rounds a number down to the nearest integer.

LCM(number1,number2, ...)
Returns the smallest positive integer that is a multiple of all the given numbers (least common multiple).

LN(number)
Returns the natural logarithm of a number. Natural logarithms are based on the constant e (2.71828182845904).

LOG(number,base)
Returns the logarithm of a number to a specified base.

LOG10(number)
Returns the base-10 logarithm of a number.

MDETERM(array)
Returns the matrix determinant of an array.

MINVERSE(array)
Returns the inverse matrix for the matrix stored in an array.

MMULT(array1,array2)
Returns the matrix product of two arrays.

MOD(number,divisor)
Returns the remainder after number is divided by divisor. The result has the same sign as divisor.

MROUND(number,multiple)
Rounds a number to a specified multiple.

MULTINOMIAL(number1,number2, ...)
Returns the ratio of the factorial of a sum of values to the product of factorials.

ODD(number)
Round a number up to the nearest odd integer.

PI( )
Returns the number 3.14159265358979, accurate to 15 digits.

POWER(number,power)
Returns the result of a number raised to a power; POWER(3,2) equals 9.

PRODUCT(number1,number2, ...)
Multiplies together all the given numbers and returns the product.

QUOTIENT(numerator,denominator)
Discards the remainder of a division, returning the integer portion.

RADIANS(angle)
Converts degrees to radians.

RAND( )
Returns a random number greater than or equal to 0 and less than 1. A new random number is returned every time the worksheet is calculated.

SERIESSUM(x,n,m,coefficients)
Returns the sum of a power series based on the formula.

SIGN(number)
Determines the sign of a number (1 for a positive number, 0 if the number is 0 and -1 if the number is negative).

SIN(number)
Returns the sine of the given angle.

SINH(number)
Returns the hyperbolic sine of a number.

SQRT(number)
Returns the square root of a positive number; SQRT(16) equals 4.

SQRTPI(number)
Returns the square root of (number * p).

SUBTOTAL(function_num,ref1,ref2,…)
Returns a subtotal in a list or database.

SUM(number1,number2, ...)
Adds all the numbers in a range of cells, SUM(3,2,6) equals 11.

SUMIF(range,criteria,sum_range)
Adds the cells that meet a specified criteria.

SUMPRODUCT(array1,array2,array3, ...)
Multiplies corresponding components in the given arrays, and returns the sum of those products.

SUMSQ(number1,number2, ...)
Returns the sum of the squares of the arguments.

SUMX2MY2(array_x,array_y)
Returns the sum of the difference of squares of corresponding values in two arrays.

SUMX2PY2(array_x,array_y)
Returns the sum of the sum of squares of corresponding values in two arrays.

RANDBETWEEN(bottom,top)
Returns a random number between the specified numbers. A new random number is returned every time the worksheet is calculated.

ROMAN(number,form)
Converts an arabic numeral to roman, as text; ROMAN(499,0) equals CDXCIX

ROUND(number,num_digits)
Rounds a number to a specified number of digits, ROUND(2.75, 1) equals 2.8

ROUNDDOWN(number,num_digits)
Rounds a number down, toward zero, ROUNDDOWN(6.2, 0) equals 6.

ROUNDUP(number,num_digits)
Rounds a number up, away from zero, ROUNDUP (6.2,0) equals 7.

SUMXMY2(array_x,array_y)
Returns the sum of squares of differences of corresponding values in two arrays.

TAN(number)
Returns the tangent of the given angle.

TANH(number)
Returns the hyperbolic tangent of a number.

TRUNC(number,num_digits)
Truncates a number to an integer by removing the fractional part of the number, TRUNC(8.9) equals 8.

STATISTICAL FUNCTIONS

Excel provides numerous statistical functions from the most commonly used SUM and AVERAGE functions, through to the cumulative beta probability density function! Some of the functions are designed for specialist use but many prove useful in every day worksheets.

AVEDEV(number1,number2, ...)
Returns the average of the absolute deviations of data points from their mean.

AVERAGE(number1,number2, ...)
Returns the average (arithmetic mean) of the given numbers.

BETADIST(x,alpha,beta,A,B)
Returns the cumulative beta probability density function, commonly used to study variation in a percentage across samples, such as the fraction of the day people spend driving.

BETAINV(probability,alpha,beta,A,B)
Returns the inverse of the cumulative beta probability density function.

BINOMDIST(number_s,trials,probability_s, cumulative)
Returns the individual term binomial distribution probability; used for problems with a fixed number of independent trials, when the outcomes of a trial is success or failure and the probability of success is constant throughout the experiment.

CHIDIST(x,degrees_freedom)
Returns the one-tailed probability of the chi-squared distribution.

CHIINV(probability,degrees_freedom)
Returns the inverse of the one-tailed probability of the chi-squared distribution.

CHITEST(actual_range,expected_range)
Returns the value from the chi-squared (c2) distribution for the statistic and the appropriate degrees of freedom.

CONFIDENCE(alpha,standard_dev,size)
Determines, with a particular level of confidence a range on either side of a sample mean. For example, if you drive to work each day, the earliest and latest you will arrive.

CORREL(array1,array2)
Uses the correlation coefficient to determine the relationship between two properties; for example, the relationship between the temperature and ice cream sales.

COUNT(value1,value2, ...)
Counts all the values that are numbers. If the value is a cell address Excel will check whether the cell contains a number and, if so, include it in the count.

COUNTA(value1,value2, ...)
Counts all the values within the list of arguments. If a value is a cell reference, Excel checks that the cell contains information and if so includes it in the count.

COVAR(array1,array2)

Returns covariance, the average of the products of deviations for each data point pair.

CRITBINOM(trials,probability_s,alpha)

Returns the smallest value for which the cumulative binomial distribution is greater than or equal to a criterion value.

DEVSQ(number1,number2,...)

Returns the sum of squares of deviations of data points from their sample mean.

EXPONDIST(x,lambda,cumulative)

Returns the exponential distribution; used to model the time between events.

FDIST(x,degrees_freedom1,degrees_freedom2)

Returns the F probability distribution; used to determine whether two data sets have different degrees of diversity.

FINV(probability,degrees_freedom1,degrees_freedom2)

Returns the inverse of the F probability distribution.

FISHER(x)

Returns the Fisher transformation at x; used to perform hypothesis testing on the correlation coefficient.

FISHERINV(y)

Returns the inverse of the Fisher transformation.

FORECAST(x,known_y's,known_x's)

Calculates, or predicts, a future value by using existing values; used to predict future sales, inventory requirements, or consumer trends.

FREQUENCY(data_array,bins_array)

Calculates how often values occur within a given range of values, returning a vertical array of numbers. As this function returns an array, it must be entered as an array formula.

FTEST(array1,array2)

An F-test returns the one-tailed probability that the variances in array1 and array2 are not significantly different; used to determine whether two samples have different variances.

GAMMADIST(x,alpha,beta,cumulative)

Returns the gamma distribution; used to study variables that may have a skewed distribution. The gamma distribution is commonly used in queuing analysis.

GAMMAINV(probability,alpha,beta)

Returns the inverse of the gamma cumulative distribution; used to study a variable whose distribution may be skewed.

GAMMALN(x)

Returns the natural logarithm of the gamma function, $G(x)$.

GEOMEAN(number1,number2, ...)

Returns the geometric mean of an array or range of positive data; used to calculate average growth rate given compound interest with variable rates.

GROWTH(known_y's,known_x's,new_x's,const)

Calculates predicted exponential growth by using existing data, returns the y-values for a series of new x-values specified by using existing x-values and y-values.

HARMEAN(number1,number2, ...)

Returns the harmonic mean of a data set. The harmonic mean is the reciprocal of the arithmetic mean of reciprocals.

HYPGEOMDIST(sample_s,number_sample,population_s,number_population)

Returns the hypergeometric distribution, the probability of a given number of sample successes, given the sample size, population successes, and population size. Used for problems with a finite population, where each observation is either a success or a failure, and where each subset of a given size is chosen with equal likelihood.

INTERCEPT(known_y's,known_x's)

Calculates the point at which a line will intersect the y-axis by using existing x-values and y-values. The intercept point is based on a best-fit regression line plotted through the known x-values and known y-values.

KURT(number1,number2, ...)

Returns the kurtosis of a data set; positive kurtosis indicates a relatively peaked distribution, negative kurtosis indicates a relatively flat distribution.

LARGE(array,k)

Returns the k-th largest value in a data set; by setting k to 5, the fifth largest value will be returned.

LINEST(known_y's,known_x's,const,stats)

Uses the "least squares" method to calculate a straight line that best fits the data.

LOGEST(known_y's,known_x's,const,stats)

Calculates an exponential curve that fits the data and returns an array of values that describes the curve (in regression analysis).

LOGINV(probability,mean,standard_dev)

Returns the inverse of the lognormal cumulative distribution function of x, where ln(x) is normally distributed with parameters mean and standard deviation.

LOGNORMDIST(x,mean,standard_dev)

Returns the cumulative lognormal distribution of x, where ln(x) is normally distributed with parameters mean and standard deviation; used to analyze data that has been logarithmically transformed.

MAX(number1,number2,...)

Returns the largest (maximum) number in the range.

MAXA(value1,value2,...)

Returns the largest value in a list of arguments. Text and logical values such as TRUE and FALSE are compared as well as numbers.

MEDIAN(number1,number2, ...)

Returns the median, the number in the middle of a set of given numbers; half the numbers have values that are greater than the median, and half have values that are less.

MIN(number1,number2, ...)

Returns the smallest (minimum) number in the range.

MINA(value1,value2,...)

Returns the smallest value in the list of arguments. Text and logical values such as TRUE and FALSE are compared as well as numbers.

MODE(number1,number2, ...)

Returns the most frequently occurring, or repetitive, value in a range of data.

NEGBINOMDIST(number_f,number_s,probability_s)

Returns the negative binomial distribution, the probability that there will be number_f failures before the number_s-th success, when the constant probability of a success is probability_s.

NORMDIST(x,mean,standard_dev,cumulative)

Returns the normal cumulative distribution for the specified mean and standard deviation. This function has a very wide range of applications in statistics, including hypothesis testing.

NORMINV(probability,mean,standard_dev)

Returns the inverse of the normal cumulative distribution for the specified mean and standard deviation.

NORMSDIST(z)

Returns the standard normal cumulative distribution function. The distribution has a mean of 0 (zero) and a standard deviation of one

NORMSINV(probability)

Returns the inverse of the standard normal cumulative distribution. The distribution has a mean of zero and a standard deviation of one.

PEARSON(array1,array2)

Returns the Pearson product moment correlation coefficient, r, a dimensionless index that ranges from -1.0 to 1.0 inclusive and reflects the extent of a linear relationship between two data sets.

PERCENTILE(array,k)

Returns the k-th percentile of values in a range, used to establish a threshold of acceptance.

PERCENTRANK(array,x,significance)

Returns the rank of a value in a data set as a percentage of the data set; used to evaluate the relative standing of a value within a data set.

PERMUT(number,number_chosen)

Calculates the number of permutations for a given number of objects that can be selected from number objects; used for lottery-style probability calculations.

POISSON(x,mean,cumulative)

Returns the Poisson distribution; used to predict the number of events over a specific time, such as the number of people entering a building in 5 minutes.

PROB(x_range,prob_range,lower_limit,upper_limit)

Returns the probability that values in a range are between two limits.

QUARTILE(array,quart)

Returns the quartile of a data set; often used in sales and survey data to divide populations into groups.

RANK(number,ref,order)

Returns the rank (size relative to other values) of a number in a list of numbers. If the list is sorted, the rank of a number is its position in the list.

RSQ(known_y's,known_x's)

Returns the square of the Pearson product moment correlation coefficient through data points in known_y's and known_x's.

SKEW(number1,number2,...)

Returns the skewness of a distribution, the degree of asymmetry of a distribution around its mean. Positive skewness indicates a distribution with an asymmetric tail extending toward more positive values. Negative skewness indicates a distribution with an asymmetric tail extending toward more negative values.

SLOPE(known_y's,known_x's)

Returns the slope of the linear regression line through data points in known_y's and known_x's.

SMALL(array,k)

Returns the k-th smallest value in a data set.

STANDARDIZE(x,mean,standard_dev)

Returns a normalized value from a distribution characterized by mean and standard deviation.

STDEV(number1,number2,...)

Calculates the standard deviation by estimating how widely values are dispersed from the average value.

STDEVA(value1,value2,...)

Calculates the standard deviation by estimating how widely values are dispersed from the average value. Text and logical values such as TRUE and FALSE are included in the calculation.

STDEVP(number1,number2,...)

Calculates standard deviation based on the entire population given as arguments.

STDEVPA(value1,value2,...)

Calculates standard deviation based on the entire population given as arguments, including text and logical values.

STEYX(known_y's,known_x's)

Returns the standard error of the predicted y-value for each x in the regression.

TDIST(x,degrees_freedom,tails)

The t-distribution is used in the hypothesis testing of small sample data sets; used in place of a table of critical values for the t-distribution.

TINV(probability,degrees_freedom)

Returns the inverse of the Student's t-distribution for the specified degrees of freedom.

TREND(known_y's,known_x's,new_x's,const)

Returns values along a linear trend.

TRIMMEAN(array,percent)

Returns the mean of the interior of a data set; used to calculate the mean taken by excluding a percentage of data points from the top and bottom tails of a data set.

TTEST(array1,array2,tails,type)

Returns the probability associated with a Student's t-Test.

VAR(number1,number2,...)

Estimates the variance based on a given sample of numbers.

VARA(value1,value2,...)

Estimates the variance based on a sample of values. In addition to numbers, text and logical values such as TRUE and FALSE are included in the calculation.

VARP(number1,number2,...)

Calculates the variance based on the entire population.

VARPA(value1,value2,...)

Calculates the variance based on the entire population. In addition to numbers, text and logical values such as TRUE and FALSE are included in the calculation.

WEIBULL(x,alpha,beta,cumulative)

Returns the Weibull distribution; in reliability analysis, such as calculating a device's mean time to failure.

ZTEST(array,x,sigma)

Returns the two-tailed P-value of a z-test. The z-test generates a standard score for x with respect to the data set, and returns the two-tailed probability for the normal distribution.

TEXT FUNCTIONS

Text functions enable you to manipulate text strings in a variety of ways.

CHAR(number)

Displays the character that represents the given number.

CLEAN(text)

Removes all the nonprintable characters from the specified text; used to remove characters that will not print when importing data from another application.

CODE(text)

Returns a numeric code for the first character in a text string. The returned code corresponds to the character set used by the computer.

CONCATENATE (text1,text2,...)

Joins several text strings together to form a single text string.

DOLLAR(number,decimals)

Converts a number to text using currency format, with the decimals rounded to the specified place. The format used is $#,##0.00_);($#,##0.00).

EXACT(text1,text2)

Compares two text strings and returns TRUE if they are exactly the same and FALSE if they differ. EXACT is case-sensitive but ignores formatting differences.

FIND(find_text,within_text,start_num)

Finds specific text from within other text. The starting position of the text found is displayed as a number representing the position from the leftmost character of the text string. For example, =FIND("smith","john smith") will return 6. This function is similar to, but unlike SEARCH, FIND is case-sensitive and does not allow wildcard characters.

FIXED(number,decimals,no_commas)

Rounds a number to a specified number of decimal places, formats the number in decimal format using a period and commas, and returns the result as text.

LEFT(text,num_chars)

Returns the first (or leftmost) character or characters in a text string.

LEN(text)

Returns the number of characters in a text string.

LOWER(text)

Converts all uppercase letters in a text string to lowercase.

MID(text,start_num,num_chars)

Returns a given number of characters from a text string, starting at the position specified.

PROPER(text)

Capitalizes the first letter in a text string and any other letters that follow any character other than a letter. Converts all other letters to lowercase letters.

REPLACE(old_text,start_num,num_chars,new_text)

Replaces part of a text string with a different text string.

REPT(text,number_times)

Repeats text a given number of times.

RIGHT(text,num_chars)

Returns the last (or rightmost) character or characters in a text string.

SEARCH(find_text,within_text,start_num)

Locates a character or text string within another text string returning the number of the character at which a specific character or text string is first found, reading from left to right.

SUBSTITUTE(text,old_text,new_text,instance_num)

Substitutes new text for old text in a text string.

T(value)

Returns the text referred to by value.

TEXT(value,format_text)

Converts a value to text using a specific number format.

TRIM(text)

Removes all spaces from text except for single spaces between words; used to trim spaces from text received from another application that may have irregular spacing.

UPPER(text)

Converts text to uppercase.

VALUE(text)

Converts a text string that represents a number to a number.

OTHER USEFUL BOOKS

Active Education, *Excel 2000 Step by Step Student Guide: Expert Skills*, Microsoft Press International, 2000

Ageloff, Roy, *New Perspectives on Microsoft Excel 2000-Advanced*, Course Technology, 2002

Banfield, Colin, *Excel 2002 for Dummies Quick Reference*, Hungry Minds Inc., 2001

Barker, Bernard, *Learn Microsoft Excel*, Pearson Publishing, 1997

Blattner, Patrick, *MS Excel 2000 Functions in Practice*, Que, 1999

Blattner, Patrick, *Using Excel 2000 Interactive Tutor (Boxed Set)*, Prentice Hall, 2000

Bloch, S.C., *Excel for Engineers and Scientists*, John Wiley and Sons (WIE), 2000

Bowcock, Stephen, and Bayfield, Nat, *Excel for Surveyors*, Estates Gazette, 2000

Brindley, Keith, *Excel 2000 Business Edition Made Simple*, Made Simple, 2000

Bryant, Michael, *Creating Spreadsheets with Excel 2000*, Cliff Notes, 2001

Bullen, Stephen, et al, *Excel 2000 VBA Programmer's Reference*, Wrox Press Ltd., 1999

Camarda, Bill, et al, *Using Microsoft Word and Excel in Office 2000: Special Edition*, 1999

Carlberg PHD, Conrad, *Business Analysis with Microsoft Excel 2002*, Que, 2001

Catapult Inc, *Microsoft Excel 5 for Windows Step by Step*, Microsoft Press International, 1994

Chester, Thomas, and Martin, Mindy, *Mastering Excel 2000 Premium Edition*, 1999

Copestake, Stephen, *Excel in Easy Steps*, Computer Step, 1997

Copestake, Stephen, *Excel 2002 in Easy Steps*, Computer Stop, 2001

Courter, Gini, *Mastering Microsoft Excel 2002*, Sybex International, 2001

Craig, Deborah, *How to Use Microsoft Excel 2000*, Sams, 1999

De Levie, Robert, *How to Use Excel in Analytical Chemistry*, Cambridge University Press, 2001

Dinwiddie, Robert, *Essential Computers: Excel: Formulas & Functions*, Dorling Kindersley, 2002

Dodge, Mark, et al, *Running Microsoft Excel 97*, Microsoft Press International, 1997

Dodge, Mark, *Excel 2000 Learning Kit*, Microsoft Press International, 1999

Dodge, Mark, *Running Microsoft Excel 2000*, Microsoft Press International, 1999

Doe, *Practical Statistics by Example*, Prentice Hall, 2002

ENI Development Team, *By Example, Self Training Guides: Excel 2000*, ENI Publishing, 1999

ENI Development Team, *Straight to the Point, Excel 2000*, ENI Publishing, 1999

ENI Development Team, *MOUS Exam, Excel 2000 Expert*, ENI Publishing, 2000

ENI Development Team, *Training CD-Roms, Excel 2000*, ENI Publishing, 2001

ENI Development Team, Gillian Cain (Translator) *On Your Side, Excel 97*, ENI Publishing, 1998

ENI Development Team, *Finding your Way, Excel 2000 Basic Functions*, ENI Publishing, 1999

Ford, Mary, *Excel '97*, Michael O'Mara, 1999

Foster, Jeremy J., *Data Analysis Using SPSS for Windows Versions 8 to 10*, Sage Publications Ltd, 2001

Fulton, Jennifer, *Sams Teach Yourself Microsoft Excel 2000 in 10 minutes*, Sams, 1999

Gillies, Alan, *Excel for Clinical Governance*, Radcliffe Medical Press, 2000

Grauer, Robert T., and Barber, Maryann, *Exploring Microsoft Excel 7.0*, US Imports & PHIPEs, 1996

Green, John, et al, *Excel 2002 VBA Programmer's Reference*, Wrox Press Ltd, 2001

Haag, Stephen, and Perry, James, *Microsoft Excel 2002-Complete*, Mayfield, 2002

Habraken, Joe, *Ten Minute Guide to Microsoft Excel 2002*, Que, 2001

Harris, Matthew, *Sams Teach Yourself Excel 2000 Programming in 21 Days*, Sams, 1999

Harvey, G., *Excel 97 for Windows for Dummies*, Hungry Minds Inc., 1997

Harvey, G., *Excel 2002 for Dummies*, Hungry Minds Inc, 2001

Heathcote, P.M., *Basic Excel 2000*, Payne-Gallway Publishers, 2001

Heathcote, P.M., *Successful ICT Projects in Excel*, Payne-Gallway Publishers, 2000

Ivens, Kathy, *Excel 2000: the Complete Reference*, Osborne McGraw-Hill, 1999

Jackson, Mary and Staunton, Mike, *Advanced Modelling in Finance using Excel and VBA*, John Wiley & Sons, 2001

Jacobson, Reed, *Microsoft Excel 2002 Visual Basic for Applications Step by Step*, Microsoft Press, 2001

Jacobson, Reed, *Microsoft Excel 2000 Visual Basic for Applications Fundamentals*, Microsoft Press International, 1999

Jinjer, Simon, *Excel 2000 in a Nutshell*, O'Reilly UK, 2000

Kantaris, N., and Oliver, P., *Microsoft Excel 2002 Explained*, Bernard Babani (Publishing) Ltd, 2001

Kassar, Barbara, *Sams Teach Yourself Microsoft Excel 2000 in 24 Hours*, Sams, 1999

Kelly, Julia, *Using Microsoft Excel 97*, Que, 1998

Ketcham, Emily, *MOUS Test Preparation Guide for Excel 2000*, Prentice Hall, 2000

Kinkoph, Sherry, *The Complete Idiot's Guide to Microsoft Excel 2000*, Que, 1999

Korol, Julitta, *Learn Microsoft Excel 2000 VBA Programming*, Wordware Publishing Inc., 2000

Lagan, Gabrielle, *Learning to use Excel for Windows 95*, Heinemann Educational Secondary Division, 1997

Langer, Maria, *Microsoft Excel X for Mac OS X*, Peachpit Press, 2002

Langer, Maria, *Excel 2001 for Macintosh: Visual QuickStart Guide*, Peachpit Press, 2001

Levine, *Statistics for Managers Using Microsoft Excel*, US Imports & PHIPEs, 2001

Liengme, Bernard V., *Guide to Microsoft Excel 2002 for Scientists and Engineers*, Butterworth-Heinemann, 2002

Liengme, Bernard V., *A Guide to Microsoft Excel for Business and Management*, Butterworth-Heinemann, 1999

McDowell, Monica, *Moving on with Exel 97*, Liberty Hall, 1998

Marmel, Elaine, *Easy Excel 97*, Que, 1998

Mayes, Shank, *Financial Analysis with Microsoft Excel*, Thomson Learning, 2000

Mansfield, Ron, *Excel 2000 for Busy People*, Osborne McGraw-Hill, 1999

Maran, *Microsoft Excel 2000 Simplified*, Hungry Minds Inc., 1999

Microsoft Press International, *Quick Course in Excel 2000*, Microsoft Press International, 2000

Middleton, Michael, *Data Analysis Using Microsoft Excel*, Duxbury, 1999

Moira, Stephen, *Teach Yourself Excel 97*, Teach Yourself, 1998

Moore, Jeffrey, H. (Editor), and Wetherford, Lawrence R. (Editor), *Decisions Modeling with Microsoft Excel*, Prentice Hall, 2001

Morris, Stephen, *Excel 97 for Windows Made Simple*, Made Simple, 1997

Morris, *Excel 2002 Made Simple*, Butterworth-Heinemann, 2002

Morris, Stephen, *Excel (Version 7) for Windows 95 Made Simple*, Made Simple, 1996

Morris, Stephen, *Teach Yourself Quick Fix: Excel 2000*, Teach Yourself, 2001

Microsoft Excel 2000 Step by Step, Catapult, Microsoft Press International, 1999

Muir, Jim, *Excel 97 Further Skills*, Continuum International Publishing Group, 2001

Muir, Jim, *Excel 7*, Continuum International Publishing Group, 1996

Muir, Jim, *Excel 2000: an Introductory Course for Students*, Learning Matters, 2001

Muir, Jim, *Excel 2000: an Advanced Course for Students*, Learning Matters, 2000

Munnelly, Brendan, *ECDL Advanced Spreadsheets*, Prentice Hall, 2002

Murach, Mike, *Work Like a Pro with Excel 5*, Mike Murach & Associates Inc., 1995

Nanda, V., *Finance & Financial Engineering with Excel*, Redmond Technology Press, 2002

Nelson, S., *Microsoft Excel 97 Field Guide*, Microsoft Press International, 2000

Nelson, S., *Excel Data Analysis for Dummies*, Hungry Minds Inc., 2002

Neufeld, John L, *Learning Business Statistics with Microsoft Excel 2000*, Prentice Hall, 2000

O'Hara, Shelley, *Easy Microsoft Excel 2000*, Que, 1999

O'Keefe, Tara Lynn, and Reding, Elizabeth Eisner, *Microsoft Excel 2000*, Thomson Learning, 2001

O'Keefe, Tara Lynn, *Microsoft Excel 2000*, Thomson Learning, 2001

O'Leary, Timothy and Linda, *Excel 2002*, Osborne McGraw-Hill, 2001

O'Mara, Michael, *Excel 2000*, 2000

Owen, Glenn, *Excel and Access in Accounting*, South Western College Publishing, 2002

Patterson, Lois, *Sams Teach Yourself Microsoft Excel 97 in 24 Hours*, Sams, 1997

Perspection Inc, *Microsoft Excel*, Sybex International, 2001

Perspection, *Excel 2002 Plain and Simple*, Microsoft Press International, 2001

Perspection, *Microsoft Excel 2000 at a Glance*, Microsoft Press International, 1999

Prince, Anne, *Crash Course Excel 95*, Mike Murach & Associates Inc., 1997

Prince, Anne, *Crash Course Excel 97*, Mike Murach & Associates Inc., 1997

Robinson, James, *New Excel Phenomenon*, Prima Games, 2001

Robinson, James, *Excel Phenomenon: The Astonishing Success Story of the Fastest-Growing Communications Company-and What It Means to You*, Prima Publishing, 1997

Robson, Andrew J., *Designing and Building Business Models Using Microsoft Excel*, McGraw-Hill Education, 1995

Robson, Andrew, *Introductory Business Statistics with Microsoft Excel*, Business Education Publishers, 1999

Roman, Steven, *Writing Excel Macros with VBA*, O'Reilly UK, 2002

Shelley, Gary B., *Microsoft Excel 2000 Comprehensive Concepts and Techniques*, Course Technology, 1999

Smith, Gaylord, *Excel Applications for Management Accounting*, South Western College Publishing, 1999

Stephen, Moira, *Teach Yourself Excel 2000*, Teach Yourself, 1999

Stultz, Russell A., *Learn Excel of Windows in a Day*, Wordware Publishing Inc., 1992

Thomas, Richard, *Microsoft Excel (Version 5)*, Nelson Thornes, 1995

Thompson, D., *A Practical Approach to Excel for Windows 95*, Bernard Babani Ltd, 1996

Thomson Learning, *First Steps: Excel 97*, 1998

Ulrich, Laurie, *Troubleshooting Excel Spreadsheets*, Microsoft Press International, 2000

Ulrich, Laurie Ann, *Troubleshooting Microsoft Excel 2002*, Microsoft Press, 2001

Ulrich, Laurie Ann, *Special Edition Using Microsoft Excel 2000*, Que, 1999

Vazsonyi, et al, *Quantitative Management Using Microsoft Excel*, Wadsworth, 2000

Walkenbach, John, *Excel 2000 for Windows for Dummies Quick Reference*, Hungry Minds Inc., 1999

Walkenbach, John, and Brian, Underdahl, *Excel 2002 Bible*, Hungry Minds, 2001

Walkenbach, John, *Excel 2000 for Windows for Dummies Quick Reference*, Hungry Minds Inc., 1999

Weale, David, *Excel 2000 Basic Skills*, Continuum International Publishing Group, 2001

Weale, David, *Excel 2000 Further Skills*, Continuum International Publishing Group, 2001

Wempen, Faithe, *Microsoft Excel 2002 Fast and Easy*, Prima Tech, 2001

Wermers, Lynne, *Illustrated – Microsoft Excel XP: Second Course*, Course Technology, 2001

Winter, Rick, *Microsoft Excel 2000 Mous Cheat Sheet*, Que, 1999

ACKNOWLEDGEMENTS

All pictures are courtesy of Foundry Arts except:

Hulton Archive: 10 (l); 29 (b) ; 43 (r); 48 (t); 54 (l); 71 (r); 85; 91 (b); 93 (b); 108 (l); 128; 132; 136; 137 (l); 156; 159; 164 (t); 166; 176

Mary Evans Picture Library: 41 (b); 99

Topham Picturepoint: 58; 64; 73 (l); 74 (b); 115 (t); 123 (r); 125 (t); 196

AUTHOR BIOGRAPHIES

S.A. MATHIESON

General Editor; Hot Tip, Hot Web Site

S.A. Mathieson is a freelance reporter specializing in I.T. He writes regularly for the *Guardian's* Online technology supplement, *Computing* newspaper and *Health Service Journal* magazine. He has previously written about using Excel, by drawing on his plentiful experience of using the software for planning his work schedule and working out his accounts.

ROB HAWKINS

How To

Rob Hawkins has been a freelance journalist since 1993, writing for computer magazines including *Computeractive*, *Webactive*, *PC Direct* and *What PC*, and for several motoring publications to cater for his interest in anything with four wheels and an engine. Since 1996 Rob has also delivered training courses covering a wide range of software including Microsoft Excel.

CAROL ELSTON

Easy, Intermediate, Advanced, Case Study, Beyond Excel

Carol Elston is an Owner Director of CATS Consulting Ltd., a company providing I.T. Training and Development solutions to the corporate market. Carol has extensive experience of working as a Training Consultant and has co-authored, designed and desktop published five I.T. text books which are used within schools and businesses to support a range of syllabi.

SUE ORRELL

Easy, Intermediate, Advanced, Case Study, Beyond Excel

Sue Orrell has 20 years experience in the field of training and education and is a Co-Director of CATS Consulting Ltd. She has been involved in organizing national teaching conferences, setting G.S.C.E and A Level examination papers and examining. She is the co-author of a market-leading G.C.S.E Psychology text book and the co-author of five I.T. text books.

INDEX